ON THE OTHER SIDE OF SORROW

BOOKS BY THE SAME AUTHOR

The Making of the Crofting Community, Edinburgh (John Donald), 1976
For the People's Cause: From the Writings of John Murdoch, Edinburgh
  (HMSO), 1986
Skye: The Island, Edinburgh (Mainstream), 1986
The Claim of Crofting: The Scottish Highlands and Islands, 1930–1990,
  Edinburgh (Mainstream), 1991
Scottish Highlanders: A People and Their Place, Edinburgh (Mainstream),
  1992
*A Dance Called America: The Scottish Highlands, the United States and
  Canada*, Edinburgh (Mainstream), 1994

ON THE OTHER SIDE
of SORROW

Nature and People in the Scottish Highlands

JAMES HUNTER

MAINSTREAM
PUBLISHING
EDINBURGH AND LONDON

First published in Great Britain in 1995 by
MAINSTREAM PUBLISHING COMPANY (EDINBURGH) LTD
7 Albany Street
Edinburgh EH1 3UG

ISBN 1 85158 765 9

A catalogue record for this book is available from the British Library

Subsidised by   THE SCOTTISH ARTS COUNCIL

Typeset in Adobe Garamond

Printed and bound in Great Britain by
Butler & Tanner Ltd, Frome and London

For
Catherine and Paul

Thar bochdainn, caithimh, fiabhrais, àmhghair,
thar anacothrom, eucoir, ainneart, ànraidh,
thar truaighe, eu-dòchas, gamhlas, cuilbeart,
thar ciont is truaillidheachd; gu furachair,
gu treunmhor chithear an Cuilithionn
's e 'g éirigh air taobh eile duilghe.

– SOMHAIRLE MACGILL-EAIN

Beyond poverty, consumption, fever, agony,
beyond hardship, wrong, tyranny, distress,
beyond misery, despair, hatred, treachery,
beyond guilt and defilement; watchful,
heroic, the Cuillin is seen
rising on the other side of sorrow.

– SORLEY MACLEAN

CONTENTS

ACKNOWLEDGEMENTS

Many people have helped make this book possible. When Professor Christopher Smout of the Institute for Environmental History at St Andrews University invited me in the spring of 1994 to prepare a paper on Highland landscape for delivery at one of the institute's seminars, he was expecting, I guess, something in the order of two or three thousand words. In the event, Chris found himself circulating – uncomplainingly – a paper which was as much as four times longer than he had anticipated. Now that the paper in question has grown into a book, it is good to have the chance to thank Chris both for his encouragement to me personally and for his wider commitment to developing the environmental history of Scotland.

As well as benefiting greatly from the discussion of my original paper at St Andrews in the summer of 1994, I profited from having the chance, later that year, to air some of my ideas at a seminar organised by the History Department in the University of Aberdeen and at a conference organised by the Department of Scottish History in the University of Glasgow.

One very helpful outcome of these gatherings, and of more informal contact with a number of friends and colleagues, was the extent to which I was plied with suggestions as to where I might look for additional information. Bob Aitken, Richard Hingley, Norman Macdonald, Andy Wightman and Professor Charles Withers took particular trouble in this regard. I was also fortunate in having the benefit of comments made on an early version of my material by Dr John Bannerman of the Department of Scottish History at the University of Edinburgh and Professor Donald Meek of the Department of Celtic Studies at the University of Aberdeen.

At a fairly early stage in my researches, I learned that the project on which I was engaged was one that dovetailed neatly with the work of Malcolm MacLean of the National Gaelic Arts Project in Stornoway. Malcolm, it transpired, was interested in having a book to place alongside a planned multi-media presentation on links between Gaelic culture and the natural environment – a presentation organised by Cailean Maclean and others in Skye. Malcolm was kind enough to suggest that my own book might be what was wanted. It was with the help of the National Gaelic Arts Project that I was able to attract some very welcome grant aid from the European Union's LIFE programme to assist with research and travel costs.

Thanks to the connection thus made between my venture and his own multi-media show, I was able to draw – once again – on Cailean Maclean's skill as a photographer. I am grateful to Cailean for providing the pictures which illustrate my book.

The book, by its very nature, is one that relies heavily on the work of other writers, past and present. I am especially grateful to Sorley MacLean for permission to use a line from his own work as my book's title. Sorley also allowed me to quote extensively from his poetry. A number of other writers and poets have been equally generous in this respect. They include Angus Peter Campbell, Hugh Fife, Sir John Lister-Kaye, Norman MacCaig, John McGrath, Alasdair MacLean, Aonghas MacNeacail, Catriona Montgomery, William Neill, Iain Crichton Smith, Derick Thomson and Adam Watson. My thanks also to Angus Macleod for having allowed me to quote from one of his letters to me.

I am grateful to Bill Campbell, Peter MacKenzie, Raymond Cowie, Richard Mellis and their colleagues at Mainstream for once more helping me to get into print.

And I am grateful, as always, to Evelyn, Iain and Anna who demonstrated admirable tolerance even when my mind no doubt seemed more occupied with the tenth century than with the twentieth.

One of the delights of researching a book of this type, as far as I am concerned anyway, is that such research provides a justification for spending hours, days or even weeks in a place which I regard as next best thing to paradise – the reading room of the National Library of Scotland in Edinburgh. My thanks are due again to the library's unfailingly helpful staff.

My thanks are due also to the two people on whose hospitality I rely in the course of almost all my trips from my Skye home to Scotland's capital. They are Catherine and Paul Boyle, my sister and my brother-in-law. To them, with love, this book is dedicated.

INTRODUCTION

Your Blooms in Agreement Like Elegant Music

Tyndrum, its indigenous architecture long since overwhelmed by as tasteless a set of buildings as one is likely to find anywhere this side of the Atlantic Ocean, is not the most obvious Scottish locality in which to begin a book about the relationship between humanity and the natural environment. A settlement's appearance and lay-out should embody some degree of feeling for that settlement's surroundings. But Tyndrum's hotels and fast-food eateries – collectively dominating the approaches to what was once a passingly attractive little village – appear to have been thrown up with practically no regard for their physical setting. Like Aviemore, another monument to poor taste and bad planning, the place contrives to be simultaneously bleak and garish. You wonder, stopping here, why Scotland sells itself so short to tourists. You wonder if we will ever do architectural justice to the Highlands. And so dispiriting is the overall effect of what you see about you that, on taking the Glencoe road and pulling up the hill out of Tyndrum, it seems hard to believe that you are about to set eyes on a scene which long ago inspired one of the finest pieces of nature poetry ever put together in the British Isles. But within four or five miles of Tyndrum, and dominating the view as you drive westwards, is Ben Dorain. And it was Ben Dorain that the eighteenth-century Highland poet, *Donnchadh Ban Mac an t-Saoir*, Duncan Ban MacIntyre, set out to celebrate in intricately crafted verse.

By Highland standards, as it happens, Ben Dorain, though impressive enough, is neither an especially high nor an especially attractive peak. Many other mountains have undoubtedly engendered every bit as much, and maybe more, affection. But no hill has been so honoured by a poet as this one was by Duncan MacIntyre. No hill has been so meticulously, so scrupulously, so lovingly described. No hill has a better claim to be mentioned on the opening page of a book intended to provide some insight into thinking about the Highland landscape.

Today, as a justifiable anxiety about this landscape's future both spreads and intensifies, Ben Dorain's literary associations are beginning to receive the recognition they unquestionably merit. Towards the start of a paper published in 1993 by Scottish Natural Heritage, for example, Professor

Christopher Smout, SNH's vice-chairman and Scotland's historiographer royal, quotes four lines from Iain Crichton Smith's modern verse translation of Duncan Ban MacIntyre's great Gaelic poem, *Moladh Beinn Dobhrain*, In Praise of Ben Dorain:

 *In flawless green raiment
  as bright as the diamond
  your blooms in agreement
  like elegant music.[1]

Professor Smout's publication, *The Highlands and the Roots of Green Consciousness*, deals mainly in external perceptions of the area to which its title refers. Duncan Ban MacIntyre is one of very few Highlanders named in the paper's pages. And MacIntyre is mentioned only in the bygoing. Professor Smout, however, is clearly taken with this Gaelic poet's work. He is especially attracted, one may safely guess, by the way in which MacIntyre's imagery anticipates a central feature of the ecological outlook which SNH, the government agency responsible for Scotland's natural environment, aspires strongly to promote. Ben Dorain's different types of vegetation, MacIntyre says, are 'in agreement'. They harmonise, as his lines put it, 'like elegant music'. This is to glimpse – metaphorically if not scientifically – the concept of the ecosystem. It is to discern that an apparent confusion of divergent species can constitute an integrated, somehow balanced, whole. Christopher Smout, though about to hurry on to other matters, accordingly pauses to hint at the possible significance of Duncan Ban MacIntyre's words. 'It is from roots like these,' the SNH vice-chairman comments, 'that an indigenous Scottish green consciousness could perhaps be traced.'[2]

With the proviso that 'green consciousness' is understood to embrace all the varied ways in which our little segment of humanity has endeavoured to engage positively and sympathetically with its natural surroundings, that sentence constitutes this book's starting point. The indigenous Scottish green consciousness postulated by Professor Smout, or so this book maintains, both exists and has roots which can be traced not just to Duncan Ban MacIntyre, though he will certainly feature in what follows, but to many other individuals even more remote from us in time.

To provide a full account of how people in Scotland have evolved a particular mode of thinking about the natural world would be a hugely

---

* Indicates material which has been translated from Gaelic.

daunting task. The following pages, therefore, contain no more than a rough outline of a very complex body of ideas. But even this quick sketch results from an attempt to get to grips with a great deal of history – any meaningful understanding of our Scottish green consciousness requires some investigation of the developing relationship between people and place in Scotland over the fifteen hundred years which separate us from the arrival here of the first folk to be known as Scots.

One might argue that the chronological scope of any such enquiry ought to be even greater; that it should start with the pioneering settlers who came to Scotland, some eight or nine millennia ago, when the ending of the last Ice Age made our country habitable by human beings. But green consciousness, to return to Christopher Smout's terminology, is essentially a cultural construct. What is at issue here, in other words, is not so much humanity's physical interaction with the natural environment as the manner in which people have responded mentally to that same environment. And the archaeological evidence on which we depend for our knowledge of Scotland's first inhabitants is necessarily of limited value in this regard. Such evidence certainly tells us something about the thoughts and emotions – as reflected, for example, in religious practices – of the peoples from whom it derives. But worthwhile insight into a society's deeper feelings is impossible in the absence of written records. Such insight, in fact, requires the survival of literary expression – literary expression, ideally, of the sort to be found in the poetry of Duncan Ban MacIntyre. That is why this book concerns itself so much with literature. And since no substantial body of Scottish literature survives from earlier epochs, the decision to begin with the fifth, sixth and seventh centuries is one that is imposed, in effect, by the nature of the available source material.

This book examines, then, a slice of time some one-and-a-half millennia in duration. The geographical limits of its subject matter are rather harder to lay down. Ireland, for reasons that will become apparent in due course, seems occasionally to loom as large as Scotland. Other, much more distant, places figure also. But the book concentrates, for the most part, on the Highlands – defined, for this purpose, in such a way as to include the Hebrides, Argyll, Arran, Bute and the entire Scottish mainland to the north and west of a line extending from the lower end of Loch Lomond to the Angus glens and thence, by way of Deeside and Donside, to the Moray Firth in the neighbourhood of Nairn. This is a big area. But a lot of Scotland lies outside its boundaries. And since what follows has already been presented as an attempt, in Christopher Smout's phrase, to trace the roots of a Scottish green consciousness, it may seem a shade arbitrary thus to exclude a substantial tract of Scotland from further consideration. A degree of bias may even be suspected on the part of an author who is himself a Highlander by birth, by residence and by inclination.

Since one of this book's objectives is to promote debate, reasoned criticism of the role here assigned to the Highlands is much to be encouraged. But as long as 'green consciousness' is understood to refer to our modern society's steadily expanding interest in nature conservation, environmental protection and other matters of that sort, no worthwhile case can possibly be made for assigning to Buchan, Fife, Galloway or the Borders, say, anything more than a small fraction of the importance which attaches, in this context, to the Highlands. Buchan, Fife, Galloway and the Borders, to be sure, are very nice; more attractive scenically, some might feel, than much of the Highlands. In relation to this book's central themes, however, such localities scarcely even register. For simplicity's sake, therefore, they are best set aside.

Reflect, for just a moment, on the various statutory designations which government and its agencies nowadays deploy in order to bestow official recognition on landscapes and habitats considered to be particularly valuable. The list of such designations is both long and growing. It includes Sites of Special Scientific Interest, National Nature Reserves, National Scenic Areas and several more besides. The protected sites which result from designation of this type are to be found, of course, all over Britain. As has been remarked repeatedly in recent years, however, an extraordinarily high proportion of them – from a United Kingdom point of view as well as from a purely Scottish one – are located in the Highlands. That is one semi-objective measurement of the region's environmental significance. It is mentioned here to help account for the high status accorded by this book to a part of Scotland which otherwise tends – usually on socio-economic grounds – to be regarded as comparatively disadvantaged.

SSSIs, NNRs, NSAs and all the rest, admittedly, are of little relevance to most of the many centuries about to be explored. Additional evidence is thus required to substantiate this book's eventual contention that the Highlands – even if the frame of reference and the basis of comparison were to be extended far beyond Scotland – have played a singularly distinctive role in the development of environmental thinking. The character of this evidence will become apparent in ensuing chapters. One of these chapters demonstrates that something approximating to a green consciousness, or at least a profound feeling for nature, can be discerned in the Highlands a thousand or so years before it can be detected in most of the rest of Europe. Another chapter contends that this same green consciousness – as indicated, for example, by the content of Duncan Ban MacIntyre's poetry – was carried forward, through the medium of Gaelic literature and Gaelic tradition, to the eighteenth century. A further chapter shows how a particular – though indubitably slanted – version of this Gaelic cultural heritage, as rendered into English by one of Duncan MacIntyre's Highland contemporaries, was decisively to shape and direct the so-called romantic movement from which the western world has derived so much of its approach to landscape and to nature.

In view of their dual role as a historically vital source of environmental awareness and a place of continuing environmental significance, it is ironic – not to say tragic – that the Highlands should have become the setting, as the twentieth century has advanced, for frequently embittered conflict between environmental organisations and those Highland communities where there survives something of that same Gaelic culture to which Scottish, British, European, even global, environmentalism owes so much. Particular disputes have turned on particular issues: on the designation of protected sites of the sort already mentioned; on the statutory safeguarding of geese and other birds; on whether or not there should be additional winter sports facilities in the Cairngorms, a large coastal quarry in Harris, afforestation in the Caithness and Sutherland flow country. The catalogue is familiar. Equally familiar is the extent to which each of these wrangles has been characterised by allegations, from the Highland side, that environmental objectors to afforestation, ski-ing or quarrying care little or nothing for those Highlanders to whom all such activity seems, rightly or wrongly, to promise economic benefits of a type which will promote community development. The record is a sad one. It is made all the sadder by environmentalist mutterings – themselves provoked, very often, by anti-environmentalist rhetoric – to the effect that Highlanders clearly have no regard for their natural environment and ought not to be entrusted, therefore, with its management.

If this book's analysis of earlier Highland attitudes is even approximately accurate, the fact that Highlanders and environmental campaigners are regularly at odds is, at first sight, as paradoxical as it is disappointing. The two groups, one might think, should be on the best of terms. That they are so often at loggerheads, a subsequent chapter suggests, is to be explained by the extent to which the wider world's understanding of the Highlands has diverged, over several centuries, from the way in which the area was – and generally still is – understood by Highlanders themselves. Environmentalism, this book argues, most certainly had Highland roots. But its development, the argument

15

continues, was such as to ensure that environmentalists were ultimately influenced much more by external – and usually romantic – perceptions of the Highlands than they were influenced by Highland realities. The result has been that the environmentalist outlook nowadays appears both alien and threatening to many of the Highland inheritors of the very Gaelic culture in which environmentalism itself, to some degree at least, originated. This is a state of affairs which, in a better-ordered world, would never have arisen. It is also a state of affairs which, now that it has arisen, demands remedial action. Hence this book's attempt to reconcile the thinking of two sets of people who have far more in common than they might readily believe.

Media reporting of the issues at stake between Highlanders, on the one side, and environmentalists, on the other, tends to utilise militaristic metaphors of the kind an earlier paragraph indulged in almost automatically. We read, or hear, of battle, conflict, attack, confrontation. We are encouraged to think, as a result, in terms of winners and of losers, in terms of victory and defeat. But war can also end in peace negotiations. Enemies can, and do, become allies. Former foes can, and do, put previous disagreement behind them in order to pursue new and larger goals. That is the approach this book urges on both parties to the hostilities in which Highlanders and environmentalists have for too long been engaged. Nor need an agreed way forward be all that difficult to map out. There is no good reason, a concluding chapter argues, as to why Highlanders and environmentalists should not rapidly unite around a single strategy for the Highland future. And in order to appreciate why some such strategy is so urgently required, it is necessary only to contemplate what has been at stake in one of the several controversies already mentioned: the much-publicised dispute revolving around proposals to open a so-called super quarry at Lingerabay on the east side of Harris.

Supporters of the Lingerabay development, which was the subject of a protracted public enquiry at the time these pages were being written, tend to concentrate, inevitably, on the jobs it could generate and on the obvious importance of such jobs to one of the most severely depopulated and socially fragile localities in the United Kingdom. Opponents of the quarry mostly point, equally inevitably, to the damage such an undertaking might easily inflict on the Harris landscape and on both the terrestrial and marine ecosystems in the projected quarry site's general vicinity.

Neither the Lingerabay enquiry nor its outcome are crucial to this book. It is worth dwelling for an instant, however, on Lingerabay's peculiarly compelling symbolism. Here is a community whose Gaelic language embodies – in the poetry of Duncan Ban MacIntyre and in the writings, too, of many other people – a deep reverence for mountains. But here also is a locality where the self-same community's long-term survival, together with the survival of its traditional culture, can plausibly be said to depend – for such is the almost unimaginable scale of the planned quarry – on the physical removal of just the sort of mountain to which Highlanders have long attached a huge emotional significance.

At Lingerabay, then, to wish to protect a hill from a quarry company is to attract accusations of conspiring in the drawn-out, but seemingly inexorable, depeopling of an island and the consequent destruction of that island's way of life. Proponents of the opposite line, however, fare little or no better. To insist that the quarry company must be allowed to create the employment its representatives have promised is at once to be portrayed as caring nothing for the mountain which will necessarily be obliterated in the process.

There could be no more convincing illustration of the extent to which a concern for community and culture, on the one hand, and a concern for the natural environment, on the other, are so readily regarded in the modern Highlands as mutually incompatible. Environmentalists and Highlanders, it might justifiably be concluded, are destined to remain forever locked in combat – one group making progress only at the expense of the other. As already indicated, however, this book takes an altogether more optimistic line. It contends that, in the Scottish Highlands anyway, people and nature can, after all, co-exist in ways which will benefit both. And it seeks to establish a basis for such co-existence in a heritage which belongs equally to Highlanders and to environmentalists. That heritage will shortly be explored in detail. But first it makes sense to investigate the origins of the Highland sensitivities which make it so difficult for environmentalists to handle episodes of the Lingerabay variety. These sensitivities date mostly from the hundred or so years following the Jacobite Rebellion of 1745.

CHAPTER ONE

Everyone Who Ever Mattered is Dead and Gone

The upper reaches of Glen Shiel, in the part of the West Highlands called Kintail, are steep and rocky. A road and a river jostle here for elbow-room as they plunge through a series of narrow gorges. Especially in winter, when deep snow drives them down from the high tops, red deer are everywhere. Now and then, in places too precipitous even for deer, you glimpse long-haired, big-horned goats. But there are few other signs of life; certainly no sign of human habitation; not even when you reach the part of the glen where the mountains, as it were, draw back a little to make room for several fields and some small areas of woodland.

This spot, so larger-scale maps tell you, is Achadh nan Seileach, a Gaelic phrase denoting both the relative flatness of the place and the presence here of willow trees. In any broadly similar part of Europe – in Norway, for example – this is where you might expect to find a village. But the Scottish Highlands, though their physical structure and their climate give them something of the appearance of the region to the west and north of Oslo, have had a very different history from Rogaland, Hordaland or Nord Trondelag. There is no settlement to be seen in the vicinity of Achadh nan Seileach. What can be seen, however, and with no great effort on your part, is a good deal of evidence that Achadh nan Seileach was not always the unpopulated locality it so clearly is today.

Leave your car by the roadside. Take a look around the grassy meadows which slope gently towards the River Shiel, its pace a lot less hectic here than further up the glen. On both sides of the river, and especially on its northern bank, you quickly come across the remains of several stone-built homes. The walls of one or two still stand some three, or four, or five feet clear of their surroundings. Others are reduced now to little more than roughly squared-off undulations in the turf.

On a fine summer's evening, with the sun picking out every detail of peaks like Sgurr an t-Searraich, Sgurr nan Saighead, Sgurr Fhuarain and Sgurr na Carnaich, this is a most attractive corner. Seating yourself on the ground with your back to what is left of the gable of a long-abandoned house, its stones still retaining a good deal of the day's heat, it is tempting to speculate – if you know a little of the place's past – that this might be the very spot once occupied by the only individuals ever to have set down in print some impression of how Achadh nan Seileach seemed before its people were expelled forever from their homes.

Samuel Johnson and James Boswell came this way in the course of the trip they made from London to the Hebrides in 1773; leaving Inverness on 30 August; spending that night at Fort Augustus; staying the following night in Glen Moriston; getting to Achadh nan Seileach – with their four horses, their servant and their two guides – on the afternoon of 1 September. An hour or two before, the party having halted to allow their horses to graze for a little, Johnson had spent some moments 'resting', as he expressed it, 'on a bank such as a writer of romance might have delighted to feign'. Romance, it should be said, held no appeal for Samuel Johnson – then one of England's best known literary figures. His, as a modern Scottish writer has remarked, was very much a 'reasoning mind'. But Johnson, though only three days out from Inverness, was already sufficiently taken with the Highlands to appreciate that his excursion had the makings of a first-rate story. While waiting for his horse to be got ready for the onward trek to Glenelg and the Skye ferry, Samuel Johnson had accordingly 'conceived the thought' of the 'narration' eventually issued as A Journey to the Western Islands of Scotland. Achadh nan Seileach, reached at the point when the notion of such a publication was thus beginning to take shape, possibly features more than it might otherwise have done in Johnson's reminiscences of his Highland jauntings. It features also in the separately produced Journal of a Tour to the Hebrides which James Boswell, Johnson's future biographer, was to bring out some time after his friend had demonstrated the existence of a huge demand for travel books about the Scottish Highlands.[1]

Auknasheals, Johnson called this 'village' which he described as 'consisting of many huts, perhaps twenty, built all of drystone, that is, stones piled up without mortar'. In Boswell's account, its author's Scots tongue being more capable than Samuel Johnson's English one of getting to grips with Gaelic pronunciation, the place is Auchnasheal – 'a kind of rural village,' as Boswell puts it, 'a number of cottages being built together, as we saw all along the Highlands'.[2]

Precisely how many people lived in Achadh nan Seileach in 1773 there is now no way of knowing; perhaps a hundred; perhaps half as many again; certainly 'considerable numbers', according to Johnson's description of the crowd which promptly surrounded him and his companions. But irrespective of its exact size, this, as Boswell comments, was clearly both a welcoming and a hospitable community:

At Auchnasheal we sat down on a green turf-seat at the end of a house; they brought us out two wooden dishes of milk which we tasted. One of them was frothed like a syllabub. I saw a woman preparing it with such a stick as is used for chocolate, and in the same manner.[3]

Achadh nan Seileach would survive for some years yet. As Johnson and Boswell were quickly to learn in the course of their 1773 travels, however, the wider Highland society to which the people of Achadh nan Seileach belonged was starting to be radically reconstructed. Not least among the causes of this reconstruction was the transformation of the Highland aristocracy – the clan chieftains of earlier times – into landowning magnates on the long-established southern model. This particular metamorphosis was greatly pleasing to the British government – its ministers being understandably anxious to integrate into the United Kingdom a still largely tribal region which, as recently as the 1740s, had been in a state of armed rebellion. But the social revolution precipitated by their traditional leadership's adoption of an openly commercial approach to land management was one which benefited very few folk of the sort who turned out to receive Samuel Johnson and James Boswell that September afternoon at Achadh nan Seileach. As chieftains-turned-landlords cast about for the revenues needed to finance the lavish lifestyles deemed appropriate to their new status, the rents which these men levied were ruthlessly jacked up. And when age-old communities like Achadh nan Seileach proved incapable of yielding the desired return, as many of them shortly did, most such communities were simply obliterated with a view to their lands being released for alternative, and much more profitable, uses.

The beginnings of these upheavals were observed with deep disgust by Samuel Johnson. Despite his having nothing but contempt for other people's attempts to portray Highlanders as having traditionally lived in a state of primeval virtue and simplicity, Johnson was enough of an old-fashioned Tory, even a Jacobite, to have hoped that the Highlands might have preserved at least a little of the pre-capitalist order. Here, he fondly believed, something other than the cash nexus – already the dominating social fact in so much of the rest of Britain – would connect folk of higher rank with those of lesser fortune. Such indeed had been the case in the era of clanship. But that era, Samuel Johnson now reported sadly, had passed into history. And all sorts of ancient ties and obligations had been discarded in the process. 'Their chiefs,' Johnson wrote of Highlanders, 'have already lost much of their influence; and as they gradually degenerate from patriarchal rulers to rapacious landlords, they will divest themselves of the little that remains.'[4]

One of Johnson's Highland contemporaries, the North Uist poet, *Iain MacCodrum*, made the same point still more bitterly:

> *The warrior chiefs are gone
> who had a yearning for the truth,
> who had regard for their faithful followers . . .
>
> Look around you
> and see the nobility
> without pity to poor folk,
>   without kindness to friends;
> they are of the opinion
> that you do not belong to the soil,
> and though they have left you destitute
>   they cannot see it as a loss.[5]

MacCodrum urged Highlanders to emigrate to North America – 'to the country of milk, to the country of honey, to the country where you may buy land to your will' – rather than submit to the tyrannical exactions of their landlords. John MacRae, a Kintail poet of the same period and a man who was himself to settle in North Carolina, was equally insistent on the need to get away:

> *Let us go and may God's blessing be with us.
> Let us go and charter a vessel.
>
> Better that than to remain under landlords
> who will not tolerate tenantry;
>
> who would prefer gold to a brave man.[6]

Johnson and Boswell had heard something of such discontents even before they reached Achadh nan Seileach. 'Of the farm which he himself occupied,' Glen Moriston's innkeeper had informed them, 'the rent had, in twenty-five years, been advanced from five to twenty pounds, which he found himself so little able to pay that he would be glad to try his fortune in some other place.' This was bad enough. What was much worse, from the standpoint of the resident population anyway, was the eventual discovery by Highland landlords that not even rent rises on such a scale were capable of producing anything like the returns to be got from the sheep farmers who began to move into the Highlands during the couple of decades following the excursion made here by Samuel Johnson and James Boswell.[7]

Immediately to the south of Glen Shiel is Glen Garry where sheep were displacing people as early as the 1780s. A 'triple rent', observed a local clergyman of the time, was then on offer for much of Kintail also. But the numerous MacLennans and MacRaes whose names are entered in Glen Shiel's eighteenth-century rentals were, for the moment, spared evictions of the kind occurring in Glen Garry. Kintail's proprietor, MacKenzie of Seaforth, according to this same parish minister, 'absolutely refused' the threefold rent increase so temptingly held out to him – 'declaring,' or so the minister continued, 'that he would never prefer sheep to men'.[8]

Such attitudes, however laudable, were not destined to endure. The Seaforth MacKenzies, being ultimately no more immune to the charms of southern money than others of their class, were soon playing their own prominent part in the events which became known as the Highland Clearances. Sheep farmers accordingly began arriving in Kintail in the early nineteenth century. To start with, admittedly, they did not have things all their own way – David Dick, who took over the lower part of Glen Shiel during this period, being the understandably outraged victim of repeated attacks on both his stock and property. 'I have had another proof of the savage brutality and barbarous ferocity of the people here in deliberately killing three of my horses this morning,' Dick wrote to MacKenzie of Seaforth on 25 June 1820. 'The fourth and only remaining one escaped alive with a fractured skull.' But David Dick was clearly not to be intimidated by Glen Shiel's original occupants, however much they tried to frighten him away. 'The question,' he commented of the people causing him so much trouble, 'seems now to be whether the property of this country is to belong to them or the lawful owners.' As to how that question would eventually be answered, there was never any doubt.[9]

So total and far-reaching were the clearances now set in train that, by the time evictions ceased, no more than fourteen of Glen Shiel's thousands and thousands of acres remained in the occupancy of descendants of the people living here at the point when Samuel Johnson and James Boswell had put in their brief appearance. Hundreds of people, one Kintail man commented in the 1840s, had been 'entirely swept away'. Many had left, in altogether desperate circumstances, for

North America. Others had been 'crowded', as a further account puts it, on to miniscule crofts or smallholdings by the shores of Loch Duich – the fiord-like Atlantic inlet you come upon when driving onwards from Glen Shiel to the Skye Bridge. Since it was invariably characteristic of nineteenth-century crofts that they were utterly incapable of providing their occupants with anything approximating to a worthwhile livelihood, the Loch Duich people – excluded now from the much more spacious lands their ancestors had worked for generations – were 'dependent for subsistence upon the laborious and uncertain pursuit of the herring fishery'. As for Achadh nan Seileach, where Johnson and Boswell had sat drinking milk in the September sun, its pastures had been given over completely to sheep and its ruins quarried for the materials that Glen Shiel's south country shepherds used to construct the many field boundary walls still to be seen by visitors to this part of the Highlands.[10]

Among the many people who emigrated from Kintail to North America in the 1830s was a man called Neil MacLennan. Neil's son, Duncan, became a tailor in Cape Breton Island, Nova Scotia. Duncan's son, named Sam, was a doctor in the Cape Breton mining township of Glace Bay. And Sam's son, Hugh, developed into one of twentieth-century Canada's more challenging, more thoughtful, novelists. This latest MacLennan was to make his fiction the vehicle for several determined efforts to delineate a Canadian national identity. But he was also to remain intensely conscious of his Scottish Highland origins:

> Whenever I stop to think about it, the knowledge that I am three-quarters Scotch, and Highland at that, seems like a kind of doom from which I am too Scotch even to think of praying for deliverance. I can thank my father for this last-ditch neurosis. He was entirely Scotch; he was a living specimen of a most curious heritage. In spite of his medical knowledge, which was large; in spite of his quick, nervous vitality and tireless energy, he was never able to lay to rest the beasties which went bump in his mind at three o'clock in the morning. It mattered nothing that he was a third-generation Canadian who had never seen the Highlands before he visited them on leave in the First World War. He never needed to go there to understand whence he came or what he was. He was neither a Scot nor was he Scottish; he never used these genteel appellations which now are supposed to be *de rigeur*. He

was simply Scotch. All the perplexity and doggedness of the race was in him, its loneliness, tenderness and affection, its deceptive vitality, its quick flashes of violence, its dog-whistle sensitivity to sounds to which Anglo-Saxons are stone deaf, its incapacity to tell its heart to foreigners save in terms which foreigners do not comprehend, its resigned indifference to whether they comprehend or not. *It's not easy being Scotch*, he told me once. To which, I suppose, another Scotchman might say, *It wasn't meant to be.*[11]

Hugh MacLennan made his own journey to Kintail in the 1950s, driving north across the English-Scottish border in an aged Vauxhall:

Next day I was in the true north of Scotland among the sheep, the heather, the whin, the mists, and the homes of the vanished races. Such sweeps of emptiness I never saw in Canada before I went to the Mackenzie River later in the same summer. But this Highland emptiness, only a few hundred miles above the massed population of England, is a far different thing from the emptiness of our own North West Territories. Above the sixtieth parallel in Canada you feel that nobody but God has ever been there before you, but in a deserted Highland glen you feel that everyone who ever mattered is dead and gone.[12]

So accustomed are we to the notion that the literary and artistic imagination should warm automatically to the Scottish Highlands, should find places like Kintail a source of aesthetic – even spiritual – satisfaction, that it comes as something of a shock to discover that Hugh MacLennan reacted very differently to what he saw of Glen Shiel; that he was glad, in the end, to be out of Scotland; pleased to be on his way back to Canada. What, then, differentiated this North American novelist from all those other visitors who, for the last two hundred years or more, have revelled in the undoubted beauty of our Highland landscape? The answer, of course, is to be found in Glen Shiel's history and in Hugh MacLennan's deep awareness of it. His response to Kintail was conditioned by his knowledge of what clearance and eviction had done both to his family and to the community of which his family had been part. Although this twentieth-century writer had been raised in a home which was separated from the Highlands by several thousand miles, as well as by three generations, he harboured what one critic has called 'a sense of belonging to a wronged people'. In Hugh MacLennan's novels this bitter inheritance is partly assuaged by the way in which the Highland-descended North Americans among his characters find a forward-looking basis for their lives in the task of constructing a new nation. But for all his pride in Canada, for all his feeling for that country, there was enough of the Highlander in Hugh MacLennan to make the actuality of a depopulated Scottish glen a desperately hard thing to accept.[13]

How to make clear the way in which our people's historical experiences continue to shape Highland sensibilities? How to explain the complex of emotions which are bound up with those landscapes where, as Hugh MacLennan wrote, you feel that everyone who ever mattered is dead and gone? Historians of the Highlands, and there have been a lot of them of late, are seldom very good on issues of this kind. Emotions of the sort revealed by Hugh MacLennan seem to make historians terribly uneasy. This is because historians, most academically-inclined historians of Scotland anyway, tend to eschew both folk tradition and imaginative literature as guides to understanding. Such historians like to focus on what seems self-evidently 'factual'; preferring to deal with the economic circumstances surrounding the Highland Clearances rather than with the not-so-measurable impact of these events on the attitudes and on the outlook of the people who were most affected by them.

The twentieth-century Highland poet and novelist, Iain Crichton Smith, translator of Duncan MacIntyre's great poem on Ben Dorain, was once asked for his opinions about historians and history. He replied:

> What many people do, if they are not inside a particular culture, is choose certain facts out of an enormous number of facts and put them together in a historical fashion. And Scotland has suffered from bad history of this kind. But what I like to think about is a kind of history lived on the bone rather than an intellectual creation, which is why I think that poets and writers are better historians, often, than the professionals.[14]

Crichton Smith went on to acknowledge that we need to have historians as well as makers of poetry and fiction. And so we do. But his underlying point, that works of literature can be better guides to the past than works of history, is one which – as indicated earlier – is particularly valid in relation to this book's central theme. The way people feel about our Highland landscape, about our natural environment, depends very largely on the mental baggage, so to speak, that they haul around with them. A great deal of that baggage, as can be seen from Hugh MacLennan's response to Glen Shiel, has been carried forward from the past. But the particular past from which it derives, whether in MacLennan's case or in the case of Highlanders more generally, is one better accessed by way of poems, songs and novels than by way of histories of the sort that Crichton Smith had in mind – those laborious exercises in 'balance' and 'objectivity' which, though wholly meritorious in their own terms, fail miserably to explain passions of the sort so strongly evident in Hugh MacLennan's comments on Kintail.

The origins of the manifestly gaping chasm between 'literary' and 'historical' interpretations of the Highland past can perhaps be traced, as Iain Crichton Smith suggests, to the fact that very little Highland history has been written from 'inside' the culture with which it purports to deal. The academic perspective on the Scottish Highlands is typically external. Being external, and making a positive virtue of a neutrality which verges at times on the amoral, most academic histories of the clearances seem either uncomprehending or insulting to Highlanders whose feelings about these events are fuelled principally by folk memory and by the various cultural expressions to which folk memory has given rise. There is nothing that is at all inevitable about this state of affairs, however. It is a function of the strangely unambitious character of most recent renderings of the Highland past. It is a function, in particular, of an apparent reluctance on the part of Scottish academics to take on board the findings of those other scholars who have attempted to get to grips with what has been done to the numerous societies elsewhere on our planet which have more recently undergone experiences similar to those which once affected the northern half of Scotland. Turn, even for a moment, to books of the type produced by a commentator like Edward Said – a man whose work deals enormously illuminatingly with what is involved in the reconstruction of personal and group identity in colonialism's psychologically shattering aftermath – and you become immediately aware of just how impoverished, by comparison, is much of our approach to Highland history. Said aspires to move from an analysis of events to an understanding of people's intellectual and emotional responses to events. And his principal guide to such responses is imaginative literature.[15]

The academic historians of the Highlands, in stark contrast, generally disregard the insights which such literature can provide. One of the most impressive and productive such historians mentions the 'theatrical works' and other literary forms which have been inspired by the Highland Clearances only as a prelude to dismissing such manifestations of human creativity as irrelevant to his concerns. All 'popular' interpretations of the Highland past are similarly cast into outer darkness by this same authority to whom 'academic writing' is invariably a better guide to a community's historical experiences than such a community's own collective memory as expressed in song or story.[16]

By such means is the university-based study of Highland history disconnected from what is actually going on in the Highlands where, on those numerous occasions when 'popular' conceptions of Highland history impact on contemporary decisions about nature conservation and associated matters, it is rather less than helpful simply to assert that Highlanders have got their own past badly wrong. So much more constructive is analysis of the sort in which Edward Said so fascinatingly specialises; analysis which, far from leaving such matters out of account, actually tries to make sense of what the generality of people feel to be significant about the means by which their communities came to be as they now are; analysis which consequently gives due weight to all the varied ways in which human beings have reacted to the destruction of community and culture in those parts of the world subjected, in the course of the last two centuries, to imperial conquest and subordination of one kind or another.

To look to former colonies for enlightenment on the Highlands, it should be stressed at this point, is not to say that northern Scotland was colonised in the way that Africa, for example, was colonised. Such was clearly not the case. It is, all the same, a highly suggestive circumstance that the British variety of imperialism, even the very vocabulary of this country's particular brand of racism and colonialism, owes a good deal of its early development to the political requirement to rationalise and justify central authority's efforts to impose its will on Scottish Highlanders – or, if not on Highlanders, then on the Irish with whom, as this book will several times repeat, Highlanders have long had much in common.

Underpinning the destruction of the largely self-governing Lordship of the Isles in the 1490s; underpinning the Statutes of Iona, the Massacre of Glencoe and other seventeenth-century attempts to break the Highland clans; underpinning the final assault on clanship in Culloden's brutal aftermath; underpinning every effort to subvert and eliminate those features of their traditional society which gave Highlanders some degree of independence and autonomy: underpinning all of this was a profound conviction, held in Edinburgh every bit as much as it was held in London, that the people thus being brought to heel were an irredeemably inferior set of human beings.

In one of those 'theatrical works' which the historian quoted earlier was so anxious to disparage, John McGrath's 1973 musical, *The Cheviot, the*

Stag and the Black, Black Oil, Lord Cask and Lady Phosphate, owners of one of the many sporting estates which have flourished in the Highlands since the nineteenth century, point their shotguns in the direction of their tenantry and sing:

> You had better learn your place,
> You're a low and servile race.[17]

Similarly disparaging refrains have echoed around the north of Scotland for at least six hundred years – ever since the Kincardineshire chronicler, John of Fordoun, writing in the 1380s, set out to differentiate 'domesticated and cultured' Lowlanders like himself from the 'wild and untamed' folk who lived beyond the Highland Line.[18]

Fourteenth-century Highlanders were thought merely 'wicked' by their critics. Sixteenth-century Highlanders were 'barbarous' as well. And much stronger language would soon follow. In the early seventeenth century, for instance, Highlanders are routinely described in the records of successive Scottish governments, as 'void of all religion and humanity'; 'given . . . over to all kinds of barbarity'; 'void of all fear and knowledge of God'; collectively responsible, in one especially comprehensive indictment, for 'most detestable, damnable and odious murders, fires, ravishing of women, witchcraft and depredations'. Such labels – as is, of course, their purpose – serve quickly to dehumanise those to whom they are attached. And such dehumanisation, in its turn, serves to render acceptable, even admirable, oppression of a kind that otherwise would tend to be regarded as quite wrong.[19]

The MacDonalds of Glencoe, to the politicians who ordered their slaughter, were a 'mere sept of thieves' – people not to be seen as inhabiting the same moral and ethical universe as their persecutors. Those other Highlanders who rallied to the Jacobite cause in 1745 seemed, to most southerners, to be similarly beyond the pale. They were 'wild and barbarous beyond expression', 'uncouth savages', 'robbers', 'hungry wolves', 'bare-arsed banditti'; a people who, as was remarked by one cabinet minister, the Duke of Newcastle, deserved only to be 'absolutely reduced'. And absolutely reduced Highlanders duly were – their failure to qualify as 'civilised' rendering them liable to treatment of a kind that eighteenth-century Britain would never have considered meting out to any of the several European nations with which the country was so frequently at war.[20]

His troops, one English officer reported from the north of Scotland in the summer following Culloden, were 'carrying fire and destruction as they passed, shooting the vagrant Highlanders that they meet in the mountains and driving off their cattle'. This was to treat Highlanders as Afghans and Zulus would one day be treated. It was to do so with the same ostensible justification – that justification, being, of course, the lowly racial status which all such peoples were allocated by their imperial masters. Nor did such stereotyping cease, in the Highland case, with the elimination of the military threat which the clans had long posed to their southern neighbours. By the later part of the eighteenth century, when the Highlands had become peaceable enough to be attracting their first tourists in the shape of travellers like Samuel Johnson and James Boswell, racist characterisations of the region's indigenous inhabitants remained as common as ever. 'The Lowlanders,' commented one Scottish writer, John Pinkerton, in the 1780s, 'are acute, industrious, sensible, erect, free; the Highlanders indolent, slavish, strangers to industry.' This distinction was to be attributed, Pinkerton thought, to the 'Gothic' origin of Lowland Scots – Goths, or Saxons, being of self-evidently finer stock than the Celts from whom Highlanders, like the Highland population's Irish counterparts, were unfortunate enough to be descended.[21]

The 'notions of racial superiority' which were thus developed by the United Kingdom's ruling orders in the course of their dealings with Ireland and the Scottish Highlands, one historian of empire has remarked, 'would easily be adapted to justify the enslavement of Africans and the conquest of the Indian subcontinent'. Nor was this a wholly one-way traffic. Just as racist gibes which were originally hurled against Celts could afterwards be directed against Africans and Asians, so new and improved taunts were increasingly imported from overseas colonies to be targeted on Celts. Such practices are particularly evident, as far as the Highlands are concerned, in the career of Patrick Sellar – the sheep farmer and estate manager who was almost singlehandedly responsible for the enforced removal of many hundreds, possibly thousands, of people from Strathnaver, the Strath of Kildonan and other parts of Sutherland in the course of the nineteenth century's second decade. To Sellar, Sutherland people seemed merely 'a parcel of beggars with no stock but cunning and laziness'. Like Highlanders generally, they were 'barbarous hordes' and 'aborigines' whose position 'in relation to the enlightened nations of Europe' was 'not very different from that betwixt the American colonists and the aborigines of that country'.[22]

In the light of Sellar's thinking, so redolent of the colonialist mentality, it becomes easier to see the relevance to Highland circumstances of Edward Said's musings on the nature of imperialism. Said, whose Palestinian origins are evident in his strong sympathy for peoples who have undergone external domination, writes thus about the general phenomenon of which the fate of the Scottish Highlands was merely one very local aspect:

> Neither imperialism nor colonialism is a simple act of accumulation and acquisition. Both are supported and perhaps even impelled by impressive ideological formations that include notions that certain territories and peoples *require* and beseech domination, as well as forms of knowledge affiliated with domination: the vocabulary of classic nineteenth-century imperialism is plentiful with such words and concepts as 'inferior' or 'subject races', 'subordinate peoples', 'dependency', 'expansion' and 'authority'.[23]

These remarks have obvious resonances in a Highland context. So do the very similar observations made in the 1930s by an Irish writer, Daniel Corkery, whose primary target, needless to say, was the British ruling-class or 'ascendancy' which had so long governed his country:

> The first article in an ascendancy's creed is, and always has been, that the natives are a lesser breed and that everything that is theirs (except their land and their gold) is therefore of little value. If they have had a language . . . it cannot have been a civilised language, cannot have been anything but a *patois* used by the hillmen among themselves; and as for their literature, the less said about it the better.[24]

This was certainly the case with regard to the Highlands. No aspect of Highland life was more consistently derided and despised, over the centuries, than the Gaelic language which Highlanders shared with the Irish and which the Scottish and English politicians who aspired to rule both Ireland and the Highlands clearly considered, quite correctly, to be a serious obstacle in the way of their plans for these places.

In 1616, when legislating for the establishment of schools in Highland parishes, the Scottish Privy Council took the opportunity to underline its position on the language issue. The 'English tongue' was everywhere to be the medium of instruction, the privy council insisted. Gaelic, being 'one of the chief and principal causes of the . . . barbarity and incivility' for which the Highlands were now a byword, was to be 'abolished and removed'. Those provisions, like lots of others couched in similar vein, were most seriously intended. Gaelic was ideally to be made extinct. And if the language has survived into modern times, as somehow it has contrived to do, this is certainly not due to any lack of commitment to its extirpation on the part of the various external authorities to whom Highlanders have been subject. The Scottish Society for the Propagation of Christian Knowledge, an educational organisation which took over in the eighteenth century where the Scottish Privy Council had earlier left off, was committed to 'rooting out' Gaelic. One wholly representative observer of the early nineteenth-century Highland scene considered it 'vain to attempt to change the current of thought and action in the Highlands while the language is allowed to remain'. And there was nothing that was unique about the Kintyre teacher who commented a little wanly in the 1880s: 'I do wish Gaelic were an unknown language.'[25]

Officially inspired hostility towards those things which were distinctively Highland did not stop, of course, with attacks on Gaelic. 'Since one of the purposes of colonial education,' Edward Said remarks of the policies pursued by the French and the British in their many overseas territories, 'was to promote the history of France or Britain, the same education also demoted the native history.' That the Highland experience was virtually identical is implicit in many comments made by Highlanders about their schooling. An especially memorable illustration of the point – and one that is particularly relevant to this book's purposes – can be found in a semi-autobiographical novel, *Highland River*. The novel's author was Neil Gunn. Gunn's subject was a north of Scotland childhood at the beginning of the twentieth century. And what is striking about that childhood is the contrast Gunn makes between the different types of knowledge available to Kenn, his novel's hero.[26]

From his family, from his community and from his natural surroundings, especially from the river of the novel's title, Kenn absorbs much that Gunn presents as rich and real and meaningful. The ambience of Kenn's school, in contrast, is both alien and threatening. There 'the master was a roaring lion in a cage':

> Nor had any of the things the master taught any joy in them. History and geography were both taken that day. The history was concerned with English kings and queens and the dates of battles. There had been Plantaganets. Now there were the Tudors. That Henry VIII had six wives did not really interest the children. They would have gaped in the same way if he had had six hundred. What was important was the exact number six. A near shot, such as seven or eight, would have made the lion roar.
>
> The geography was an even worse ordeal because, as it happened, they were dealing with that portion of the British Isles that contains

a great number of towns, each with its 'most important industry'. Some of the towns, like Birmingham or Nottingham, had several industries. Kenn's memory was his weakest part and he was capable of transposing small arms and lace with an air of innocent calm.

He got thrashed twice.[27]

In such a setting, as Said and others point out, to attempt to recover and reinterpret sympathetically the much-derided 'native' past is to engage in an act of protest, even of rebellion. So it was in African and Asian colonies where the beginnings of the independence struggle were necessarily bound up with efforts to rehabilitate those cultures and histories which the imperialist schools had ignored or suppressed. So it was in Ireland where the intellectual origins both of Sinn Fein and of the Easter Rising – the one a party seeking political autonomy and the other an armed insurrection which helped secure eventual self-government – are to be found in that country's growing interest, from the later nineteenth century onwards, in its ancient Gaelic heritage.

Irish developments had their parallels in Scotland, especially northern Scotland. John Murdoch, a Highland land reformer who knew Ireland well and who kept in close touch with a number of leading Irish nationalists, made this comment to a royal commission which was established in 1883 to look into the causes of crofting discontents:

> The language and lore of the Highlanders being treated with despite has tended to crush their self-respect and to repress that self-reliance without which no people can advance. When a man was convinced that his language was a barbarism, his lore as filthy rags, and that the only good thing about him – his land – was, because of his general worthlessness, to go to a man of another race, what remained . . . that he should fight for?[28]

It thus seemed obvious to John Murdoch – just as it gradually came to seem obvious to those men and women who would one day rid Africa and Asia of their colonial regimes – that any set of people, if they were to be 'prosperous, comfortable and independent', must 'respect themselves' and 'must set full value on what belongs to them'. The state schools established in the Highlands and Islands in the wake of the Scottish Education Act of 1872, in Murdoch's opinion, were of no help in this connection. It was bad enough that they were 'imparting instruction in a foreign language'. It was still more deplorable that, as a result of their neglecting both Gaelic and the cultural heritage to which Gaelic gave access, these same schools were 'inspiring' Highland children 'with respect and love for any place but their own'. What was needed, Murdoch thought, was something entirely different. Highlanders had to be made to feel that 'they themselves, and the things which belong to them, are of greater value in the world than they have for some time been taught to regard them'.[29]

At the end of the twentieth century, when Gaelic-medium primary schools are proliferating across the Scottish Highlands, this seems comparatively uncontroversial. But such was not at all the case in Murdoch's lifetime. Then the Irish, with whom this Highland radical so warmly identified, were routinely depicted as apes and chimpanzees in a British pictorial press – which had eagerly gulped down, if it had not fully digested, Charles Darwin's theory of evolution. Then newspaper editorials dealt habitually in the notion that Highlanders, just like the Irish, were a less-developed species whose many difficulties were to be attributed, for the most part, to their own innate failings. Then the idea that Gaelic-speakers possessed a worthwhile history was one that, from a southern perspective, seemed very little short of an absurdity.[30]

Change was a long time coming. The school Neil Gunn depicts in *Highland River* was probably not untypical of the early twentieth-century Highlands. It was to have its mid-twentieth-century counterparts also. In a poem significantly entitled *A Proper Schooling*, the Skye-born poet, Aonghas MacNeacail, precisely delineates – and angrily protests against – the way in which the Scottish education system, even in the 1950s, made a clear distinction between his own people's past and the other, allegedly more important, pasts which dominated his school's history syllabus:

> *it wasn't history but memory
> the day Kirsty baptised the factor
> with piss from a pot she took from the backroom
> to the meeting up on the brae of the croft
> not spilling a single drop
>
> it wasn't history but memory
> the day the township's warriors stood
> on the banks of the glen river
> confronting the sheriff's surly troops
> who marched that far then returned without dipping a toe
> clutching their wads of eviction orders.[31]

Aonghas MacNeacail's 'memories' concern, as it happens, the land agitation which John Murdoch did so much to promote – that protracted battle for security of tenure which, when it was finally won by crofters in 1886, brought clearance and eviction to an end. These were momentous times in the Highlands. And MacNeacail – who has written elsewhere that it took him 'many years . . . to put together fragments of the myth and lore which underlay my language and my being' – is here explicitly seeking to incorporate into 'history' his own Skye community's collective experience of a crofting campaign which was decisively and permanently to curtail the power of landlords. That campaign, from Aonghas MacNeacail's standpoint, is every bit as important a part of the past as the English history forced on Kenn in *Highland River*. Indeed it is much more important. For if today's Highlanders are made fully aware of what was accomplished by their ancestors, so MacNeacail implies, then today's Highlanders will be more readily persuaded to assert themselves politically on their own account.[32]

MacNeacail's ambition thus 'to shape a weapon' from the Highland past is shared by another modern poet, Angus Peter Campbell from South Uist. Campbell, reflecting in adult life on a schoolroom experience which must have closely paralleled the humiliation endured by Neil Gunn's Kenn, wishes he had then understood what he now understands about his people's history:

> and oh that I would have known
> of Columba and Alasdair MacColla
> or screamed of the MacMhuirichs . . .
> but all I knew
> was that my Gaelic father was only a joiner
> and that my Gaelic mother scrubbed floors
> in a polished English world.[33]

Columba, MacColla and the MacMhuirichs – the first, the great sixth-century churchman known to Gaels as *Colum Cille*, the second a seventeenth-century general who fought alongside the Marquis of Montrose, the third the bardic family who served the medieval Lords of the Isles – are here called forth to give the lie to the idea that both Gaelic and the folk who speak it are, in some inescapable way, unworthy. What is being resisted, then, is a process which theorists of colonial revolution, most notably Frantz Fanon, have dubbed inferiorisation. This process – which Fanon describes in terms which are very close to those employed by both John Murdoch and Neil Gunn – belittles practically everything about a colonised people. Not just their language, but their entire culture, their music, their traditions – all those things, in short, which render them distinctive – are scorned, derided, denigrated. The colonised community's sense of identity is thus diminished. And those individuals who together constitute that same community – the African in his school just like Kenn, or Neil Gunn, in his – have their self-esteem diminished, their self-confidence eroded.[34]

Inferiorisation triumphs completely, of course, when the subjects of colonial rule begin actually to believe its endlessly repeated insistence on their intrinsic incapacity; when it is taken for granted, by the subject people as well as by those who rule over them, that a colonising country's culture, language and general ethos are indeed superior to those of the society which has been colonised. Frantz Fanon, a Caribbean psychologist who participated in the Algerian war of independence, would have recognised just such acceptance of their own subordinate status in those Highlanders who, over the years, have condemned and resisted the emergence of Gaelic-medium schools and the beginnings of television broadcasting in Gaelic. But Fanon would have recognised also what it is that has impelled poets like Campbell and MacNeacail to reach back into their people's history for the means to combat such defeatism. 'The passion with which contemporary Arab writers remind their people of the great pages of their history,' Frantz Fanon comments, 'is a reply to the lies told by the occupying power.' Substitute 'Highlander' or 'Gael' for 'Arab', and that sentence, set down by Fanon in the 1960s, goes some considerable distance to explaining why the more mature Angus Peter Campbell should so earnestly wish that his younger self had been in a position to 'scream of the MacMhuirichs'.[35]

Fanon accepts that a knowledge of long-vanquished societies can very readily be dismissed as being of no practical utility today. To those who make such points, however, he makes this reply:

I am ready to concede that on the plain of factual being the past existence of an Aztec civilisation does not change anything very much in the diet of the Mexican peasant of today. I admit that all the proofs of a wonderful Songhai civilisation will not change the fact that today the Songhais are underfed and illiterate, thrown between sky and water, with empty heads and empty eyes. But . . . this passionate search for a national culture which existed before the colonial era finds its legitimate reason in the anxiety shared by native intellectuals to shrink away from that Western culture in which they all risk being swamped. Because they realise they are in danger of losing their lives and thus becoming lost to their people, these men, hot-headed and with anger in their hearts, relentlessly determine to renew contact once more with the oldest and most pre-colonial springs of life of their people.

Let us go farther. Perhaps this passionate research and this anger are kept up or at least directed by the secret hope of discovering beyond the misery of today, beyond self-contempt, resignation and abjuration, some very beautiful and splendid era whose existence rehabilitates us both in regard to ourselves and in regard to others. I have said that I have decided to go farther. Perhaps unconsciously, the native intellectuals, since they could not stand wonderstruck before the history of today's barbarity, decided to go back farther and to delve deeper down; and, let us make no mistake, it was with the greatest delight that they discovered there was nothing to be ashamed of in the past, but rather dignity, glory and solemnity.[36]

These passages were written with the Third World very much in mind. But they have their Highland applications also. Just as colonial revolutionaries were made more steadfast in their purposes by finding that their supposedly worthless past was characterised, after all, by dignity, glory and solemnity, so Highlanders who have learned of Columba and Alasdair MacColla – Highlanders who, as Angus Peter Campbell puts it, can scream of the MacMhuirichs – are arguably much more likely to possess both the motivation and the self-confidence they will need if they are to put right the many things which, over the last two centuries, have gone so badly wrong in Highland Scotland. Not least among the matters urgently requiring such attention, so this book claims at all events, is the tripartite relationship between Highlanders, their natural surroundings and the environmental movement.

Environment and landscape have featured only obliquely in the course of this excursion from Glen Shiel and Achadh nan Seileach – by way of the writings of Hugh MacLennan, Edward Said and Frantz Fanon – into contemporary Highland literature. But one or two of the difficulties in the way of getting an agreed environmental strategy for the Highlands have become a little clearer all the same. Highland landscapes, it has been demonstrated, mean very different things to different people. The unpopulated character of these landscapes, it has been shown, are every bit as symbolic of the eradication of human communities as they are suggestive of wild nature. And the elimination of humanity from so much of the Highlands, it has been stressed, has been merely the most dramatic manifestation of exploitative processes which have also subverted an entire culture. Already it begins to be apparent why Highlanders can be so easily aggravated by those environmentalists who, knowing little of Highland history, tend to see in localities such as Achadh nan Seileach nothing more than 'unspoiled' country of a sort that ought to be kept always in an uninhabited condition.

Reflecting in 1982 on some of the problems inherent in promoting economic expansion in societies which are still experiencing traumas of the sort produced in Scotland by the clearances, the World Bank observed:

> A tribal population confronted with development or modernisation often experiences loss of self-esteem; its members feel a deprivation of their sense of self-worth and a devaluation of their own identity. Loss of self-esteem may result from explicitly critical or negative evaluations of the tribal culture by the agents of change or members of the dominant society. Belittling the tribal population as ignorant, dirty or backward is common . . . Development itself may be phrased in terms that implicitly, if not explicitly, devalue the tribal culture . . . Tribal traditions and knowledge are stigmatised and simply replaced by the dominant culture. Seldom are traditional tribal values acknowledged or are attempts made to perpetuate them.[37]

The World Bank, for all its capitalist credentials, is there endorsing a large part of the Frantz Fanon critique of colonialism. And its strictures deserve to be taken on board by environmentalists as much as by developers. This may seem an odd comment to make in view of the fact that the World Bank – the principal source of funding, very often, for large-scale dams and other projects which have caused a lot of environmental havoc in various Asian, African and Latin American countries – has been much criticised by the international environmental movement. But environmentalists are arguably every bit as prone as Patrick Sellar's modern counterparts to ignore or undervalue cultures and traditions which they do not fully understand. And for all that the modern Highlands are very far removed from situations of the sort the World Bank customarily addresses, the region's history has been such, as this chapter has now emphasised sufficiently, to give the bank's remarks some relevance to Highland circumstances. The most successful strategies for the Highlands – in the environmental sphere as well as in the developmental one – are likely to be those which are framed in such a way as to draw on the cultural traditions of the area with which they deal.

Nor need this be at all constraining. As was stressed in this book's introduction, Gaelic culture has habitually placed an extraordinarily high value on the natural environment. It is remarkably easy, therefore, to make connections between modern environmental concerns and longstanding Highland attitudes to land, to landscape and to nature. To appreciate the full extent of what is possible, however, it is necessary to leave aside more recent history and, taking Frantz Fanon's good advice to heart, to go far back and to delve deep. The era to which this book now turns, then, is the one to which Angus Peter Campbell refers when wishing that, as a boy, he 'would have known of Columba'. Here, some fifteen hundred years ago, one finds the Highland equivalent of those other historical epochs which Fanon had in mind when remarking that 'there was nothing to be ashamed of in the past, but rather dignity, glory and solemnity'. Here, too, one discovers the ultimate origins of the Scottish green consciousness with which this book began.

CHAPTER TWO

The Glory of Great Hills is Unspoiled

On the island side of Clachan Bridge, the enormously hump-backed structure which links Seil with the Argyll mainland, the Easdale road picks its way delicately between shallow inlets and grass-covered hills. White-painted houses are scattered all along a sheltered shoreline. And so small-scale is this landscape that the altogether wider view which opens suddenly to the west and south-west comes as something of a shock. Out there is the Atlantic Ocean. Also out there, though only visible on good days, are the Garvellochs – a set of wave-battered islets of the sort that you would expect to have been forever left to seals and seabirds.

But here and there across these strung-out scraps of land, and especially on Eilean an Naoimh, the most southerly of them, there are to be seen the remnants of human habitation – not, as at Achadh nan Seileach, the ruins of nineteenth-century homes, but structures which are far, far older. The dwellings which still stand on Eilean an Naoimh were built more than a thousand years ago. And it is no small testimony to the skill of their builders, folk who employed no mortar, that this low island's clustered huts – their shapes reminiscent of beehives – have so successfully stood up to storms for so very many centuries.[1]

There is nothing that is unique about these carefully constructed shelters. If you were to make a voyage all along the length of the immensely intricate and jagged western coastlines both of Scotland and of Ireland – starting, say, at the northernmost tip of the Hebrides and finishing in County Cork or County Kerry – you would discover lots of former settlements of the Eilean an Naoimh type. You might begin with North Rona, an island so tiny and so remote that it can seldom be seen from either Lewis or Sutherland, the nearest pieces of inhabited land. You might take in some of the many other – and scarcely more accessible – fragments of rock and heather to be found in the wide sounds which separate larger islands like Skye, Mull, Jura, Islay, Harris and the Uists both from each other and from the Scottish mainland. You might visit Inishmurray in Donegal Bay or Skellig Michael which projects, like an inverted cone, from the waters to the south-west of Valencia. And at each and every landfall you would find more buildings of the sort that have endured on the Garvellochs.

What would be your most enduring memory of such a journey? The feel and smell and sound of the sea would obviously linger in your mind. But possibly making an even more indelible impression would be those huge Atlantic skies on which there is continually played out the meteorological drama that results from weather front after weather front advancing from the ocean. Something of this drama's character was captured by Neil Gunn in words he wrote in 1937 at the end of a trip from Skye to Eigg:

> The wind became intermittent and the colours in the sea varied and fascinating. Towards the west, where the blue sky was widening, the water was living amarynth; east and south it was a leaden rolling waste. The cloud formations were of great complexity, from pure white puffs in the distant blue, airy as meadowland dreams, through swirls and wind-drawn white augers overhead, to the sombre pall that lay on Skye and the inky gloom that blotted out the south-west ... There was a splendid exhilaration in this width and expanse, an expanse rendered all the vaster by the hazed islands and the immense stretch of the mainland Highlands now rising out of the thinning clouds far to the east and south'ard. Something here very much grander, more impressive, than any circle of horizon when no land is seen.[2]

It is remarkably easy, when trying to turn any such scene into words, to resort to the language of the Celtic Twilight – a literary school this book will get around in time to criticising rather harshly. Twilight authors – always more at home with shadow than with substance – were inclined to attach a mystical significance to the effects produced by light on cloud and water. In truth, all such phenomena can be explained without resorting to the supernatural. Their origins are mostly to be found in the extraordinary translucence of an atmosphere which, especially when the wind blows from the west or from the north, is almost wholly free of smoke, dust, fumes and other debris of that kind.

What Robert Louis Stevenson called 'the inimitable brightness of the air', then, is one of the most striking features both of the Hebrides and the adjacent mainland. Hence these lines by a Lewis-born poet, Derick Thomson:

*Probably there's no other sky in the world
  that makes it so easy for people
  to look in on eternity;
  you don't need philosophy
  when you can make do with binoculars.[3]

There are plenty of times in the Highlands, of course, when lowering cloud combines with rain and wind to produce zero visibility. But when the good days come along, and in the end they always do, you find yourself, if not exactly in touch with eternity, then certainly much more aware than usual of your natural surroundings – the clarity of these surroundings being all the more apparent after a spell of dull and stormy weather.

This heightening of perceptions, it seems more than probable, must have been experienced particularly strongly by those individuals who elected, at various periods in the past, to live in isolation on the remotest Hebridean islands. Such was certainly true of the naturalist and pioneering ecologist, Frank Fraser Darling, who, when he made this entry in his diary on 14 July 1938, was permanently resident on North Rona:

Enormous waves broke against the cliffs and the water was churned to white foam . . . The sound and the scene were awe-inspiring. It was the sort of sea of which people often say, 'Nothing could survive in this terrible surf.' So you would think, but there, close into the rocks and where the waves broke most fiercely, were our friends the great seals. They were not battling against the seas, but taking advantage of them for play . . . They were leaping to the surface, nearly a hundred of them, enjoying the deep rise and fall of the sea and the spray of the shattered waves. They were living joyfully and I, in my way, rejoiced with them. The sky had become a brilliant blue, the wind was dropping and, as usually happens, the surf began to get bigger. The whiteness of it shone in the sunlight and the movement and the sound of it all were glorious.[4]

A very similar testimony to the influence islands can exert on the imagination is to be found in a poem written many hundreds of years prior to Frank Fraser Darling getting to North Rona. This poem was written by a man of the sort responsible for what Fraser Darling – on inspecting a North Rona equivalent of the ancient huts on Eilean an Naoimh – called the 'finest example' of drystone walling he had ever seen. And the poem, like the walling, is the work of an outstanding craftsman:

*Delightful I think it to be in the bosom of an isle, on the peak of a rock that I might often see there the calm of the sea.

That I might see its heavy waves over the glittering ocean, as they chant a melody to their Father on their eternal course.

That I might see its smooth strand of clear headlands, no gloomy thing; that I might hear the voice of the wondrous birds, a joyful tune.

That I might hear the sound of the shallow waves against the rocks; that I might hear the cry by the graveyard, the noise of the sea.

That I might see its splendid flocks of birds over the fullwatered ocean; that I might see its mighty whales, greatest of wonders.[5]

The Gaelic-speaking monks who created verses of this type – and who created also so many stone cells like the one that so impressed Frank Fraser Darling on North Rona – were remarkably at home in lonely places. Their stonework survives on islands of the sort already mentioned. What does not survive are the equivalent dwellings constructed from timber in the woods where numbers of these monks also established hermitages. But whether they lived among forests or on the edge of the Atlantic, these determinedly ascetic individuals, as is readily apparent from their writings, developed what was – from a European standpoint anyway – a wholly new relationship with nature.

Western civilisation, until the eighteenth century, mostly tended to treat wild nature as something to be feared – something, ideally, to be beaten down, conquered and subdued. The Greeks, being a mountain people, had some degree of positive feeling for the hills around them. But the Romans – for all that poets like Virgil and Horace were given to idealising those pastoral and farmed countrysides which had already been domesticated by Italian agriculturalists – regarded untamed territory with a deep repugnance. Typical of the products of such thinking are those Latin verses which consider it a 'serious defect' – and one which ought, by implication, to be quickly set to right – that so much of the earth was 'greedily possessed by mountains and the forests of wild beasts'.[6]

This adversarial approach to nature was to be reinforced, if anything, by Christianity. The Bible, as a result of its stressing humanity's God-given right of dominion over the rest of the divine creation, encourages a dim view to be taken of any components of the natural order which manage, as it were, to maintain their independence. Such was the way, at least, in which the scriptural message was initially interpreted – not just by the Romans but also by many of the Germanic peoples who were to come to prominence in much of Western Europe, including a large part of the British Isles, in the wake of Rome's collapse. These peoples, after all, had traditionally lived in some considerable dread of the dangers thought, by no means without reason, to lurk in still-unsettled country. That much is apparent from the Anglo-Saxon epic, *Beowulf*, where mountains and wooded places are invariably characterised as dismal, dark, wolf-haunted, weird and frightening. Wilderness, it is thus made clear by their earliest literature, held absolutely no appeal for England's founding fathers. And in the case of woodland, in particular, most English people, over several hundred years, saw little reason to challenge the longstanding identification of unbridled nature with all that was menacing, fierce and disruptive. Thus the very word 'savage' – applied so frequently, as the preceding chapter showed, to Scottish Highlanders – had its origins in a Latin term, *silva*, meaning forest. To cut down trees was consequently to expand civility and culture – the prevalent state of English opinion on such issues being highlighted, as late as the seventeenth century, by a poetical dictionary which suggests that woods are most appropriately described as dreadful, uncouth, melancholy or gloomy.[7]

The sheer staying power of such ideas makes all the more remarkable the sentiments contained in thousand-year old poems like the following:

> *May-time, fair season, perfect its aspect; blackbirds sing
> a full song, if there be a scanty beam of day.
>
> Summer brings low the little stream, the swift herd makes for
> the water, the long hair of the heather spreads out, the weak
> white cotton-grass flourishes.
>
> The harp of the wood plays melody, its music brings perfect
> peace; colour has settled on every hill, haze on the lake of full
> water.
>
> The corncrake clacks, a strenuous bard; the high pure
> waterfall sings a greeting to the warm pool; rustling of rushes
> has come.

Light swallows dart on high . . . The hardy cuckoo sings,
the speckled fish leaps . . . The glory of great hills is
unspoiled.

Delightful is the season's splendour, winter's rough wind has
gone; bright is every fertile wood, a joyful peace is summer.[8]

You sense in these verses something of the sheer relief with which Frank
Fraser Darling, many centuries afterwards, would greet the return of spring
to the particular corner of the Highlands — it was not North Rona, this
time, but somewhere almost equally inaccessible — where he was trying to
set up home:

The first day of May will long remain in my memory, for to begin
with it was gloriously calm and mild. When you have had a long
period of wind and wild weather and it is followed by a perfect day,
activity seems to be frozen and all you can do is lie about and heal
your battered self in the quiet of it all. The morning had brought the
welcome sound of common sandpipers to the lochans, that long-
continued piping which is as moving to me as any music Pan
himself might make. The sun shone through the canvas of the tent
in the early hours, and I lay basking in it and listening to the
sandpipers before I rose. This, I thought, was spring at last, and I let
my imagination play with the picture of that active little mite
standing on a stone at the edge of the sunlit water, his head and beak
nodding and tail flirping, and then the ecstatic, vibrant flight over
the lochan wih a paen of his piping.[9]

Nature's sounds, then, were as important as its sights to Fraser Darling.
So they were also to the unknown poet who first set down these lines:

*Swarms of bees, beetles, soft music of the world, a gentle
humming; wild geese, barnacle geese, shortly before All
Hallows, music of the dark torrent.

A nimble singer, the combative brown wren from the hazel
bough, woodpeckers with their pied hoods in a vast host.

Fair white birds come, cranes, gulls, the sea sings to them, no
mournful music; brown fowl out of the red heather.

46

The voice of the wind against the branchy wood, grey with cloud; cascades of the river, the swan's song, lovely music.[10]

Such poems — composed originally in Gaelic — date from the eighth, ninth and tenth centuries. Their touch is sure and delicate. They indulge neither in elaborate description nor in introspective moralising. They deal sometimes in memorable images: 'the harp of the wood plays melody'; 'the corncrake clacks, a strenuous bard'. But there tends to be about them something of that spare simplicity which was also to be characteristic of much later Gaelic verse and which Iain Crichton Smith captures perfectly in these lines of his own:

There is no metaphor. The stone is stony . . .
The rain is rainy and the sun is sunny.
The flower is flowery and the sea is salty.[11]

But what matters most about such early Gaelic poetry, as far as this book is concerned, is the enormously sympathetic tone which it adopts when dealing with wild nature. This, in the context of its own time and in the context of very many later centuries also, was little short of revolutionary. No wonder, then, that Kuno Meyer, one of the earliest translators of such verse into English, should have commented in 1913:

In nature poetry the Gaelic muse may vie with that of any other nation. Indeed, these poems occupy a unique position in the literature of the world. To seek out and watch and love nature, in its tiniest phenomenon as in its grandest, was given to no people so early and so fully as to the Celt.[12]

Meyer, in fact, exaggerated slightly. Eastern peoples like the Chinese and the Japanese, whose Buddhist and Shinto religions emphasise the essential unity of all living things, possess a literary tradition very similar to the one that had its origins in places like Eilean an Naoimh. Among green mountains, asserts a Chinese poet of the eighth century, there is to be found 'a heaven and earth beyond the world of men'; a place where one's soul 'is quiet'; a spot where 'peach blossom follows the moving water'. In such surroundings, another eighth-century Chinese poet comments, there is both delight and spiritual satisfaction to be got from tracking 'a stream to its fountainhead' or simply sitting on a rock 'to watch the clouds gather at sunset'. The Gaelic-speaking monks who were just then making very similar observations, you feel on glancing at this

Chinese poetry, would have instinctively identified with sentiments like these.[13]

In the slightly more limited setting of the British Isles, or even Europe, however, Kuno Meyer was surely right to emphasise the sheer distinctiveness of the lyrics he translated. Nor is it so surprising as it might seem initially that Gaels should have been so far in advance of so much of the rest of the world in this respect. Today, when the various dialects of Gaelic are spoken by a mere handful of people on the Atlantic fringes of Scotland and Ireland, it is easy to be unaware that the language was not always the highly marginalised tongue it has now become. Because we mostly assume Gaelic to be of no very general significance, we readily overlook the fact that Gaelic-speakers, as has been commented recently by a German historian, Michael Richter, 'developed a written culture at an earlier stage than most other European peoples'. We tend to miss the point that, though they were the work of men who inhabited isolated islands or who lived alone in forests, the Gaelic poems quoted in this chapter were not at all the products of a primitive or unsophisticated society. Although they had chosen – for a time at least – to become hermits, the men who shaped such poems belonged to communities where there had developed modes of thought and forms of expression which, if we exclude only the overarching achievements of the Greeks and the Romans, were such as to have made these communities the originators of what was, to cite Richter again, the 'most significant European culture' of the Christian era's early centuries.[14]

This culture had its origins, of course, in Ireland. It was imported into Scotland by those Gaels – as Irish people then called themselves – who began moving from Ulster to Kintyre, Islay and adjacent localities at about the time the Roman Empire was beginning to disintegrate. Rome, though it had ruled much of mainland Britain, had never brought the Irish under its jurisdiction. But Ireland, in the early part of the fifth century, had nevertheless become Christian. And in their successful fusing of Christianity with older Celtic tradition is to be found the distinguishing feature of the civilisation which the Gaels now began to develop both in Ireland and in Scotland.

Crucial to this civilisation was a commitment to monasticism. But monasteries of the Celtic type are not to be confused with their medieval successors. They left, for instance, no great architectural monuments along the lines of those resulting from the much later abbeys of the Scottish border country. This is because the Gaels, in contrast to many other early Christians, had not inherited the temple-building traditions of more Mediterranean-orientated peoples. Their churches, just like the monastic settlements which developed around these churches, were consequently very modest. The typical place of worship was built largely of timber. Only occasionally – and mostly in those places where wood was simply unobtainable – was it constructed from stone. Always it was fairly small. And the other buildings which went up in such a church's immediate vicinity – a refectory, a guest-house, a school perhaps and certainly a clutter of those little cells or huts inhabited by individual monks – were similarly unpretentious.[15]

One of the most famous and most influential of all such monasteries was the one established in the sixth century by the Ulster churchman, *Colum Cille*, St Columba, on the Hebridean island of Iona. Nowadays, our civilisation being so closely bound up with great cities, it is extremely hard for us to think of places like Iona as anything other than peripheral. We mostly go to such localities in search of peace and quiet, not mental stimulation. The development and interchange of new ideas we associate with towns. But in Columba's time, and for some centuries afterwards, the monastic community which developed in Iona was one of Europe's leading intellectual centres – a source of literacy, of learning and of several innovative strands of thought.

Iona's steadily expanding missionary effort brought Christianity both to the Pictish realms and to the kingdom of Northumbria – the Picts being a Celtic people who then occupied most of what is now Scotland and the Northumbrians, whose territories stretched from the Forth to the Humber, being Germanic incomers who had migrated westwards from the continent. Nor were Pictland and Northumbria the limits of Iona's influence. Gaelic-speaking monks were to bring both their faith and their scholarship to several of the continental kingdoms founded by the Roman Empire's barbarian invaders. Thus it came about that the Carolingian Renaissance, the name given by historians to the cultural upsurge which so transformed Western Europe in the ninth century, can be attributed in no small part to men who – though they spent much of their lives at the Aachen court of the Frankish emperor Charlemagne – began their careers in monasteries of the kind Columba had created on Iona.[16]

A key focus of Iona's monastic life, in Colum Cille's time and later, was the building known as the *scriptorium* – a word meaning place of writing. Here both Columba himself and perhaps hundreds of his contemporaries and successors helped to turn out the intricately illuminated scriptures now considered to be one of the marvels of their age. The highly ornamented pages of these gospel books, in the opinion of a leading twentieth-century art historian, Kenneth Clark, 'are almost the richest and most complicated pieces of abstract decoration ever produced'. And from a time some eight hundred years earlier than Clark's there comes an equally striking tribute. It is to be found in the writings of Giraldus of Wales, a leading cleric of that period. The volume to which his passage refers was very probably the Book of Kells which is held today by Trinity College, Dublin, and which was almost certainly created, or so the current consensus has it, on Iona.[17]

A mightily impressed Giraldus commented:

> This book contains the harmony of the four evangelists according to Jerome, where for almost every page there are different designs, distinguished by varied colours. Here you may see the face of majesty, divinely drawn, here the mystic symbols of the evangelists, each with wings, now six, now four, now two; here the eagle, there the calf, here the man, there the lion and other forms almost infinite. Look at them superficially, with an ordinary casual glance, and you would think it an erasure, not tracery. Fine craftsmanship is all about you, but you might not notice it. Look more keenly at it, however, and you will penetrate to the very shrine of art. You will make out intricacies so delicate and subtle, so exact and compact, so full of knots and links, with colours so fresh and vivid, that you might say all this was the work of an angel and not of man. For my part, the oftener I see the book, and the more carefully I study it, the more I am lost in ever fresh amazement.[18]

The Book of Kells and other equally striking versions of the scriptures, it is readily apparent to the modern eye, drew on design traditions which were common to the various Celtic peoples who were dominant in much of Western Europe prior to the rise of Rome. But these traditions, in the Iona monastery and in its sister institutions, were brought to a wholly new pitch of perfection:

> They began with the barest patterns
> Of design, in their minds, and then
> Something converted them into artists
> With an exalted lyric gift.
> What this something was
> No one can claim perfectly to know.
> Some of them were reported as believing
> In assistance from the angels.
> Whatever the source, the result was some
> Of the most beautiful work the world has ever seen.[19]

These lines were written by twentieth-century Scotland's greatest poet, Hugh MacDiarmid. In them, as in so much of his work, he was looking for inspiration – both of the artistic and the political variety – to those Gaelic-speaking folk who, as the previous chapter demonstrated, were so widely and so persistently considered, both by Lowland Scots and by the English, to have contributed practically nothing of value to the sum of human experience. MacDiarmid, being the sort of man he was, took great pleasure in adopting a position wholly at odds with the conventional one. Scotland, he came to believe, would never find cultural purpose or salvation in anything other than its Gaelic heritage – a heritage which, MacDiarmid thought, reached back to the Book of Kells and its creators.[20]

This book returns to Hugh MacDiarmid in due course. For the moment, it suffices to have registered the fact that Gaelic-speaking Highlanders – those 'aborigines' whom men like Patrick Sellar took such pleasure in evicting from their ancestral lands – could lay claim, after all, to a substantial record of achievement. Nor was that achievement confined to art and literature. The Gaels or the *Scoti,* as this people were habitually called in the Latin of the chroniclers who first set down their history, both created the Scottish kingdom and provided that kingdom with its monarchs. Thus it came about that Scotland, for the first few centuries of its existence, was a predominantly Gaelic-speaking country ruled by Gaelic-speaking kings. These kings, however, are not this book's concern. The development of its arguments depends much less on great men and their doings than it does on those monastic hermits who sought spiritual salvation in places like Skellig Michael, the Garvellochs and North Rona.[21]

Although Christianity differs so markedly from most other world religions – particularly Buddhism and Hinduism – in the separation that it makes between humanity and nature, the first Christians, like the Jews to whose own faith Christianity owed so much, looked to the wilderness as a place where an individual might most readily be alone with God. What the Bible means by wilderness, of course, is desert of the sort which has been common in the Middle East since long before Abraham moved out of Ur. And the original role of this type of arid wasteland in processes of spiritual renewal, one suspects, had less to do with its natural charms than with the fact that it offered very little in the way of distractions from the prayer and meditation thought to be the key to self-renewal. It was to such terrain, at all events, that various Old Testament prophets habitually retreated. It was in such terrain also, no doubt, that Jesus himself once engaged in wrestling with his conscience – in the shape sometimes of the devil – for, as Matthew tells us, 'forty days and forty nights'.[22]

It is by no means surprising, therefore, that Middle Eastern Christianity – especially in Syria and Egypt in the centuries prior to these countries yielding very largely to the still newer religion of Islam – should have developed its own tradition of seeking spiritual solace in wild places. Nor is it any more surprising, given the nature of the trade routes connecting Ireland with the Mediterranean, that the idea of the wilderness retreat should eventually have been adopted so enthusiastically by some of the sterner spirits within the monastic communities which had earlier been established in localities like Iona.[23]

These communities, as already mentioned, were nothing if not basic in their lifestyle. But the monastic existence was positively luxurious in comparison with that now adopted by the many individual monks who, having turned their backs more or less completely on their fellow human beings, departed, either by themselves or in small groups, for the wild places which both Ireland and Scotland could so plentifully offer. 'Labouring with their hands,' runs a typical passage from an early account of what it meant to be a hermit in such circumstances, 'they tilled the earth with a hoe. Rejecting all animals, they possessed not so much as one cow. And if any offered them milk or butter they received it not.' Such solitaries, then, practised a strict self-sufficiency; subsisting largely on what they could grow themselves; supplementing the output of their little gardens with fruit, eggs, honey and other natural produce of that kind. One hermit is described as drinking only 'pure water', eating nothing but 'nuts of the wood and plants of the ground', having 'no bed but a pillow of stone under his head and a flag under him'. Many others were every bit as scornful of comfort.[24]

Today, in the western world anyway, the only people who choose to live in so elemental a fashion are those so-called 'deep ecologists' who reject even the most far-reaching variants of conventional environmentalism as involving too many compromises with a civilisation they regard as utterly beyond redemption – and who consequently tend to take themselves off to mountain and forest locations where they try to enter into something approximating to a personal relationship with nature.

Deep ecology has been celebrated thus by an American poet, Robinson Jeffers:

Civilised, crying to be human again: this will tell you how.
Turn outward, love things, not men, turn right away from
    humanity.

Lean on the silent rock until you feel its divinity.
Make your veins cold, look at the silent stars, let your eyes
Climb the great ladder out of the pit of yourself and man.[25]

Although no Celtic monk would have been so uncaring of his
Christianity as to discern the divine – other than indirectly – in an
inanimate piece of stone, there is clearly much in deep ecology that is
reminiscent of the thinking of the men who once inhabited the
Garvellochs. Deep ecology, for instance, advocates its own modern
variant of the hermitage. 'The more we know a specific place intimately
– know its moods, seasons, changes, aspects, native creatures – the more
we know our ecological selves'. So writes one deep ecologist. And if 'soul'
or something like it were to be substituted for that sentence's last two
words, it would readily have found an audience in the ninth-century
world of Gaelic-speaking solitaries like Declan:

> For he was in his own dear cell which he had built for himself. It is
> between the wood and the sea in a narrow, secret place above the
> ocean-edge. A clear stream of water flows from the hill into the sea
> and trees encircle it beautifully . . . He dearly loved his cell in which
> he could be . . . alone with God.[26]

The more one discovers about Declan and his fellows, in fact, the more
they seem to have in common with the much more recent originators of
contemporary environmentalism. Here, for example, is Henry David
Thoreau, the New Englander who, in 1845, did so much to initiate the
modern cult of wilderness by deciding to live alone in a shack which he
built for himself on the shores of Walden Pond, near Concord,
Massachussetts:

> Sometimes in a summer morning . . . I sat in my sunny doorway
> from sunrise till noon, rapt in reverie, amidst the pines and hickories
> and sumacks, in undisturbed solitude and stillness, while the birds
> sang around or flitted noiselessly through the house.[27]

In their own very similarly situated woodland huts, so you gather from
hints dropped in their verses, the Gaelic-speaking clerics of some eleven
or twelve centuries ago were every bit as given as Thoreau to sitting
quietly listening to 'the trilling of birds' from some nearby 'woodland
thicket'. Nor were such men content merely to commune with nature.
They observed it closely also – almost, it is no very great exaggeration to

remark, with the determined accuracy of a modern field naturalist. Thus the 'nimble' bee is described, in one early poem, as regularly making 'a great journey in the sun'; flying long distances in search of honey; returning, at last, to join 'his brethren in the hive'. Birds were equally closely scrutinised. You read of one monk leaving his cell specifically to watch a lark. You come across another who compares the highly territorial blackbird with an especially isolationist hermit. The blackbird's distinctive song, this poet comments, serves the same purpose as the bell which a solitude-seeking monk takes care to keep to hand. Both are sounded with the aim of warning off approaching strangers.[28]

It is possible to detect various literary influences in this extraordinarily early nature poetry. The men responsible for its production were as highly educated, after all, as anyone in the Europe of their time. Many of them, being widely read in Latin, would have been well acquainted with the Roman authors whose works were copied and recopied in monastery *scriptoria*. Others – and this may be of more significance – were very probably among those monks who first rendered into written Gaelic a substantial selection of the tales, legends and sagas which their people had previously transmitted orally from one generation to the next. Much of this material makes imaginative use of language. And the very act of transcribing it – a process which was, in itself, revolutionary in a society formerly incapable of making a permanent record of its speech – might easily have helped unleash new forms of creativity.[29]

But the particular poetry which emerged in places like Eilean an Naoimh, as hinted at the beginning of this chapter, very probably owed rather more to the physical circumstances in which it was conceived than it did to the various cultural and intellectual influences operating on the minds of its originators. The 'almost impersonal clarity' which Iain Crichton Smith discerns in this poetry, or so it seems reasonable to theorise, surely derives – in part at least – from the fact that it reflected the experiences of men who had chosen to live in wild places entirely by themselves. These men, admittedly, left no personal memoirs of how it felt to be alone with nature in a setting such as that provided by the Garvellochs. But the content of their poetry is such as to indicate that their responses to their surroundings were by no means dissimilar to those of much more recent Highland solitaries.[30]

Few recent writers have been so merciless as Alasdair MacLean in their debunking of romantic stereotypes of what it means to be by oneself in a place battered ceaselessly – or so it seems when winter gales are at their worst – by storm and wet. There is absolutely nothing in the way of lyrical evocation of the self-sufficient existence in MacLean's grimly unsentimental account of life on the Ardnamurchan croft he inherited in the 1970s from his father. Rather the reverse. But for all the harshness of his time there, the wide view westwards from his coastal home could occasionally impact on Alasdair MacLean with a quite startling force. One such moment occurred at the end of one of those 'appalling' days so common in the Highlands; a day of 'long curtains of rain sweeping across the hillside'; a day when, towards evening, the clouds start suddenly to break:

> Since I had not been out of doors at all I went to the garden gate as the first few thistledowns of darkness began to seed the air. I went to lean and to ponder and I leaned long and pondered hard. I think I added a little to my store of riches though I should be in difficulties were I asked to state exactly where the profit lay. At last I watched night take the islands, blue becoming indigo becoming velvet black, these poor terms standing for a thousand delicacies of colour, till all labelling was lost in the general anonymity of night.[31]

That passage, of course, tells one as much about Alasdair MacLean as it does about the landscapes, or the seascapes, he was looking out on. But it is hard to believe that his mental processes would have been quite the same had his garden gate given access to a suburban street or, for that matter, to a neatly farmed countryside of the southern variety. The same is true of Gavin Maxwell's reaction to Isle Ornsay, just off the southern coast of Skye:

> Here, it seemed to me, where the rocks and the white stone buildings were the only solid things in a limitless bubble of blue water and blue air, one might be able to live at peace again, to recover a true vision long lost by now in the lives of other humans and in the strifes of far countries; here one might set back the clock and re-enter Eden.[32]

Gavin Maxwell, writing in the 1960s, was famously given to searching for spiritual solace in exactly those Highland localities where the Gaelic-speaking hermits of a thousand and more years before had tried to discover the same thing. When a student, he once wrote, he had been 'an earnest member of the Celtic fringe, avid for tartan and twilight'. Much of this, of course, was afterwards discarded. But Maxwell remained sufficient of a mystic to make his Isle Ornsay Eden readily dismissable as just another outgrowth of romanticism run riot. It is not so simple, however, to set aside Maxwell's conviction that total isolation can be a hugely liberating experience.[33]

To be bereft of social intercourse when living in a busy town or city, Gavin Maxwell conceded, can be profoundly depressing:

> But to be quite alone where there are no other human beings is sharply exhilarating; it is as though some pressure has suddenly been lifted, allowing an intense awareness of one's surroundings, a sharpening of the senses and an intimate recognition of the teeming sub-human life around one.[34]

Both his books and the films which were based on them made Gavin Maxwell's name familiar to millions. The authors of the eighth- and ninth-century Gaelic poems featured in this chapter will forever be anonymous – their individual identities being now beyond recovery. But so striking is the extent to which Maxwell and his hermit predecessors share a common attitude both to wild country of the Highland type and to the creatures which inhabit all such country that it seems unnecessarily perverse to deny the possibility – already raised in relation both to deep ecology and to a nineteenth-century environmentalist like Thoreau – of the Gaelic-speaking world having long ago anticipated modes of thought which we mostly categorise as relatively recent.

The way in which the Celtic church's hermits identified with birds, with mammals, even with insects, is especially indicative of their ability to shake off the constraints of their own time. Again the earliest Gaelic poetry makes the point. 'They lived so much among the wild creatures,' it was noted of this poetry's authors by one of the first modern commentators on their work, 'that they became almost one with them, almost own brother to them, as it were hardly conscious that there was any distinction of genus.' To accord such recognition to animals is highly unusual even today. Hence the fascination engendered by the manner in which Gavin Maxwell was prepared to share his life with otters. And in the past, of course, such a breaking down of the barriers between species was infinitely more exceptional – animals being generally regarded, by our western civilisation at any rate, as having no status beyond that bestowed on them by their biblically-ordained function of helping to meet humanity's needs for food, for furs, for leather and for other materials of that sort.[35]

To one of Protestant Christianity's principal founders, John Calvin, a man whose doctrines were destined to come to prominence in the Highlands, it seemed beyond argument that 'the end for which all things were created was that none of the conveniences and necessaries of life might be wanting to man'. And Calvin's Scottish disciples, well into the twentieth century, were still insisting that 'the world exists for our sakes and not for its own'. The Celtic church, however, held an altogether less utilitarian, less exploitative, view of nature. Remarking that the weather of 917 had been so bad as to cause much 'mortality of cattle', one Gaelic-speaking chronicler of that remote period takes care to add – with an evident sense of regret – that 'the sound of a blackbird or thrush was scarcely heard that year'. And this concern for wildlife is reflected still more strongly in the 'lives', or biographies, which Celtic monks compiled by way of honouring their church's saints. Thus Columba is said to have cared for an injured crane. Comgall is trusted by the swans which come to him when he calls. Ciaran makes friends with a fox and a badger. Maelanfaid is reported never to have killed 'any animal little or big'. And Moling, we learn, 'nurtured animals both wild and tame in honour of their Creator'.[36]

Consider, for a moment, Frank Fraser Darling's account of an early summer's morning on a Hebridean island:

> I am lying in sunlight by lapping water, where bright green blades of flags come through the sodden ground at the water's edge. Here is a tiny rowan tree in leaf, making a continual change of pattern against the sky as the breeze crosses its leaves. Bracken is uncurling all around me and I can see the blue carpet and smell the sweet nostalgic scent of the bluebells . . . A brilliantly coloured fly hovers before the bells of a flower and settles on a stalk. I am struck by its iridescence in the sunlight.[37]

The saints of the Columban church, or so it seems reasonable to deduce from what has been demonstrated of their outlook, could readily have written something very similar. So, too, could the nameless ninth-century monk who – while getting on with his copying on a summer's morning of the kind, no doubt, described by Fraser Darling – paused long enough to note in Gaelic beside his Latin text: 'Pleasant to me is the glittering of the sun today upon these margins.' One senses even in such casual comments – and others could be cited – something of the sheer delight which the men who made them clearly took in natural phenomena.[38]

Nothing that has been said so far, it is important to get straight at this stage, proves the existence of a uniquely caring or protective attitude towards the natural environment on the part of the Gaelic-speaking society which began to be established in the Highlands during the fifth and sixth centuries. The nowadays common belief that pre-industrial communities lived totally in harmony with their surroundings is one that probably owes more to our guilty feelings about the undoubted damage which we are presently inflicting on the earth than it does to the way our remoter ancestors actually behaved. Their impact on nature was certainly a lot less than ours. But this might well have been due principally to their having had no access to technologies of the kind required to produce environmental disasters of the sort with which we have become all too familiar. The relative lack of such disasters in earlier ages is certainly not to be attributed to an instinctive ecological awareness on the part of men and women who necessarily lived close to nature. Right across the world, after all, peoples armed only with spears, bows and arrows proved perfectly capable of exterminating entire animal species. And Scotland, where humanity had been present for several millennia before the arrival of the Gaels, had undoubtedly been affected in a very fundamental way by successive generations of hunters and farmers. Even in the time of Colum Cille, then, as a later chapter will have cause to emphasise, the Highlands are not to be imagined as a pristine wilderness. Nor should every Highlander of that period be presumed to have shared beliefs of the kind that took some men to the Garvellochs.[39]

To be a churchman in the Gaelic-speaking world of the eighth century, say, was as much to be in a minority as to be a churchman today. To be a hermit of the Eilean an Naoimh sort – and the bulk of the early poetry in which this chapter deals was almost certainly composed by just such hermits – was to be in an altogether smaller minority still. It is a fair assumption, therefore, that an average member of the society in which there first began to emerge something approximating to a Scottish green consciousness was no more likely to have espoused that green consciousness than the typical twentieth-century Scot is likely to be intellectually in thrall to thinking of the kind associated with contemporary deep ecologists. This is not to say, however, that modern environmentalists – and especially those with a particular interest in the Highlands – have nothing to learn from the more secular, more mundane, concerns of the civilisation from which the Garvelloch hermits so steadfastly turned aside.

This civilisation's basic unit was the *tuath*. Perhaps as close an approximation as has ever existed – in the British Isles at any rate – to the small, self-governing and largely self-contained community which some ecologists and environmentalists nowadays propound as the ideal

58

alternative to our industrial society, the tuath, although ruled by a king, was not a kingdom in the commonly accepted meaning of that word. It was seldom more than a few hundred square miles in extent. It consisted of only a few thousand people. And it contained neither towns nor cities – the Gaelic-speaking world being, in its origins, entirely rural.[40]

While the 'bioregional' social structures postulated by green political theory might approximate in scale to the tuath, and while their economies might be similarly agrarian, few modern environmentalists would take kindly to the way the tuath actually operated. Although its king – just like the clan chief of much later times – was by no means all-powerful, the tuath was neither democratic nor egalitarian. It was, on the contrary, aristocratic, hierarchical and founded very largely on those kinship principles which were to remain the key social determinant in the Highlands until the old order was finally destroyed in the eighteenth century. The tuath, then, was organised – just like the clan of subsequent centuries – in such a way as to facilitate its mobilisation in times of war. Its king was also its military commander. Its higher ranking nobles, many of whom were closely related both to their king and to each other, were its senior officers. Its freemen-farmers were its NCOs. Its lower orders were the equivalent of a modern army's private soldiers. The latter, some of whom were every bit as lacking in status as the serfs who were to constitute feudalism's labouring class, consequently had far fewer rights than the warrior caste who were their rulers. But the tuath, despite its many inequalities, was no straightforward tyranny. Its leading men, including its kings, were subject to laws which were already ancient when they began to acquire a written Gaelic form during the seventh and eighth centuries. The resulting law tracts, as is to be expected of rules designed to govern the conduct of a society which looked primarily to the land and the sea for its livelihood, have a lot to say about natural resources. Their approach to such resources is one that retains relevance in the Highlands to this day.

The Gaelic law tracts, like the early Gaelic poems quoted elsewhere in this chapter, were preserved in Ireland rather than in Scotland. But the distinction between what is Irish and what is Scottish is one that made little or no sense to Gaels until comparatively recently. 'Gaelic-speaking Scotland and Ireland,' comments the leading authority on these matters, 'constituted a single culture province down into the seventeenth century.' This meant that Gaelic law, like Gaelic literature, was by no means limited to Ireland – the entire social order established in Scotland by the Gaels being modelled on Irish patterns. Organised, to begin with, in the way outlined in the preceding paragraph, that social order, even when modified substantially in later centuries, accorded considerable weight to the *aes dana*, meaning men of learning. This was a group whose existence is evident not only in Ireland but in those other Celtic societies whose fate it was to be submerged in the Roman Empire.[41]

Among the continental equivalents of the Irish aes dana were the priests called druids by the Romans. Julius Caesar, who tangled repeatedly with such druids in the course of his conquest of Gaul, left this account of them:

> The druids are concerned with the worship of the gods, look after public and private sacrifice and expound religious matters. A large number of young men flock to them for training and hold them in high honour. For they have the right to decide nearly all public and private disputes and they also pass judgement and decide rewards and penalties in criminal and murder cases and in disputes concerning legacies and boundaries.[42]

Other Roman and Greek writers make very similar comments. Most agree with Caesar that prospective druids underwent an extremely rigorous training lasting for as many as twenty years. Some, however, distinguish more carefully than Caesar between the different types of learned individual who, in the Gaelic-speaking world, were to be subsumed under the general heading of aes dana. As well as venerating druids, in Caesar's sense of priests and law-givers, the continental Celts, according to observers like Strabo, Diodorus and Athenaeus, honoured also bards whose responsibilities clearly overlapped with those of druids proper and who are generally said to have combined the functions of poet, historian and tradition-bearer. Christianity, of course, was to deprive the druids of their priestly powers by introducing new forms of worship. But what is particularly striking about the aes dana as a whole is the way in which their more secular roles were to survive virtually unaltered from one generation to the next. Thus the Gaelic bards of the seventeenth-century Highlands performed much the same tasks as their Irish and Gaulish predecessors of some two millennia before. Continuity of this kind was commonplace. It is particularly evident, as this book often emphasises, in the relationship between Gaels and their natural environment.[43]

Take woodland, for example. Economically it was a vital source of raw materials in places like the Highlands for practically the whole of the period covered by this book:

Picture a specific but not untypical Highland scene of the not so distant past – a township of a few families, near the shore of a loch, on gentle ground at the foot of wooded hills. On the loch there are boats made of oak and pine, with oars and rudders of ash. Above the beach there are meadows hedged by hawthorn and holly. In the midst of the meadows are the houses with beams of oak and thatch supports of hazel, with furniture of elm and alder, and baskets of willow and bowls of elder. By the houses are rowans and there are cherry trees and blackthorns and elders for fruit. A river flows by the houses and there is a mill with a waterwheel of alder. Nearby are the osier-beds and along the banks are coppiced alders. The land rises to open pasture then to copses of hazel. Then there are oaks and huge ash trees, then pines and juniper on rocky knolls surrounded by seas of birch, rising high up the hills to the high crags where rowans grow. From those wild woods of oak and pine and elm and ash and birch and hazel and holly, the people of the township take timber and fuel, dyes, fertilisers and food . . . They relied upon the trees and their way of life allowed for and demanded the indefinite flourishing of the trees.[44]

Given its huge day-to-day importance, it is not at all surprising that woodland should have loomed large in Celtic culture from the very earliest times. Along with springs and rivers, which were equally essential to life, trees were commonly thought sacred by pre-Christian Celts. One Roman writer, Lucan, notes of the Gauls that 'they worship the gods in woods without making use of temples'. Other classical authors stress the part played by oak groves, in particular, in druidic ritual. Nor was the coming of Christianity noticeably to diminish the high regard in which woods and trees were held both in Celtic Ireland and Celtic Scotland. Thus the conviction that the planting of a rowan beside a house will help ward off misfortune is one that lingers in the Highlands still. Other trees were long believed to have their own equally powerful, and equally magical, properties.[45]

In view of such carryovers from the pagan past into a world which owed its literacy to its newfound Christianity, there is something symbolically appropriate about the fact that the Gaelic alphabet – A *ailm*, B *beith*, C *coll*, D *darach*, E *eadha* – was itself connected, for mnemonic purposes, with the names of trees. These same trees feature frequently in the literature which the new alphabet made possible:

*Oak, bushy, leafy,
  you are high above trees;
  hazel-bush, little branchy one,
  sweet-smelling with hazel nuts.

  Alder, you are not spiteful,
  lovely is your colour,
  you are not like the prickly hawthorn
  where you are in the gully.

  Apple-tree, little apple-tree,
  violently everyone shakes you;
  rowan, little berried one,
  lovely is your bloom.

  Yew, little yew,
  you are conspicuous in graveyards;
  ivy, little ivy,
  you are familiar in the dark wood.

  Holly, little shelterer,
  shutter against the wind;
  ash, baneful,
  weapon in the hand of a warrior.

  Birch, smooth, blessed,
  proud, melodious,
  lovely is each entangled branch
  at the top of your crest.[46]

Although that very ancient poem concentrates on the appearance of the different trees it praises, there is implicit in it the basis of a way of classifying tree species in accordance with the different uses to be made of them. Just such a classification can be found in the Gaelic law tracts where woodland – because of its importance to the workings of the tuath – is considered at some length.

Woodlands are mostly treated by the law tracts in much the same way as hill pastures. They are consequently seen as common property. It follows that the materials to be got from any woodland were available to all the inhabitants, certainly all the freemen, of the particular tuath which contained the woodland in question. On this point the law tracts are

55655655555555555556555555555555555555555

specific. They list, for instance, what it is exactly that the generality of people may take from those forests to which they have access:

> *The night's supply of kindling from every wood.
> The cooking material of every wood.
> The nutgathering of every wood.
> The framework of every vehicle, yoke and plough.
> Timber of a carriage for a corpse.
> The shaft fit for a spear . . .
> The tapering wood of the three parts of a spancel.
> The making of hoops (for barrels).
> The makings of a churnstaff.[47]

The fact that woodlands were communal assets did not imply, however, that they were liable to uncontrolled depredation. Again the law tracts are clear on the point. Indeed it is when their authors turn to the means by which forests are to be conserved for future generations that the strictly hierarchical outlook of the tuath is seen to have been applied, as was hinted in the poem quoted earlier, to trees as well as to human beings.

The relevant passages in the law tracts list twenty-eight species of tree, shrub and plant which are then divided into four categories of seven species each – the four overall categories corresponding to degrees of social ranking in the communities where the law tracts originated. First come *airig fedo*, nobles of the wood, comprising trees like oak, hazel, holly, yew, ash, pine and apple. Next in line are *aithig fedo*, freemen or commoners of the wood, including alder, willow, hawthorn, birch, elm and wild cherry. Third and fourth in general standing are *fodla fedo* and *losa fedo* which consist of blackthorn, aspen, juniper, bracken, bog myrtle, gorse, bramble, heather, broom and other species of that sort. Their status corresponds to that of serfs and slaves. And just as it was a lesser offence to do harm to a serf than to a nobleman, so the penalty for damaging gorse and brambles, say, was a lot less severe than that arising from the unlawful removal of an oak, an ash or a pine. Anyone who engaged in the illicit destruction of one of those superior trees risked a fine equivalent to the value of two-and-a-half milk cows. But a small amount of bracken, which was used for bedding animals, might be taken almost with impunity.[48]

The Gaelic law codes – which are, incidentally, the first documents of this type to be set out in any European language other than Greek or Latin – deal in cows-as-currency for the simple reason that they were intended to regulate an essentially pastoral economy in which cattle were the primary source of wealth. Nor were cow-based valuation systems to be rapidly abandoned. As late as the seventeenth century, more than a thousand years after the law tracts were first given written form, it was still possible in the Highlands to place a 'price' of sixty milk cows on an especially precious manuscript. And what was true of the way in which the law tracts reckoned fines was even truer of their approach both to woodland and other natural resources. The notion that such resources ought to belong to the generality of people in a given locality, rather than to privileged individuals, is one that Highlanders have still not given up.[49]

The tuath of the early Gaelic world was not at all a communist society. Its farms, for instance, were occupied by particular families whose tenurial position the law tracts guaranteed. But the people of the tuath, as demonstrated by the way they managed woodland, made a marked distinction between what had been artificially created and what existed naturally. Both a cultivated field and the cultivator's home were clearly in the first category. Forests, mountains and the wild animals they supported were clearly in the second. It was consequently unlawful to take corn from your neighbour's field. But it was perfectly acceptable – provided that due attention was paid to the need to ensure that long-term output was sustained – to take supplies of timber, nuts and other commodities from a wood. It was equally acceptable for individuals to go where they pleased in hill country and to take the game such country supported – provided again that such resources were not exploited to excess. Much the same sort of thinking was applied to watercourses – an important source of food. Thus a man, though not entitled to take as many river fish as he liked, was certainly permitted to net or trap the occasional salmon for his family's consumption.[50]

Anyone who knows the modern Highlands will recognise in that last stipulation the remote origins of the enduring conviction that, irrespective of our modern society's remarkably draconian laws on poaching, there is nothing morally wrong in taking 'a fish for the pot'. Folk memory – not just in this instance but in the still more generally applicable Gaelic proverb to the effect that everyone has a right to a deer from the hill, a tree from the forest and a salmon from the river – has both preserved the ethics of the tuath and employed these ethics in such a way as to provide a principled basis for actions which Scots law nowadays places on much the same basis as theft.[51]

'It is not easy to convince a Highlander that a landlord has a better right to a deer, a moorfowl or a salmon than he has himself,' one pro-landlord commentator noted despairingly in 1802, 'because he considers them the unconfined bounty of heaven.' The fact that the persistence of such sentiments made it practically impossible to stamp out poaching seemed bad enough to the possessing classes. But what was still more worrying, from the estate-owning point of view, was the ease with which this kind of thinking could be incorporated into attacks on the entire institution of unrestricted private property in land.[52]

Speaking at a Highland Land League meeting in Skye in the 1880s, a crofter demonstrated something of the possibilities in this regard:

> *The fish that was yesterday miles away from the land was claimed by the landlord the moment it reached the shore. And so also were the birds of the air as soon as they flew over his land. The law made it so, because landlords were themselves the lawmakers, and it was a wonder that the poor man was allowed to breathe the air of heaven and drink from the mountain stream without having the factors and the whole of the county police pursuing him as a thief.[53]

The Highland Land League was an intensely radical organisation. It aspired to create a better future for those Highlanders who had survived the clearances. And it succeeded in so doing. As is shown by its Gaelic slogan, *Is treasa tuath na tighearna*, however, the Land League had strong roots in the past. Because it is usally translated into English as 'The people are mightier than a lord', that slogan seems to have a determinedly democratic, even a socialist, ring to it. But though 'tuath' can certainly be rendered as 'people' in this forward-looking way, the Land League also wanted to be seen to be enforcing traditional rights of which Highlanders had been deprived by the men responsible for evictions of the sort which devastated Achadh nan Seileach. 'The landlord class,' one leading reformer observed, 'have been but the usurpers of the right which the people . . . once possessed in the soil.' The royal commission which looked into crofting grievances in 1883 was to hear a lot of testimony to much the same effect.[54]

This testimony, just like the equally long-lived insistence that every Highlander was entitled to the odd deer or salmon, derived ultimately from the world of the tuath. Then the occupants of land were thought to have claims on that land which transcended those even of their king. Such claims, of course, are accorded no place in the externally imposed legal systems which have held sway in the Highlands in recent centuries. But this has never stopped Highlanders clinging stubbornly to much earlier formulations. Thus eighteenth-century tacksmen – those substantial tenants who were the first to feel the full force of the wind of change which Samuel Johnson and James Boswell found blowing in the

Highlands – were reported to 'look upon' their farms as 'their right of inheritance'. So insistent were such men on their entitlement to what amounted to permanent tenancies that they commonly 'refused to take a written lease' on the grounds that the acceptance of such leases, which were for a stipulated period only, amounted to an admission that landlords could, if they wanted, go so far as to remove a farm's occupants. Such removals, needless to say, went ahead in any case. But when a later generation of proprietors tried to buy off the Land League by granting leases to crofters who had previously been offered no such concessions, this offer, too, was turned down. To take such leases, the Highland Land League resolved, would be 'inconsistent' with its demand for security of tenure – such security being useless, so the Land League argued, unless it was effectively perpetual.[55]

When the royal commission of 1883 eventually reported on the underlying causes of the crofting unrest which was then convulsing the Highlands, its report included these words:

> The opinion so often expressed before us that the small tenantry have an inherited inalienable right to security of tenure in their possessions . . . is an impression indigenous to the country, though it has never been sanctioned by legal recognition and has long been repudiated by the actions of the proprietor.[56]

Such comments testify both to the sheer longevity of values which had endured in the Highlands for a millennium and to the fact that these values are of more than academic interest. Thanks to the Highland Land League, after all, various ideas which owe a good deal more to customary Gaelic law than they do to modern jurisprudence were incorporated into United Kingdom statute by the Crofters Act of 1886. The concept of security of tenure might have been one which, under the name of *duthchas*, had for ages been preserved only in the minds of those Highlanders who refused to abandon such seemingly anachronistic notions even when clearance and eviction were at their most unstoppable. But for all that many landlords were appalled by such developments, a nineteenth-century parliament was persuaded that crofters should indeed have the security they desired. That is why, since 1886, landlords have had little control over crofters. That is why the affairs of crofting townships, including the rules of succession to crofts and the regulation of common grazings, are today governed in accordance with principles which would be instantly recognisable to the men who framed the Gaelic law tracts of so long ago. And that is why environmentalists should possibly take rather more interest than they mostly do in Highland history.

It proved possible in the nineteenth-century Highlands to reinstate ancient notions concerning land tenure. Might it not prove just as possible in future to incorporate other equally long-lived ideas into strategies for the Highland environment? Might it now be time to restore a communal interest in the management of salmon, game, woodland, even mountains? Should campaigners for the expansion of community forestry in the Highlands – of whom there are more with every year that passes – be looking to the Highland past for ideas as to how such an objective might be accomplished? And should sporting rights really continue forever to be limited in ways which the Highlanders of a thousand years ago would have considered quite inconceivable?

The future, of course, cannot be a recreation of the distant past. And this book, when it gets round to making some suggestions as to how the Highlands might move forward, will certainly not advocate the restoration of the tuath. But on looking round the northern half of Scotland in the twentieth century's closing decade, it is depressingly apparent just how unprepared we are to make the case for freedoms which our Gaelic-speaking ancestors took more or less for granted.

When, in 1993, a number of environmental groups – the John Muir Trust, the Mountaineering Council of Scotland, the Ramblers Association and the Scottish Wild Land Group – concluded an access agreement with the owners of a particular Highland estate, much was made of the breakthrough which the agreement supposedly represented. And from the essentially southern perspective of the environmentalists concerned, this much-acclaimed 'Letterewe Accord' – which gives climbers and hill-walkers a conditional right of entry to the estate of the same name – might well have seemed a considerable advance. From a Highland standpoint, however, such agreements ought always to be as suspect as the leases which the Highland Land League was so careful to reject. For if it is accepted that access to our mountains is in the gift of landlords, no matter how benevolent, it follows that these same landlords may one day deny such access. No such denial ever could, or should, seem reasonable to Highlanders.[57]

Here, by way of reinforcing that point, is one more poem. In its surviving form – though it is probably much older – it was written during the middle ages in the literary Gaelic that was common then to Ireland and the Highlands. The spot the poem describes has long been thought to be Glen Etive in Argyll:

> *Glen of cuckoos and thrushes and blackbirds, precious is its
> cover to every fox; glen of wild garlic and watercress, of
> woods, of shamrock and flowers, leafy and twisting-crested.
>
> Sweet are the cries of the brown-backed dappled deer under
> the oakwood below the bare hilltops, gentle hinds that are
> timid lying hidden in the great-treed glen.
>
> Glen of the rowans with scarlet berries, with fruit fit for every
> flock of birds; a slumbrous paradise for the badgers in their
> quiet burrows with their young.
>
> Glen of the blue-eyed vigorous hawks, glen abounding in
> every harvest, glen of the ridged and pointed peaks, glen of
> blackberries and sloes and apples.[58]

Nobody whose feeling for the Highlands has been shaped by words of
that sort is ever likely to take kindly to the thought that a monied
individual – even one ostensibly imposing his or her restrictions with a
view to protecting our natural environment – should have any
entitlement to say who should, or should not, walk in places like Glen
Etive.

CHAPTER THREE

The Hind is in the Forest as She Ought to Be

On leaving Inversanda, where the Ardnamurchan road swings sharply away from the shore of Loch Linnhe and heads westwards into Glen Tarbert, you become immediately aware, especially if the day happens to be wet, of just how stark the Highland scene can be. Trees are rareties in this landscape. Its sour and skimpy soils grow little besides deer grass. Huge boulders lie everywhere. The glaciers which deposited these boulders here, you might imagine, have absented themselves only temporarily.

But beyond Glen Tarbert is Strontian. And Strontian is the gateway to a very different type of country. This is *Suaineart ghorm an daraich*; green Sunart of the oaks; one of the very few parts of modern Scotland where it is possible to form some idea of why it was that oakwoods seemed so special to the Celts. Go to Ariundle, a National Nature Reserve a mile or two up the Strontian River. Go there, if possible, on one of those brilliantly sunny days which occur often in the Highlands during May and June. Take in the sights and sounds and scents of an ancient woodland as it comes into leaf. Then you will understand just what inspired this eighteenth-century poem in praise of the first month of summer:

*Each grove, close and secret,
    has its mantle of green,
    the wood-sap is rising
    from the roots at the bottom,
    through arteries twisting
    to swell out the growth;
    thrush and cuckoo at evening
    sing their litany above.

Month of plants and of honey,
    warm, with grasses and shoots,
    month of buds and of leafage,
    rushes, flowers that are lovely,
    wasps, bees and berries,

mellow mists, heavy dews,
like spangles of diamonds,
a sparkling cover for earth.[1]

The poet who composed these verses, knew Strontian and its neighbouring oakwoods very well. *Muideartach dubh dana nan gheur-fhacal,* he once called himself; the bold, dark Moidartman of the sharp words. But to other Highlanders, then and later, he was *Alasdair MacMhaighstir Alasdair,* Alexander MacDonald, son of Master, or *Maighstir,* Alexander MacDonald – Maighstir denoting the fact that the elder MacDonald was a clergyman. Brought up in his father's manse at Dalilea beside Loch Shiel and sent for a time to university, Alasdair MacMhaighstir Alasdair, though of elevated rank because of his descent from both the chiefs of Clanranald and the Lords of the Isles, was nothing if not down-to-earth in his appearance. 'In person,' one contemporary recorded, 'MacDonald was large and ill-favoured. His features were coarse and irregular. His clothes were very sluggishly put on and generally very dirty. His mouth was continually fringed with a stream of tobacco-juice of which he chewed a very great quantity.' But none of this, in the end, was significant. What mattered most about Alasdair was his Gaelic poetry. And that was quite outstanding.[2]

MacDonald's greatest asset was his ability to turn natural phenomena into words. Something at least of this is evident in Iain Crichton Smith's translation of *Birlinn Clann Raghnaill,* Clanranald's Galley, in which Alasdair describes a storm encountered by his chieftain's ship while its crew were voyaging from South Uist to Ireland:

*The sea gathered round about it
    a black cloak,
a rough, ruffled, swarthy mantle
    of ill-look.

It swelled to mountains and to valleys
    shaggy-billowed,
the matted humpy waters rearing
    up to hillocks.

The blue waves were mouthing chasms,
    horned and brutish,
fighting each other in a pouring
    deathly tumult.

> It needed courage to be facing
>   such tall towerings,
> phosphorescent flashes sparking
>   from each mountain.
>
> Grey-headed wave-leaders towering
>   with sour roarings,
> their followers with smoking trumpets
>   blaring, pouring.[3]

In a twentieth-century novel by Fionn MacColla, a writer to whom this book will return, *Birlinn Clann Raghnail*, on its being recited by one of the novel's characters, becomes the means by which English-speaking readers are introduced to the link which MacColla discerns between the Gaelic language and the natural environment in which that language has developed:

> The old man warmed as he proceeded; a flush rose to his cheeks, the eyes glowed in his head; and in a deep and resonant voice he gave the great, mouth-filling words. The liquid lines rose and fell and flowed and ebbed till the mighty sea herself was in the room, heaving up and sinking, breaking at the tops of billows into fragments glittering in sun-sparkle, rushing up long beaches and chittering among the pebbles, dashing with huge anger against tall cliffs and snarling round the roots of black, wet rocks. The sea, the sea was in it, the restless sea, the tireless one, the calm sea that lulls and laps and hushes, the greedy sea, cruel sea howling and gaping for bodies of men. And the soul of man was in it, loving the smiling sea, glaring under fearless brows at the roaring, wrathful sea, going down, clutching, in green waters, biting the seaweed in his teeth – but never conquered![4]

'There's the Gaelic for you,' MacColla has the narrator of the poem comment in conclusion. 'That's a bit out of the poem Alasdair MacMhaighstir Alasdair made on the birlinn of Clan Ranald. And if there is the like of it in any language in the world, let the man that knows it stand to his feet.'

MacDonald's talents were to be at the disposal of a whole array of causes. Gaelic itself was one. Another was Jacobitism. For Alasdair, as well as serving in the largely Highland army which followed Prince Charles Edward Stuart into England, found time to fashion poems which come as close as anyone has ever got to explaining what exactly motivated the many Highlanders who participated in that doomed adventure. Having hurried to Loch nan Uamh to greet Prince Charles on his arrival there in July 1745, MacMhaighstir Alasdair, as he himself recalled, spent the immediately ensuing weeks in 'an intoxication of battle and happiness'. Charles, to Alasdair, was more, much more, than Stuart claimant to the British throne then occupied by the Hanoverian King George II. The Jacobite prince's real significance, from Alasdair's point of view, was largely Highland – Charles's role in his poetry being that of a messiah come to deliver Highlanders from forces which, by Alasdair's time, were already imperilling the existence both of the Highland clans and of the traditional Gaelic culture with which clanship was so inextricably bound up.[5]

From this book's standpoint, however, Alasdair MacMhaigstir Alasdair's nature poems are of more importance than his Jacobitism. And of these poems by far the best is *Oran an t-Samhraidh*, Song of Summer. Two of its verses, in Derick Thomson's translation, were quoted at the beginning of this chapter. Here are two more:

> *Lithe brisk fresh-water salmon,
>   lively, leaping the stones;
>   bunched, white-bellied, scaly,
>   fin-tail-flashing, red spot;
>   speckled skin's brilliant hue
>   lit with flashes of silver;
>   with curved gob at the ready,
>   catching insects with guile.
>
> May, with soft showers and sunshine,
>   meadows, grass-fields I love,
>   milky, whey-white and creamy,
>   frothing, whisked up in pails,
>   time for crowdie and milk-curds,
>   time for firkins and kits,
>   lambs, goat-kids and roe-deer,
>   bucks, a rich time for flocks.[6]

Said traditionally to have been composed at Glencripesdale on the Morvern shore of Loch Sunart, Alexander MacDonald's *Oran an t-Samhraidh* – which was itself to result in a host of Gaelic imitations – is generally reckoned to have had its choice of subject matter determined, partly at least, by the work of a Borders-born poet, James Thomson. Thomson, who left his Roxburghshire birthplace for London in 1725 and who went on to write the words of *Rule Britannia*, was about as far as it was possible to be from Alasdair MacMhaighstir Alasdair both in his literary style and in his politics. But Thomson's long and convoluted poems on the year's successive seasons, published between 1726 and 1730, were to enjoy a massive following. And there seems little reason to doubt that the university-educated MacDonald was familiar with their content.[7]

As one modern critic has remarked, however, Alasdair MacMhaighstir Alasdair's work shows none of the 'sentimental and didactic bias' which one finds both in Thomson and in those other self-consciously pastoral poets who were now emerging in an England which was finally discovering the beauties of the natural world. *Oran an t-Samhraidh*, unlike the Thomson equivalent, is characterised by 'intellectual precision and . . . crystalline excitement'. Here is a Highland nature poet who exhibits nothing of the cultured detachment so conspicuously favoured by his English contemporaries – Alasdair, in the words of one historian of Scottish literature, describing nature 'with so much absorption that his own personality is dropped entirely out of view'. In his ability thus to merge – indeed identify – with his surroundings, as in his equally striking capacity to evoke these surroundings by means of a wealth of meticulously noted detail, Alasdair MacMhaighstir Alasdair is very much in the tradition, of course, of the hermit poets of a millennium earlier. This is not to say that Alasdair knew of these poets or their work. And it is certainly not to claim that he had much in the way of sympathy for the Columban church's more ascetic principles – some of his verse being vigorously bawdy and erotic. But Alasdair MacMhaighstir Alasdair clearly shared that church's feelings for wild nature. And given the extent to which this most remarkable of poets was steeped in a culture which made such a virtue of its own continuity, it would have been astonishing if he had not thus inherited something of what had gone before.[8]

Much had changed in the thousand years which separate Alasdair MacMhaighstir Alasdair from his monastic predecessors. Not for several centuries, as Alasdair himself lamented, had Scots been ruled by Gaelic-speaking kings. Indeed the Gaelic language, despite its earlier expansion into the Lowlands, had become increasingly restricted to the area behind the Highland Line. Nor were Gaels left to their own devices even here. A whole succession of increasingly assertive Scottish governments had endeavoured, from the fifteenth century onwards, to impose their will completely on the Highlands. Prominent among the consequent casualties, as noted in this book's first chapter, was the Lordship of the Isles – a semi-autonomous principality which, in the absence of Gaelic-speaking monarchs, had provided Gaelic Scotland with a vitally important cultural focus.

When Alasdair MacMhaighstir Alasdair was growing up at Dalilea, around the beginning of the eighteenth century, the lordship's extinction was already two hundred years in the past. But its memory lingered still. Nowhere was that memory nurtured more determinedly than among the various component elements of Clan Donald to which Alasdair himself belonged. Because MacDonalds had controlled the Lordship, MacDonald power, MacDonald prestige also, had waned greatly with its fall. A good deal of subsequent Highland rebelliousness – up to and including the enthusiastic participation of Alasdair's own people, the Clanranald MacDonalds, in the last Jacobite rising – can consequently be traced to the stubbornly enduring conviction, particularly among the different MacDonald groupings in the Hebrides and on the West Highland mainland, that Clan Donald's vanished greatness might yet be restored.

Much was thought to have been shattered quite irrevocably, as a bard of the time so hauntingly lamented, with the collapse of the Lordship:

*Alas for those who have lost that company; alas for those who have parted from that society; for no race is as Clan Donald, a noble race, strong of courage.

There was no counting of their bounty; there was no reckoning of their gifts; their nobles knew no bound, no beginning, no end of generosity.

In the van of Clan Donald learning was commanded, and in their rear were service and honour and self-respect.

For sorrow and for sadness I have forsaken wisdom and learning; on their account I have forsaken all things; it is no joy without Clan Donald.[9]

These verses proved unduly pessimistic. The Scottish crown's destruction of the Lordship of the Isles was certainly a prominent landmark on the road that was to culminate in Culloden and the Highland Clearances. But the Gaelic civilisation established in Scotland by men like Colum Cille was to exhibit quite remarkable powers of endurance. Not only did this civilisation outlast the lordship's demise. It also proved capable of surviving still more devastating blows.

In 1601, at the Battle of Kinsale, an English army completed the Elizabethan conquest of Gaelic Ireland. Scotland's Gaels were thus deprived of what had long been, in a very real sense, their spiritual home. And England's ever more effective efforts to eliminate Ireland's Celtic culture, not least by ending the allegedly subversive influence of that country's Gaelic bards, were shortly to have their Highland parallels in the determined assaults which Scottish governments now launched against both clans and clanship.

Prominent among such assaults were the edicts known as the Statutes of Iona. Promulgated on Colum Cille's island in 1609, these consisted of various measures designed to wean Highland aristocrats away from their Gaelic inheritance by obliging them, for instance, to curtail their patronage of poets. Measures of this sort – as can be deduced from the conduct of chieftainly families during the Highland Clearances – were one day to have the intended effect. But this was by no means a foregone conclusion at the time of their implementation. What was most striking about the Highlands in the seventeenth century, and even in the early eighteenth century, was the extent to which the region's clan-based society continued stubbornly to resist the many attempts being made to disconnect it from its past.

The various MacDonald chieftains of Alasdair MacMhaighstir Alasdair's time, for instance, continued to think it worth their while to claim descent from Conn of the Hundred Battles, a shadowy Irish king of maybe fifteen hundred years before. The consequent sense of the Highland present being no more than a perpetuation of the distant past was heightened by the extent to which the Fenians and other mythical figures featured in popular tales so lengthy, according to one nineteenth-century folklorist, as to occupy 'a night or even several nights in recital'. Such tales had been ancient even when the monks of the Columban church had begun to take them down in writing. But so similar was the world of the Highland clan to the much earlier era in which the Fenian sagas had originated that these sagas seemed every bit as meaningful to MacMhaighstir Alasdair's generation as they had done to the Gaelic-speaking settlers who had originally imported all such lore from Ireland into Scotland. The typical Fenian tale, after all, was populated largely by warrior chiefs, their bards, harpists and other retainers. The upper echelons of a Highland clan consisted of exactly the same sort of people.[10]

The aes dana of early Irish society are readily recognisable in the lawmen, the musicians and the poets maintained by the Lordship of the Isles. And for all that the lordship's fall left such learned orders in an increasingly exposed position, the various – and all too often feuding – chieftains who inherited the lordship's territories also inherited at least something of its commitment to preserving Gaelic culture. 'The Hebrides are a forest of learned men,' declaimed one poet of the period around 1600. Nor was this mere wishful thinking. Island castles like Dunvegan, stronghold of Skye's MacLeod chiefs, are known to have contained all sorts of artists and performers. Itinerant bards, in particular, were both welcome and rewarded. For more than a century after the removal of their Irish counterparts in the decades following Kinsale, therefore, Highland poets – their conduct thus doing nothing to lessen the hostility shown towards them by southern politicians – were in a position to insist, as they had always done, on the need to sustain and nurture the very social structures which clanship's external enemies and critics were so anxious to see overthrown.[11]

As had equally been the case in the Celtic societies known to Julius Caesar, Highland bardic verse existed primarily to praise, exalt and honour the eminent men to whom bards owed their livelihood. To be a bard was thus, by definition, to be on the side of what was clearly sanctioned both by custom and belief. As can be seen from the extent to which bardic poetry deals in courage, in daring and in other characteristics of that kind, such poetry's values were those of the long-dead hero kings whom its practitioners commonly cited by name. Seventeenth-century Highland chiefs were carefully flattered by poets who compared them with other men – sometimes real, sometimes legendary – who had died more than a millennium earlier. And the archaic atmosphere thus fostered was both maintained and heightened by the deliberate use of antique language – the Gaelic of bardic poetry remaining loyal to its Irish roots long after the spoken Gaelic of the Highlands had begun to develop its own distinctive forms.[12]

To become a bard, then, it was necessary to undergo a long and very rigorous training. To learn both to read and to write classical Gaelic script was basic to this education. It was equally essential to commit to memory an enormous amount of historical and genealogical information. And as if that were not enough, the aspiring bard had finally to become technically proficient in the highly formulaic types of verse in which the profession had composed its poetry for many centuries.[13]

Prior to the English conquest and their ensuing abolition, the leading bardic schools had been in Ireland. And there were Highland families whose sons had been sent to such schools, generation after generation, over periods extending, in some instances, to several centuries. The most important of these families were the MacMhuirichs. This bardic dynasty's progenitor – himself a prominent poet – had come to Scotland from Ireland in the thirteenth century. His descendants had served first the Lords of the Isles and then, following the lordship's demise, the chiefs of the Clanranald MacDonalds. For some sixteen or seventeen generations, in other words, the MacMhuirichs had been central to the life of the Gaelic Highlands. And there is consequently no more poignant testimony to the Highland people's eventual fate than the sad little story taken down from Lachlan MacMhuirich, last representative of the once renowned MacMhuirich line, by men who made the journey from Edinburgh to Lachlan's Uist home in search of the ancient Gaelic manuscripts which his family were known to have previously possessed in quantity.

The year was 1800. The Highland Clearances had begun. The commonest opinion of Gaelic culture was Patrick Sellar's – this being that no such culture ever had existed. And as Lachlan MacMhuirich now made clear to the visiting scholars who had tracked him down to ask about the 'books' or manuscripts his ancestors had helped compile, the growing marginalisation of Gaelic had inevitably resulted in the loss of much that was quite simply irreplaceable:

> None of these books are to be found this day . . . He had seen one or two of them cut down by tailors in order to make measures . . . He himself had some of the skins or parchments in his custody after his father's death, but because he had not been taught to read them, and had no cause to set any value on them, they were lost.[14]

In *Neil MacVurich's Lost Poems*, its title referring to the vanished works of one of the MacMhuirich family's seventeenth-century representatives, a modern Scottish poet, William Neill, reflects thus on that passage:

> After the generations passed,
> his seed, lowered from bards to tailors,
> found the old vellum lying in a chest.
>
> History robbed them of learning
> in their own ancient tongue.
> No harm it seemed to them
> to cut up hide in tapes to measure cloth.

Be sparing of your sneers.
They could not read.
Blame those who read
and smother poets with a boor's indifference.[15]

That Lachlan MacMhuirich should have been the first senior member of
his family in possibly eighteen generations to be illiterate is a measure of
just how effective a demolition job had been done, by the start of the
nineteenth century, on the social order which had prevailed for so long in
the Highlands. It is a measure also of what was actually meant by the
'progress' which men like Patrick Sellar claimed to be bringing to the
region. Where there had been a tradition of learning and of scholarship
reaching back to the monks of Iona and the hermits of the Garvellochs,
there was now a demoralised, half-starved, dejected and largely leaderless
people who were being forcibly expelled from one township after another
in order to make way for farms of the sort which, at this point, took the
place of Achadh nan Seileach. In these circumstances, as one nineteenth-
century Gaelic poet commented, 'It is not surprising that the sweet
mother tongue should die. The deer in the wilderness do not speak and
the white sheep have no language.' Nor is it surprising either that a
twentieth-century Canadian novelist, on driving into Kintail and
thinking about his great-grandfather's enforced emigration from this now
largely empty quarter, should have commented that in a deserted
Highland glen you feel that everyone who ever mattered is dead and gone.
During the greater part of the period since so many of Alasdair
MacMhaighstir Alasdair's political hopes were extinguished at the Battle
of Culloden, the Highlands have not been a place to encourage much in
the way of optimism.[16]

It is indicative of the revolutionary nature of the many changes occurring
in the eighteenth-century Highlands that, by the century's end, a Gaelic
poet should have been honouring foxes in much the same way as his
MacMhuirich predecessors had honoured the great men of earlier times.
These great men, this poet implies, are no more. Clan chieftains have been
transformed into landlords. And whole communities have consequently
been eradicated:

*The villages and shielings
where warmth and cheer were found,

have no houses save the ruins,
and no tillage in the fields.
Every practice that prevailed
in Gaeldom has been altered,

and become so unnatural in the places
that were hospitable.[17]

Oran nam Balgairean, Song to the Foxes, this poem is entitled. Although it is by no means the most significant of the works of *Donnchadh Ban Mac an t-Saoir*, Duncan Ban MacIntyre, the man with whom this book began, it is somehow appropriate that MacIntyre, perhaps the most environmentally aware of Gaelic poets, should have wished a long life to foxes on the grounds that they were taking a welcome toll of the cheviot and blackface flocks which, by the eighteenth century's closing decades, were beginning to replace human beings in so much of northern Scotland. If there is one creature which is symbolic both of the ecological and of the social damage done to the Highlands by the clearances, that creature is the sheep. Its grazing habits have left large tracts of territory almost as bereft of vegetation as they are bereft of people. And as a whole succession of twentieth-century conservationists have clearly recognised, any successful strategy for the environmental renewal of the Scottish Highlands will have as one of its central objectives a permanent reduction in sheep numbers.[18]

That is an issue for a later chapter. What matters at this stage is the extent to which Duncan Ban MacIntyre, like Alasdair MacMhaighstir Alasdair, developed Highland thinking about nature in ways which ensured that such thinking was available to the later generations who were to undertake the task of reassembling a Highland identity from the wreckage left by the clearances. Because twentieth-century Gaelic poets like Sorley MacLean were to immerse themselves in the works of their eighteenth-century predecessors, and because these eighteenth-century poets, in their turn, were influenced by the way much earlier generations had thought about the natural environment, it is possible – as will be illustrated in due course – to detect something of the remote past in even the most recent Highland evocations of woodland and the like.

Although modern Highland writers frequently acknowledge the influence on them of Duncan Ban MacIntyre and several of his contemporaries, it is rather harder to pin down what it was that Duncan Ban MacIntyre derived from centuries prior to his own. One thing is clear about those centuries, however. The natural environment – for all that it might not have been quite as important a literary theme in the medieval period, for instance, as it had been when Gaelic was just starting to acquire a written form – had never ceased to fascinate Highlanders. A poet, even when writing about entirely different matters, would look almost automatically to his natural surroundings when in search of an appropriate simile:

> *White the swan, and white the seagull,
>   white the snow as it falls in February,
>   white the cotton-grass over the heather,
>   whiter than that my love's skin.[19]

An equally common characteristic, as in this sixteenth-century example, was to commence the poetic evocation of an especially favoured locality with a list of the wild creatures which inhabited it:

> *Sweet-tongued the eagle on its slopes,
>   sweet its cuckoos and its swan,
>   a hundred times sweeter than these the cry
>   of the fine-speckled, spotted calf of the deer.[20]

In the bardic schools, meanwhile, there was maintained the age-old Celtic practice of identifying certain human characteristics with particular elements of the natural order. Thus salmon stood for wisdom while trees, for their part, were frequently symbolic both of a chief's impressive genealogy and of the protection which he offered to his clan. A great man, of course, was most properly compared with the 'noble' trees of the ancient law tracts – with the oak, the pine and other species of that kind. Such trees, if illustrative of a man who had attained age as well as social standing, were invariably represented as lofty, spreading, fully grown. But a newly slain warrior, especially if killed in his youth, might readily be portrayed as a sapling stripped artificially of its foliage – neither the young tree nor the young man being destined to come to maturity.[21]

What was true of the bardic tradition was equally true of the less formal songs, poems and stories to be heard wherever Highlanders gathered round a fireside. Natural phenomena were always among the popular culture's more important sources of inspiration. Thus one very old Gaelic song, of which a sound recording exists in Edinburgh

University's School of Scottish Studies, imitates birds so effectively, or so a modern authority has commented, that 'the dividing lines between birdsong, music and speech are impossible to determine'. Another such song, this one a lullaby, tells where birds make their nests:

> *The nest of the raven
> is in the hawthorn rock.
>
> The nest of the ptarmigan
> is in the rough mountain.
>
> The nest of the blackbird
> is in the withered bough.
>
> The nest of the pigeon
> is in the red crags.
>
> The nest of the cuckoo
> is in the hedge-sparrow's nest.
>
> The nest of the lapwing
> is in the hummocked marsh.
>
> The nest of the kite
> is high on the mountain-slope.
>
> The nest of the red-hen
> is in the green-topped heather.
>
> The nest of the curlew
> is in the bubbling peat-moss.
>
> The nest of the oyster-catcher
> is among the smooth shingle.
>
> The nest of the heron
> is in the pointed tree.
>
> The nest of the stonechat
> is in the garden dyke.

The nest of the rook
is in the tree's top.[22]

This single song lists some two dozen birds in all. It does so, very noticeably, in the closely observed, almost matter-of-fact, manner adopted by the hermit-poets of the seventh and eighth centuries. It is this same manner – this marriage, you might almost say, of the literary with the scientific – which one finds in Duncan Ban MacIntyre's depictions of the hills between Tyndrum and Bridge of Orchy. Both in *Oran Coire a' Cheathaich*, Song to Misty Corrie, and *Moladh Beinn Dobhrain*, Praise of Ben Dorain, MacIntyre painstakingly catalogues plant after plant, species after species with the 'intent delicacy', the 'precision', the 'attentiveness' which might once have been displayed, as Iain Crichton Smith observes in one of his own poems, by a 'Celtic monk carving a Celtic cross':

Natural as a lark he sang his song
and patient too as a scientist who would marry
music to fact, research to a musical tongue.[23]

'As a nature poet,' Smith writes elsewhere of Duncan Ban MacIntyre, 'he is unmatchable.' And by way of corroborating that particular verdict, it is worth quoting once again from Crichton Smith's own English-language version of *Beinn Dobhrain*. MacIntyre is here describing the deer he came to understand, appreciate, even love, as a result of his employment as a stalker:

*Pleasant to me rising
at morning
to see them the horizon
adorning.

Seeing them so clear,
my simple-headed deer
modestly appear
in their joyousness.

They freely exercise
their sweet and level cries.
From bodies trim and terse,
hear their bellowing.

A badger of a hind
wallows in a pond.
Her capricious mind
has such vagaries!

How they fill the parish
with their chorus
sweeter than fine Irish
tunes glorious.

More tuneful than all art
the music of the hart
eloquent, alert,
on Ben Dorain.

The stag with his own call
struck from his breast wall –
you'll hear him mile on mile
at his scale-making.

The sweet harmonious hind –
with her calf behind –
elaborates the wind
with her music.

Palpitant bright eye
without squint in it.
Lash below the brow,
guide and regulant.

Walker quick and grave,
so elegant to move
ahead of that great drove
when accelerant.

There's no flaw in your step,
there's all law in your leap,
there's no rust or sleep
in your motion there.

Lengthening your stride,
intent on what's ahead,
who of live or dead
could outrace you?[24]

Not the least astonishing thing about Duncan Ban MacIntyre is the fact that he was illiterate. The bards who preceded him, admittedly, are described by their contemporaries as having constructed their compositions entirely in their heads – usually when lying down in darkened rooms. But all such bards, as previously emphasised, were highly skilled in penmanship – taking care to inscribe their newly crafted poems on vellum of the kind poor Lachlan MacMhuirich had seen so casually destroyed. MacIntyre, in contrast, relied on others to take down his work from his dictation. Neither a bard of the old school, nor, like Alasdair MacMhaighstir Alasdair, a well-connected and formally educated spokesman for the Jacobite gentry, MacIntyre can be seen as representative of the people on whom Gaelic was henceforth to depend for its survival – those crofters and others who, in the course of the next two centuries, would take such pleasure in his songs. Born in 1724 in a tiny township on the south shore of Loch Tulla, itself a couple of miles north of Bridge of Orchy, he was to eke out a precarious existence as a gamekeeper prior to his leaving the Highlands altogether in the 1760s – a period when, as indicated by the tenor of MacIntyre's own lines in praise of foxes, the enforced depopulation of the glens was just beginning to get underway.[25]

Duncan Ban MacIntyre was influenced certainly by Alasdair MacMhaighstir Alasdair – turning out his own *Song of Summer* in emulation of Alasdair's earlier masterpiece. He was influenced also, no doubt, both by the bardic heritage – his *Beinn Dobhrain* being designed to honour a mountain in terms which might previously have been applied to a great chieftain – and by the traditional tales and folksongs which he would have heard while growing up beside Loch Tulla. But Duncan Ban MacIntyre, as Iain Crichton Smith remarks when writing of *Beinn Dobhrain*, brought to his poetry a new clarity of vision which was very much his own:

It is clear why MacIntyre is regarded as a great Gaelic poet. Nowhere else in Scottish poetry do we have a poem of such sunniness, grace and exactitude maintained for such a length, with such a wealth of varied music and teeming richness of language. The whole poem has about it the authentic feel of authoritative genius. The detailed

84

obsession, the richly concentrated gaze, the loving scrutiny, undiverted by philosophical analysis, has created a particular world, joyously exhausting area after area as the Celtic monks exhausted page after page in the *Book of Kells*. And indeed it is that splendid word 'illumination' we should be using about this poem.[26]

Picking up on the fact that *Beinn Dobhrain*, is constructed on the same principle as pibroch, the classical music of the Highland bagpipe, Norman MacCaig, another modern Scottish poet with his own strong interest in the Highlands, has written:

> A mountain is a sort of music: theme
> And counter theme displaced in air amongst
> Their own variations.[27]

That brings this book back to its opening pages. For what is significant about Duncan Ban MacIntyre, in relation to the origins of the Scottish green consciousness which Professor Christopher Smout sees MacIntyre as having helped in some way to originate, is not just his achievement as a poet – great though that achievement was. What matters equally is MacIntyre's detailed understanding of the natural environment. Rather like another eighteenth-century figure with whom he otherwise had nothing much in common, this figure being Gilbert White, a Hampshire vicar, Duncan Ban MacIntyre discerned, in outline anyway, just what it means to think about the world ecologically. That is why *Beinn Dobhrain* can more meaningfully be compared with White's *Natural History of Selborne* than with nature poetry of the sort which William Wordsworth and other English romantics were soon to be producing in such quantity.

Wordsworth's 'nature' is essentially a spiritual concept. His natural world is to be experienced emotionally much more than it is to be methodically observed in the fashion pioneered by Gilbert White and other early naturalists. MacIntyre's verse, in contrast, is never introspective. It is certainly the product of Duncan Ban's strong feelings for the hills he knew so well. But it depicts those hills in terms which are strictly naturalistic. Hence the link between MacIntyre's Argyll and Gilbert White's Selborne. White, by setting birds and mammals firmly in their habitats, is groping towards the essence of ecology. MacIntyre, in poems like *Beinn Dobhrain*, is doing the same thing. Not only does he demonstrate a close knowledge of deer and their behaviour. He makes connections between deer and the particular grasses and herbs on which they graze. And he insists, as mentioned in the course of this book's

introduction, on the overarching significance of the much wider entity –
the ecosystem – of which deer, vegetation, even the mountain itself, are
simply the component parts:

> *The hind is in the forest
> as she ought to be,
> where she may have sweet grass,
> clean, fine-bladed;
> heath-rush and deer's hair grass,
> herbs in which strength resides,
> and which would make her flanks
> plump and fat-covered;
> a spring in which there is
> abundant water-cress,
> she deems more sweet than wine,
> and would drink of it;
> sorrel and rye grass
> which flourish on the moor,
> she prefers as food
> to rank field grass.
> Of her fare she deemed
> these the delicacies:
> primrose, St John's wort
> and tormentil flowers;
> tender spotted orchis,
> forked, spiked and glossy,
> on meadows where, in clusters,
> it flourishes.
> Such was the dietary
> that would increase their strength,
> that would pull them through
> in the stormy days;
> that would upon their back
> amass the roll of fat,
> which, over their spare frame,
> was not cumbersome.[28]

There were other eighteenth-century Gaelic poets who wrote evocatively
of their surroundings – among them *Rob Donn*, Robert MacKay, and
Uilleam Ros, William Ross, the one from Sutherland, the other from
Strath Suardal in Skye. But none – not even Alasdair MacMhaighstir

Alasdair who was, to some extent, the model for them all – could quite match MacIntyre's descriptive talents or quite equal the sheer profundity of his insights into what it is that makes wild nature work the way it does. It seems all the more tragic, therefore, that the poetic tradition which Duncan Ban MacIntyre had brought to so magnificent a culmination – this Gaelic tradition which had its origins in places like Eilean an Naoimh – was now to be largely ignored by a wider world which, by the end of MacIntyre's long life, was just beginning to appreciate the Scottish Highlands in a wholly novel way.

Duncan Ban MacIntyre died in Edinburgh in 1812. He had lived there since 1767. For much of this period he had served in the town guard which the Scottish capital's wealthier residents employed to protect themselves from the city's criminal fraternity. That some at least of eighteenth-century Edinburgh's many literary grandees would have encountered Duncan Ban MacIntyre in the course of their perambulations around the town is absolutely certain. That they would have paid him no very great attention is a pretty fair assumption. Town guards and literary Edinburgh quite simply did not mix.[29]

This was a great pity. For literary Edinburgh – despite its longstanding dislike of Scotland's Gaelic-speaking population – was suddenly starting to be terribly excited by the Highlands. Literary Edinburgh, in fact, was soon to be undertaking its own enthusiastic explorations of Gaelic tradition. But the variant of that tradition which literary Edinburgh was afterwards to noise around the world was one derived from sources other than the work of men like Duncan Ban MacIntyre. This meant, among other things, that external images of the Scottish Highlands – even when they began, as they now did, to be much more positive than previously – still diverged as sharply as ever from the way in which the Highlands were generally regarded by people actually living among the hills and glens which writer after writer was shortly to be glorifying in best-selling English prose. This cultural divide was to have far-reaching consequences. Among these consequences, as already hinted more than once, has been the remarkable extent to which twentieth-century environmental organisations have managed, on occasion, to offend and alienate the Highland communities with which they necessarily come in contact.

Modern environmental thinking, as the following chapter will attempt to demonstrate, owes no small debt to eighteenth-century Edinburgh's approach to the Highlands. But this approach, as will be seen, was one which tended either to ignore the Highlanders of the time or to be desperately pessimistic about their future prospects. When Highlanders – on their recovering the collective self-confidence which had taken such a knock in the era of Culloden and the clearances – finally began to assert their own interests and to promote their own interpretation of their Gaelic heritage, therefore, one of their immediate targets was that very image of the Highlands with which the environmental outlook has, from the outset, been inextricably bound up. The causes of disagreement between environmentalists and Highlanders can thus be seen to extend far beyond the detail of the various conflicts mentioned by way of introduction to this book. Ultimately at issue in such battles are two quite different perspectives on the Highlands and their future. This book's concluding chapter will suggest that these perspectives can, in the end, be reconciled. First, however, it is necessary to understand a little more about them.

CHAPTER FOUR

Oh for the Crags that are Wild and Majestic!

On leaving Kingussie and heading north through Badenoch on a road which is one of the busiest tourist routes in Scotland, you briefly glimpse a Georgian mansion on a hillside to your left. This is Balavil House which, because its windows face the Cairngorms, rising steeply to the east, enjoys views as spectacular as any in the Highlands. But what gave a particular pleasure to the man for whom Balavil House was built, or so it is tempting to deduce from what is known of that man's character, was the almost condescending way his fine home would originally have overlooked a less impressive set of dwellings just a mile or so away across the River Spey. James MacPherson had been born over there at Invertromie in 1736. And though his father was closely related to Ewen MacPherson of Cluny, chief of Clan MacPherson, the young James's circumstances had been extremely modest – so modest as to make it unlikely that anyone, not even James himself, foresaw the slightest possibility of his ever being able to afford a house as striking as the one at Balavil.

The MacPhersons being every bit as staunchly Jacobite as Alasdair MacMhaighstir Alasdair's Clan Donald kinsfolk, this part of Scotland, when James MacPherson was growing up here, was not the sort of place where people very readily prospered. Badenoch, at that time, was more a military frontier than a tourist destination. Not far from Invertromie were Ruthven Barracks – a government garrison complex which was intended to keep Highlanders in order but which, in the event, was burned by Prince Charles Edward Stuart's rebel soldiers in the early part of 1746. Nor was the eventual crushing of the prince's army to bring immediate peace to Invertromie and its neighbouring localities. MacPherson of Cluny – although he had taken a leading part in Charles Edward Stuart's rising and although he was known to be hiding out in Badenoch – was never found by the government troops who spent several years pursuing him. These troops, needless to say, took out their consequent frustrations on such lowlier MacPhersons as they could conveniently lay their hands on. The outcome, or so it was remarked by one of Cluny's senior clansmen, included 'murders, burnings, ravishings, plunderings' on a scale that was exceptional even by the unexacting standards of the period.[1]

James MacPherson, a boy of ten when Culloden was fought, no doubt witnessed something of these horrors. But neither he nor his counterparts elsewhere in the Highlands were to make it their business to avenge this latest Jacobite defeat. The previous generation of Gaelic-speaking gentry, the class into which James had been born at Invertromie, had frequently been every bit as fanatically Jacobite as Alasdair MacMhaighstir Alasdair whose own family belonged to this same middle-ranking segment of the clan-based society from which Charles Edward Stuart had obtained so much support. But that society, by the middle of the eighteenth century, was at last beginning to disintegrate. And Jacobitism, within a few years of Culloden, was clearly finished as a serious political force. Both James MacPherson and his similarly situated contemporaries, if they were to do anything substantial with their lives, had no alternative but to break completely with a lot of what had gone before. Soon many of these young men were openly ingratiating themselves – perhaps ignobly but, from their standpoint, realistically – with the new ruling order which had so forcibly been imposed on the Highlands. That ruling order naturally welcomed all such converts to its cause. Hundreds, even thousands, of well-born Highlanders – individuals of the sort who had once rallied to Charles Edward Stuart – were shortly to be serving an expanding British Empire as army officers, colonial officials, entrepreneurs. They were to be making their way in the world, in other words, by means very much like those adopted by James MacPherson who was eventually to move to England where he became, in quick succession, an imperial civil servant, a pro-government pamphleteer, an MP and the London representative of the Nabob of Arcot. These, of course, were highly lucrative positions. Hence MacPherson's ability, on his retiring to the Highlands in the 1780s, to find the sizable sums required to pay for his grand house at Balavil.

What gives James MacPherson his huge relevance to this book's central theme, however, is not his later – and highly successful – career as a Scotsman come to England on the make. What matters about MacPherson, in the context of an analysis of changing attitudes to Scotland's natural environment, is a flimsy volume he published in 1760 while still in his early twenties. MacPherson, at this point, was teaching in Badenoch to which he had returned in 1756 after a stint at university in Aberdeen. Aspiring to make a name for himself as a writer, the young man from Invertromie had already published a number of poems. These had attracted little interest. But his 1760 effort, *Fragments of Ancient*

Poetry Collected in the Highlands of Scotland, was to catapult its author to practically unprecedented literary fame. What James MacPherson was apparently making available to his readers – by means both of his 1760 collection and two very similar books which followed in 1762 and 1763 – were the poems of a Gaelic bard who had died some fifteen centuries earlier. This bard's name, it seemed, was Ossian. And that name, like James MacPherson's own, was now to wing its way across the world. Not just in Scotland and England, but in Germany, France, Italy, Spain, Russia, the United States and a host of other countries, the Highlands thus acquired a renown and a reputation they have never since quite lost. But the Highlands which more and more people now heard about, read about, thought about and wrote about were James MacPherson's Highlands. And James MacPherson's Highlands were a most peculiar kind of place.

The Highlands as depicted in MacPherson's pages owe very little to the Highlands as described, in MacPherson's own lifetime, by men like Alasdair MacMhaighstir Alasdair and Duncan Ban MacIntyre. They owe equally little to the Gaelic-speaking world as portrayed by those hermit-poets whose writings date from the period in which MacPherson's Ossianic outpourings are ostensibly located. Neither the 'sunniness' which Iain Crichton Smith discerns in *Beinn Dobhrain* nor the sheer *joie de vivre* which you get in the earliest Gaelic poetry are anywhere to be found in James MacPherson:

I sit by the mossy fountain; on top of the hill of winds. One tree is rustling above me. Dark waves roll over the heath. The lake is troubled below. The deer descend from the hill. No hunter at a distance is seen; no whistling cowherd is nigh. It is midday: but all is silent. Sad are my thoughts alone.[2]

MacPherson's Highlands, then, are irredeemably cheerless, gloomy, desolate, even haunted:

From the wood-skirted waters of Lego, ascend, at times, grey-bosomed mists . . . Wide over Lara's stream is poured the vapour, dark and deep: the moon, like a dim shield, is swimming through its folds. With this clothe the spirits of old their sudden gestures on the wind when they stride, from blast to blast, along the dusky night. Often, blended with the gale, to some warrior's grave they roll the mist, a grey dwelling to his ghost, until the songs arise.[3]

The songs MacPherson has in mind, you can be sure, will not be happy ones:

Autumn is dark on the mountains; a grey mist rests on the hills. The whirlwind is heard on the heath. Dark rolls the river through the narrow plain. A tree stands alone on the hill and marks the grave of Connal. The leaves whirl around with the wind and strew the grave of the dead. At times are seen here the ghosts of the deceased, when the musing hunter alone stalks slowly over the heath. Appear in thy armour of light, thou ghost of the mighty Connal! Shine, near thy tomb, Crimora! Like a moonbeam from a cloud.[4]

The wind which swirled around the grave of Connal was as nothing to the storm that was to break around the head of James MacPherson within months of this material's publication. Was MacPherson, as he first implied and afterwards insisted, no more than a translator of very ancient Gaelic poetry? Or was he, as Samuel Johnson and many others were soon to assert, simply defrauding his huge public by palming off as antiquated epics what were, in truth, the products of his own imagination?

There is no simple answer to these questions. The eighteenth-century Highlands were certainly well supplied with stories and poetry dealing with the very remote epoch which Ossian – a familiar name in Fenian legend and tradition – had supposedly set out to chronicle in Gaelic epics which MacPherson, in turn, had supposedly converted into English. A good deal of this material was eventually recorded systematically by folklorists whose own interest in the Highlands was stimulated, in large part, by the controversy surrounding James MacPherson's work. And much of what was afterwards collected in this way was clearly well known to MacPherson himself. As well as taking a close interest in such lore as was available in Badenoch, then a wholly Gaelic-speaking district, the young MacPherson made various forays into the West Highlands and the Hebrides. He had access, it is now conceded even by his critics, to some at least of those Gaelic manuscripts which had not fallen victim to the destructive processes described by Lachlan MacMhuirich. MacPherson's Ossianic writings, then, are by no means their author's own invention. They are founded on very ancient Gaelic myth of the sort MacPherson claimed to be translating. But the undoubted basis of authenticity on which James MacPherson constructed his prose poems was just that, a basis and an underpinning. The finished product was, in large part, his own work.[5]

This, however, did little to reduce MacPherson's impact on the wider western world. That world had for some time been dominated intellectually and philosophically by the increasingly scientific and rationalist mentality associated with what afterwards became known as the Enlightenment. Economies were expanding. Cities were growing. Society as a whole, or so Enlightenment thinkers generally considered, was steadily advancing. Humanity, in consequence, was taking charge of its own destiny. Nature was yielding up its secrets. The universe was to be understood and analysed mathematically. The superstitions and credulities of earlier ages were no longer to be taken seriously. People – certainly the people who most mattered – were increasingly committed to the values of a civilisation which took something of a self-righteous conceit in the extent to which its leading intellects appeared to be escaping from the constraining influences of a more tradition-ridden past.

But any movement of this kind tends eventually to produce a backlash. And just such a backlash duly took shape in a growing conviction that material progress, far from being a force for liberation, was destroying and corrupting all that was best about mankind. Human beings, it began to be argued vigorously by mid-eighteenth-century philosophers like Jean-Jacques Rousseau, had once been virtuous, upstanding, brave and pure. But civilised man's increasingly complex institutions, together with the money and possessions being flaunted on all sides, had hopelessly subverted those naturally occurring characteristics. A new austerity was consequently called for; a new readiness to acknowledge that affluence was frequently synonymous with decadence; a new willingness to learn from those simpler societies which Enlightenment opinion automatically dismissed as primitive. All that was tribal and primeval – whether it was to be found among eighteenth-century North America's native peoples or among Europe's own much earlier inhabitants – was thus in vogue, by the 1760s, as it had never been before.[6]

To adherents of this cult of the 'noble savage', and there were growing numbers of such adherents both in Scotland and the rest of Britain, James MacPherson's books seemed a heaven-sent confirmation of their most passionate beliefs. The world evoked by MacPherson's renderings of the poems of Ossian was a world as far removed as it was possible to be from the one inhabited by the many comfortably-off individuals who now felt their lives, as a result of what was being said so stridently by Rousseau and his followers, to be seriously lacking in the more heroic virtues. This lack MacPherson's publications helped – at least vicariously – to make good. Here was nobility. Here was courage. Here were men with whom it was a real thrill to identify:

As a hundred winds on Morven; as the streams of a hundred hills; as clouds fly successive over heaven; as the dark ocean assails the shore of the desert: so roaring, so vast, so terrible the armies mixed on Lena's echoing heath. The groans of the people spread over the hills: it was like the thunder of night when the cloud bursts on Cona and a thousand ghosts shriek at once on the hollow wind.[7]

No wonder that Napoleon, that archetypal man of action, was reputed to have carried an edition of Ossian with him on his campaigns. No wonder that Edinburgh's intelligentsia, those self-styled *literati* who had made Scotland's capital an internationally significant centre of learning, should have been equally enthralled. The Edinburgh of Adam Smith and David Hume might not have condescended to notice the great Gaelic poet – Duncan Ban MacIntyre – who was actually living in its midst. But James MacPherson was to experience no such rejection. The 'artless song of the savage', as discerned in *The Iliad* and *The Odyssey* by the Edinburgh historian and pioneer sociologist, Robert Ferguson, seemed readily discernible in Ossian also. MacPherson, as a result, found Edinburgh's doors thrown open to him. Just as the literati were afterwards to patronise the 'heaven-taught ploughman', Robert Burns, so they now took a slightly off-putting delight in flattering and befriending a previously obscure schoolteacher from Badenoch.[8]

Both Robert Burns and James MacPherson, in their different ways, provided eighteenth-century Edinburgh – or so eighteenth-century Edinburgh told itself – with direct access to the 'natural' sentiments which were then so much in fashion. But this was not the only service rendered by MacPherson, in particular, to a Scottish establishment which, despite its apparently unshakeable belief in its own significance, was prone to occasional anxiety about Scotland's long-term prospects. The country, since 1707, had been united with England. And Scotland's governing classes had no intention of imperilling this economically vital link. To have done so would have been to place their own prosperity in jeopardy. But neither were mercantile and middle-class Scots at all enamoured by the prospect of their national identity being submerged in that of England. What such Scots ideally needed, then, was a means of asserting their Scottishness in a wholly non-challenging manner. It was just such a means that James MacPherson now provided.

By enabling his patrons to lay claim to a heroic heritage on a par with that of Greece, MacPherson hugely boosted the collective ego of the men who mattered in the Scotland of his day. At a time when – thanks to Rousseau – all of Europe was in search of just such primeval glories, Scots found themselves the possessors of ancient epics of a kind that could be placed alongside those of Homer. This was something in which Scotland could take pride. This was something which reinforced the country's claim to be distinctive. But this was also something which – precisely because the world of Ossian was so far removed from eighteenth-century actualities – could readily furnish Scotland's rulers with a wonderfully unthreatening national identity. Scotland's genuinely historical heroes, such as Robert Bruce or William Wallace, could be cultivated only at the risk of raising questions as to what had happened to the independence for which such men had fought. To make too much of them – unless one wanted, Fanon-like, to conjure up the past in aid of revolutionary struggle – could well be awkward. MacPherson's mist-enveloped warriors, however, could be celebrated safely. They stood for no cause other than the one of making Scotland out to be a place that was not quite the same as England.

James MacPherson, then, began the process of providing modern Scotland, and not least Lowland Scotland, with the slightly bizarre self-image which the country has kept polished ever since. Because of its Ossianic origins – and in spite of the mutual hostility which had previously characterised relations between Lowland Scots and their northern neighbours – this self-image has been mostly Highland in character. It has habitually dealt, as all the world knows, in kilts, in pipe bands and in cabers. None of these, of course, are actually featured in James MacPherson's publications. But all such emblems nevertheless serve to reinforce the essentially Ossianic, and still astonishingly powerful, notion of Scotland as a wholly 'Highland' country. Nor does modern Scotland's 'Highlandness' begin and end with tartan. Ours is a country, as all the world also knows, of bens and glens as well as bagpipes. That the world has known this for so long is due in large part to the work of James MacPherson.

James MacPherson's books were to go through hundreds of editions in dozens of languages. The English essayist and critic, William Hazlitt, writing in 1818, thought that 'the principal works of poetry in the world' were 'Homer, the bible, Dante and, let me add, Ossian'. Goethe, Herder, Schiller and numerous other eminent literary figures were almost as unstinting in their praise. Rather like J. R. R. Tolkien's twentieth-century fantasy, *Lord of the Rings*, which owes a recognisable debt to MacPherson and which was similarly to fulfil the romantic cravings of an age that had become a little disenchanted with its own prosperity, Ossian thus acquired cult status. But Tolkien's Middle Earth, other than in the psychedelic fantasies of 1960s hippies high on pot, had no reality beyond the printed page. The Highlands, in contrast, were very solidly in existence. It was possible to visit the area in search of the eerily enticing scenes which MacPherson had so graphically described. And though MacPherson's Ossianic landscapes were scarcely less illusory than Tolkien's, it was all too easy for people to visualise the Highlands not as the Highlands actually were but as MacPherson had imagined them to be. When, at the beginning of the nineteenth century, therefore, their homeland became the setting for poems and romances even more successful than MacPherson's, Highlanders found themselves condemned to live simultaneously, as it were, in two parallel universes. One of these universes was the grimly matter-of-fact Highlands which were characterised by clearance, poverty and growing social dislocation. In the alternative Highlands, on the other hand, these things did not impinge. Their history, if it had not exactly ended, had become stuck firmly in an era which, if a bit more recent than the Ossianic one, was equally escapist.[9]

That such was so was due to Walter Scott. 'By far the greatest creative force in Scottish literature,' Edwin Muir wrote of him. And so he was. This meant that when Scott took over MacPherson's Ossianic backdrops for his own dramatic purposes, Highland hills, Highland lochs, Highland woods, even Highland weather, became still more inescapably associated with the moody grandeur in which Walter Scott delighted every bit as much as James MacPherson:

> The stag had eve had drunk his fill,
> Where danced the moon on Monan's rill,
> And deep his midnight lair had made
> In lone Glenartney's hazel shade;
> But, when the sun his beacon red
> Had kindled on Benvorlich's head,
> The deep-mouth'd bloodhound's heavy bay
> Resounded up the rocky way,
> And faint, from farther distance borne,
> Were heard the clanging hoof and horn.[10]

These lines, which could once have been recited by practically any Scottish schoolchild, are from the opening stanzas of *The Lady of the Lake* which Scott published in 1810. The poem's action takes place in the Trossachs – mostly in the vicinity of Loch Katrine. And though Scott apparently intended his narrative to be a 'vivid and exact description' of

TORRIDON, WESTER ROSS (CAILEAN MACLEAN)

KYLE OF TONGUE, SUTHERLAND (CAILEAN MACLEAN)

LOCH CILL CHRIOSD, ISLE OF SKYE (CAILEAN MACLEAN)

IONA AND ITS ABBEY CHURCH (CAILEAN MACLEAN)

ST KILDA (CAILEAN MACLEAN)

CALLANISH, ISLE OF LEWIS (CAILEAN MACLEAN)

ARDNAMURCHAN POINT (CAILEAN MACLEAN)

BUACHAILLE ETIVE MOR, GLENCOE (CAILEAN MACLEAN)

Opposite: LOCH BOISDALE, SOUTH UIST (CAILEAN MACLEAN)

HIGHLAND WOOD IN SPRING (CAILEAN MACLEAN)

the Highlands as they were in the sixteenth century, the period in which *The Lady of the Lake* is set, it is immediately apparent that the poem's world exists primarily in Scott's imagination:

> With boughs that quaked at every breath,
> Grey birch and aspen wept beneath;
> Aloft, the ash and warrior oak
> Cast anchor in the rifted rock;
> And, higher yet, the pine tree hung
> His shatter'd trunk, and frequent flung,
> Where seem'd the cliffs to meet on high,
> His boughs athwart the narrow'd sky.
> Highest of all, where white peaks glanced,
> Where glist'ning streamers waved and danced,
> The wanderer's eye could barely view
> The summer heaven's delicious blue;
> So wondrous wild, the whole might seem
> The scenery of a fairy dream.[11]

That last line is crucial. By Gaelic poets like Duncan Ban MacIntyre, landscape was celebrated for its own sake and in recognition of its own importance. In Walter Scott's work, however, landscape is always a means to an end. His trees, cliffs, and mountains clearly have a basis in reality. But Scott felt free to rearrange nature in such a way as to create 'the scenery of a fairy dream'. And the technique is one he utilised in his novels every bit as much as in his poetry:

> It was towards evening as they entered one of the tremendous passes which afford communication between the High and Low Country; the path, which was extremely steep and rugged, winded up a chasm between two tremendous rocks, following the passage which a foaming stream, that brawled from below, appeared to have worn for itself in the course of ages. A few slanting beams of the sun, which was now setting, reached the water in its darksome bed, and showed it partially, chafed by a hundred rocks, and broken by a hundred falls.[12]

The point of that paragraph from *Waverley*, Walter Scott's first novel, is to make readers properly aware of the huge distinction between the Highlands, as described by Scott at any rate, and the much more workaday world which these same readers actually inhabited. Like many of the nineteenth-century prints and paintings which it did so much to inspire, Scott's fiction quite deliberately heightens hills, widens rivers and generally creates the impression of a territory containing absolutely nothing of the commonplace. As for the Highlanders one meets in *Waverley*, they are, if anything, still more picturesque than their surroundings:

> He started at the sight of what he had not yet happened to see, a mountaineer in his full national costume. The individual Gael was a stout, dark, young man, of low stature, the ample folds of whose plaid added to the appearance of strength which his person exhibited. The short kilt, or petticoat, showed his sinewy and clean-made limbs; the goatskin purse, flanked by the usual defences, a dirk and steel-wrought pistol, hung before him; his bonnet had a short feather, which indicated his claim to be treated as a Duinhe-wassel, or a sort of gentleman; a broadsword dangled by his side, a target hung upon his shoulder, and a long Spanish fowling-piece occupied one of his hands.[13]

Walter Scott, it should be said, knew both the Highlands and Highlanders extremely well. He understood Highland history. His novels – not just *Waverley* and *Rob Roy* but others also – deal very plausibly with the workings of the clan-based society which is recreated in their pages. What Scott's fiction neither examines nor concedes, however, is the possibility that Gaelic civilisation, for all the catastrophes which had befallen it since Culloden, might still have a future. In this Scott followed James MacPherson. The 'popularity' of MacPherson's writings, Walter Scott was to note towards the end of his life, had helped convince him that 'Highland subjects' were worth tackling. But these subjects, if they were to appeal to the mass audience which Scott always wanted to attract, had to be treated very carefully. The reading public could certainly be persuaded to take an interest in Highlanders. James MacPherson had proved as much. But the Ossianic phenomenon had also shown, as Scott would have been well aware, that the public liked its Highlanders kept safely in the past.[14]

The melancholy which so pervades MacPherson's work is quite inseparable from his conviction that the Gaelic world was doomed:

> How long in Moi-lena shall we weep? How long pour in Erin our tears? The mighty will not return. Oscar shall not rise in his strength. The valiant must fall in their day and be no more known on their hills. Where are our fathers, O warriors! The chiefs of the

time of old? They have set like stars that have shone. We only hear the sound of their praise . . . Thus shall we pass away; in the day of our fall. Then let us be renowned when we may; and leave our fame behind us, like the last beams of the sun, when he hides his red head in the west . . . The days of my years begin to fail. I feel the weakness of my arm. My fathers bend from their clouds to receive their grey-haired son.[15]

There is detectable in such passages something of the feelings experienced by James MacPherson as a result of his youthful exposure to the consequences of Culloden. The society which shaped MacPherson had collapsed around him in the 1740s. And for all that MacPherson was ultimately to walk away from its wreckage, with a view to making his career in England, he was clearly affected very deeply by clanship's sudden and complete distintegration. That much is evident from the despairing hopelessness which oozes from every nook and cranny of his Ossianic landscapes.

Ironically, however, nothing did more to ensure the commercial success of James MacPherson's Highlanders than the fact that these same Highlanders were safely dead and buried. You cannot very well romanticise a people who might be about to endanger your existence. That is why the only emotions which Highlanders aroused outside the Highlands, prior to Culloden, were those of fear, suspicion, even hatred. And that is why the military conquest of the Highlands was an essential prelude to the Ossianic craze. The Edinburgh intellectuals who were both to make a god of Ossian and to treat MacPherson as his prophet would most certainly have done neither of these things if there had been the slightest prospect of a set of real-live Gaelic warriors coming once more marching up their city's High Street in the way that Charles Edward Stuart's Highland army had done in 1745. Absolutely central to the cult of Ossian, therefore, was the fact that, by the 1760s, Highlanders no longer threatened to disturb the wellbeing of the middle-class men and women who bought James MacPherson's books.

Walter Scott appreciated this as much as anyone. Reflecting on the immense public appeal of *The Lady of the Lake*, which sold the then enormous number of 20,000 copies in its first year, he openly acknowledged that 'the richer and wealthier part of the kingdom' would have been 'indisposed to countenance a poem the scene of which was laid in the Highlands' had the 'feuds and political dissensions' of an earlier period not been permanently ended at Culloden. Nor was Scott in the business of unsettling his southern readers by suggesting to them, even at a remove of more than half a century, that there was anything fundamentally wrong about the way that Highlanders had been treated in the 1740s. As *Waverley* amply demonstrates, Scott identified emotionally with the Jacobite cause and with that cause's many Gaelic-speaking adherents. But he identified a lot more strongly, and in an altogether harder-headed fashion, with the commercially driven society to which both he and his readers actually belonged. And this society, as Scott clearly understood, would have been dealt a potentially devastating blow had Jacobite Highlanders somehow managed to win their war with Hanoverian Britain.[16]

Edward Waverley, the young and rather ineffectual English officer at the centre of Walter Scott's first novel, becomes romantically infatuated with the Highlands. He attaches himself, as a result, to Charles Edward Stuart's army. But when that army goes into action against General Sir John Cope's forces on the outskirts of Edinburgh in September 1746, Waverley begins to be confronted by several home truths:

> Waverley could plainly recognise the standard of the troops he had formerly commanded, and hear the trumpets and kettle-drums sound the signal of advance, which he had so often obeyed. He could hear, too, the well-known word given, in the English dialect, by the equally well-distinguished voice of the commanding officer for whom he had once felt so much respect. It was at that instant that, looking around him, he saw the wild dress and appearance of his Highland associates, heard their whispers in an uncouth and unknown language, looked upon his own dress, so unlike that which he had worn from his infancy, and wished to awake from what seemed at the moment a dream, strange, horrible and unnatural.[17]

On reading this, you feel Scott, as it were, come tapping slyly on your shoulder. And, just like Waverley, you feel the spell which Scott himself has cast begin at last to break. Highlanders, you realise, for all their primitive charm, could not be permitted to get in the way of progress. Theirs, you are inclined to agree with Waverley, was a heroic, strangely captivating, lifestyle. But it was also, as Scott has finally got round to reminding you, a barbaric and outmoded one. So Culloden, you conclude, was maybe for the best. And not just Culloden either. For if you were one of the thousands who read *Waverley* in the year or so following the novel's publication in the summer of 1814, that gentle tapping on your shoulder – as well as adding to your enjoyment of Scott's fiction – might well have helped forestall such unease as you might otherwise have experienced on learning of the eviction of so many families from Strathnaver. For what was the expansion of sheep-farming but one more manifestation of civilisation's onward march? And what were the clearances but one more instance of the price the world has to pay for such advancement?

Walter Scott's swashbuckling clansmen and Patrick Sellar's 'aborigines', then, are arguably the two sides of a single coin. Highlanders, from Scott's perspective every bit as much as Sellar's, were fated, if not to vanish from the earth, then certainly to be extinguished as a culturally distinctive people. And even if Highlanders were to disappear entirely, what then? The empty glens which so depressed a man like Hugh MacLennan, those glens where this Canadian thought that everyone who ever mattered was now dead and gone, were not to be viewed in such a light by more than a tiny minority of their visitors. Where MacLennan was to see a depopulated and deserted countryside, Patrick Sellar and his successors were to see thriving sheep farms or flourishing deer forests. Where a North American novelist was to be saddened by thoughts of what had been destroyed, a million other tourists were to be captivated by landscapes possibly made more, not less, appealing by a sense of their having once been home to a race which Walter Scott, like James MacPherson, had imagined to be doomed.

Many years after the event, the Edinburgh publisher, Robert Cadell, was still recalling the 'extraordinary sensation' caused in 1810 by the publication of Scott's *Lady of the Lake*:

> The whole country rang with the praises of the poet. Crowds set off to the scenery of Loch Katrine, till then comparatively unknown; and, as the book came out just before the season for excursions, every house and inn in that neighbourhood was crammed with a constant succession of visitors.[18]

Nearly twenty years later, as noted by the eminent judge and diarist, Henry Cockburn, Loch Katrine and its surroundings were as popular as ever:

> The inn near the Trossachs could, perhaps, put up a dozen, or at the very most, two dozen of people; but last autumn I saw about one hundred apply for admittance, and after horrid altercations, entreaties and efforts, about fifty or sixty were compelled to huddle

together all night. They were all of the upper rank, travelling mostly in private carriages, and by far the greater number strangers. But the pigs were as comfortably accommodated. I saw three or four English gentlemen spreading their own straw on the earthen floor of an outhouse with a sparred door and no fireplace or furniture.[19]

All this activity was put down by Cockburn to Scott. 'His genius,' the diarist commented, 'immortalises the region.' And what *The Lady of the Lake* had done for the Trossachs, it soon became apparent, Scott's subsequent writings were to do for the rest of the Highlands. 'Every London citizen,' Scott himself observed a little ruefully, 'makes Loch Lomond his washpot and throws his shoes over Ben Nevis'.[20]

Not only had Scott almost singlehandedly conjured the Highland tourist industry into existence. He had also helped to determine, as Robert Louis Stevenson so plainly recognised when writing of the Trossachs, what it was that people believed themselves to be seeing when, drawn north by Scott's novels and poems, they first ventured into the Highlands:

> I suppose the Trossachs would hardly be the Trossachs for most tourists if a man of admirable romantic instinct had not peopled it for them with harmonious figures, and brought them thither with minds rightly prepared for the impression.[21]

It was certainly the case that earlier visitors to the Highlands – people not 'rightly prepared', in Stevenson's phrase, for the experience – had found the region anything but enticing. Samuel Johnson, journeying down Glen Shiel in the direction of Achadh nan Seileach, remarked of scenes that have since featured on innumerable postcards: 'An eye accustomed to flowery pastures and waving harvests is astonished and repelled by this wide extent of hopeless sterility.' The English military men who had preceded Johnson were equally uncomplimentary. These soldiers came from a country where much less lofty peaks than Scotland's were routinely described as 'warts', 'wens' and 'blisters'. And Highland hills thus seemed to them 'most horrible'. Mountains were not so much beguiling as 'frightful'. The highest summits were so many 'monstrous excrescences'.[22]

The extent to which external perceptions of the Highlands had changed by the early nineteenth century was indicative of more than Walter Scott's huge influence – although his role was critically important. Scott, and before him James MacPherson, were part and parcel of a much wider romantic movement which, having begun as a critique of

Enlightenment attitudes, had gone on to become something of an intellectual orthodoxy in its own right. At the heart of romanticism – as is evident from the writings of its many literary exponents – was a re-evaluation of humanity's relationship with nature, especially wild nature. A thousand years on from the Gaelic-speaking hermits who had first thought to seek spiritual renewal in places like the Garvellochs, western civilisation had at last begun to follow where the Columban church had led. This did not happen overnight, of course. The English-speaking world's deepseated suspicions of nature – as shown by Samuel Johnson's *Dictionary of the English Language* having defined wilderness as 'a tract of solitude and savageness' – were to endure well into the eighteenth century. By the beginning of the nineteenth century, however, the Johnson line already seemed completely out of date. To Lord George Byron, romanticism's archtetype, only an untamed landscape could have any real appeal:

> England! thy beauties are tame and domestic
> To one who has roved o'er the mountains afar;
> Oh for the crags that are wild and majestic!
> The steep frowning glories of dark Loch na Garr.[23]

Mountain landscapes of the sort which had previously been feared and detested were thus subjected by romanticism to a process which has, without hyperbole, been likened to 'divinisation'. The fact that the Highlands consequently came to be valued by southerners in a wholly new way, however, was of no real benefit to Highlanders other than those who began to profit from the developing tourist trade. As interest grew in landscapes of the Highland type, so the people who lived among such landscapes tend to drop more and more from view. That is why the typical romantic writer – as opposed to Samuel Johnson, for example – is so poor a source of information about Highlanders. Johnson might have had practically no regard for Highland hills. He might have had equally little regard for the claims being made on behalf of Gaelic tradition by James MacPherson and his backers. But he was fascinated by human beings; how they lived; what they thought; why they acted as they did. Johnson's Highlanders are real-life individuals. The Highlanders who feature in the poetry of William Wordsworth, on the other hand, are something else entirely:

Behold her, single in the field,
Yon solitary Highland lass!
Reaping and singing by herself;
Stop here, or gently pass!
Alone she cuts and binds the grain,
And sings a melancholy strain . . .

Will no one tell me what she sings?
Perhaps the plaintive numbers flow
For old, unhappy, far-off things,
And battles long ago:
Or is it some more humble lay,
Familiar matter of today?
Some natural sorrow, loss or pain,
That has been, and may be again?[24]

Samuel Johnson, had he wanted to know what a reaping girl's Gaelic song was all about, would have stopped his horse and – with an interpreter's assistance if need be – would have asked her to tell him. But it much better suits Wordsworth's purposes to impose his own Ossianic-inspired fantasies on the subject of his poem. Since nothing would be nicer than to think of her exacting such a posthumous revenge on all Wordsworthians, past, present and future, it is much to be hoped that the 'solitary Highland lass' was, in fact, singing one of Alasdair MacMhaighstir Alasdair's earthier ballads. As it is, however, we are forever stuck with her dwelling habitually on 'old, unhappy, far-off things', on 'sorrow, loss or pain'. Wordsworth, having steeped himself in the works of James MacPherson, inevitably expected Highland songs to be mournful. He equally expected the typical Highland glen to be practically devoid of habitation. That, as is evident from Wordsworth's thoughts on the supposed burial place of Ossian, was part of what it was that gave such places their romantic fascination:

Does then the Bard sleep here indeed?
Or is it but a groundless creed?
What matters it? I blame them not
Whose Fancy in this lonely Spot
Was moved; and in such way expressed
Their notion of its perfect rest.
A convent, even a hermit's cell,
Would break the silence of this Dell:

104

It is not quiet, it is not ease;
But something deeper far than these:
The separation that is here
Is of the grave; and of austere
Yet happy feelings of the dead:
And, therefore, was it rightly said
That Ossian, last of all his race!
Lies buried in this lonely place.[25]

This notion of wild country being all the more captivating as a result of its associations with a dead or dying culture was one which was to have applications far beyond the Highlands. It was to have such applications, most of all, in the United States where both James MacPherson and Walter Scott were to have enormously enthusiastic followings. Thomas Jefferson, an early US president, found MacPherson's books 'a source of daily pleasure' and considered Ossian 'the greatest poet that has ever existed'. Nor was Jefferson the only American to be thus inspired by Scottish literature. James Fenimore Cooper, his country's first great novelist and the first literary figure to appreciate the fictional possibilities of the US frontier, was not only to model himself explicitly on Scott. He was to turn Indians into Ossianic figures. That much is obvious from the closing paragraphs of *The Last of the Mohicans:*

Chingachgook grasped the hand that, in the warmth of feeling, the scout had stretched across the fresh earth, and in that attitude of friendship these two sturdy and intrepid woodsmen bowed their heads together, while scalding tears fell to their feet, watering the grave of Uncas like drops of falling rain.

In the midst of the awful stillness with which such a burst of feeling, coming, as it did, from the two most renowned warriors of that region, was received, Tamenund lifted his voice to disperse the multitude.

'It is enough,' he said. 'Go, children of the Lenape, the anger of the Manitto is not done. Why should Tamenund stay? The palefaces are masters of the earth, and the time of the Red Man has not yet come again. My day has been too long. In the morning I saw the sons of Unamis happy and strong; and yet, before the night has come, have I lived to see the last warriors of the wise race of the Mohicans.'[26]

Both that scene and its language are drawn directly from MacPherson. And not only do Cooper's Indians talk like Ossianic Highlanders. They similarly invest landscape, though in this case American landscape, with a tragic, but nevertheless romantic, ambience which stems ultimately from their own extinction. For just as it is the destiny of Highlanders in *Waverley* to be defeated by the superior civilisation which they have dared to challenge, so it is the destiny of native Americans in *The Last of the Mohicans* to give way, in the end, to whites:

> Where are the blossoms of those summers! Fallen, one by one. So all of my family departed, each in his turn, to the land of spirits. I am on the hilltop, and must go down into the valley; and when Uncas follows in my footsteps, there will no longer be any of the blood of the Sagamores, for my boy is the last of the Mohicans.[27]

North America's English-speaking colonists had begun by both fearing and loathing the forests and mountains which so hemmed in their farms and townships. Wild country was routinely described here, just as it had previously been in Europe, as 'hideous', 'howling', 'gloomy', 'brutish', 'dismal' and 'terrible'. The typical frontiersman, advancing across the Applachians and into the plains beyond, looked forward happily to the distant day when 'populous cities, smiling villages, beautiful farms and plantations' would take the place of 'solitude and savageness'. An unsettled territory, then, was reckoned to have no intrinsic worth. Like a wild horse, it gained value only by being tamed. Hence the sheer novelty of James Fenimore Cooper's portrayal of the American wilderness both as a place of beauty and as a place which enabled people to discover their innate moral worth.[28]

Cooper's fictional heroes – the frontier scout, Hawkeye, and Hawkeye's Indian allies, Chingachgook and Uncas – were clearly thought by their creator to derive their strength of character from their closeness to the very environment which the territorial expansion of the United States was to do so much to destroy. And though Cooper, whose novels date from the period between 1820 and 1840, was not actually to argue that wilderness was consequently deserving of protection, other Americans – many of them as imbued as Cooper was himself with the ideals of European romanticism – were shortly to be doing just that. Foremost among these pioneer environmentalists was Henry David Thoreau whose mission, as he told a Massachussetts audience in 1851, was 'to speak a word for nature, for absolute freedom and wildness'. James Fenimore Cooper had arguably done as much. But Thoreau now went further. 'In wildness,' he claimed, 'is the preservation of the world.'[29]

These were not mere words. By glorifying the self-same New England forests which earlier Americans had found so threatening, and by staging his own personal retreats into the woods around his native Concord, Henry David Thoreau made a decisive contribution to the emergence of the modern ecological outlook. A highly skilled naturalist, he combined the scientific study of plants and animals with a growing conviction that people ought to discard the material encumbrances which had become inseparable from a supposedly civilised existence. Only by such radical means, Thoreau considered, could humanity recapture the primeval nobility which was to be seen most clearly, Thoreau insisted, in the works of James MacPherson. 'Ossian seems to speak a gigantic and universal language,' Thoreau wrote in the course of one of his wilderness excursions. MacPherson's 'stern and desolate poetry', he continued, was hugely superior to most English literature. The writings of Chaucer, 'and even of Shakespeare and Milton', seemed strangely effete by comparison. This, Thoreau thought, was because such poets were not in sympathy with nature. 'The bard has in great measure lost the dignity and sacredness of his office . . . The poet has come within doors and exchanged the forest and crag for the fireside.'[30]

Just as Thoreau was to admire MacPherson, so Thoreau, in his turn, was to be greatly esteemed by the man who, more than any other, was to make wild country positively regarded by Americans. This was John Muir, the crusading writer and publicist whose name will always be coupled with California's Yosemite Valley which, in 1890, thanks very largely to Muir's promptings, Congress agreed to safeguard and protect for all time coming. The resulting Yosemite Act – because it recognises wilderness to have a significance which can transcend people's freedom to exploit natural resources – signalled a substantial stride along the road which James Fenimore Cooper and Henry David Thoreau had started to map out. The Yosemite Act did something more, however. It demonstrated what could be accomplished by a determined effort to mobilise public opinion in support of nature conservation. And it is in this sense that John Muir – who organised a tremendously successful public relations campaign on Yosemite's behalf – can be seen to have invented environmental lobbying of the sort that was eventually to transform the western world's attitude to nature.

John Muir had been born in Dunbar in 1838 and had emigrated to Wisconsin with his parents in 1849. 'When I was a boy in Scotland,' Muir wrote long afterwards, 'I was fond of everything that was wild, and all my life I've been growing fonder and fonder of wild places and wild creatures.' Muir, it appears, never lost his Scottish accent. Nor did he ever cease to take pride in his background – going so far as to ascribe his strong feelings for landscape, and especially his love of mountains, to the fact that his ancestors included Highlanders. Intellectually, however, he was shaped primarily by a romanticism still more all-embracing than Thoreau's. Natural objects, to Muir, were 'the terrestrial manifestations of God'. Nature was a 'window opening into heaven'. To venture deep into hill country was at once to be restored both psychologically and spiritually:

> Climb the mountains and get their good tidings. Nature's peace will flow into you as the sunshine into the trees. The winds will blow their freshness into you, and the storms their energy, while cares will drop off like autumn leaves.[31]

This was a philosophy which John Muir was to expound in a long series of increasingly influential books. One of these, *My First Summer in the Sierra*, consists principally of the journal which Muir kept in the course of his initial foray into the Californian mountains. The year is 1869 and with every day that passes, Muir's narrative explains, the country works its soothing charms on his mind. June, in particular, 'seems the greatest of all the months' the 31-year old Muir has so far lived through. Each sunrise brings another 'reviving' morning. 'Down the long mountain slopes the sunbeams pour, gilding the awakening pines, cheering every needle, filling every living thing with joy.' But every Eden has its serpent. And Yosemite's appeared to Muir some three weeks into August.[32]

The day in question had begun promisingly enough. Muir had set out for Mono Lake by way of Bloody Canyon Pass:

> Near the summit, at the head of the pass, I found a species of dwarf willow lying perfectly flat on the ground, making a nice, soft, silky grey carpet, not a single stem or branch more than three inches high . . . A little higher, almost at the very head of the pass, I found the blue arctic daisy and purple-flowered bryanthus, the mountain's own darlings, gentle mountaineers face to face with the sky, kept safe by a thousand miracles, seeming always finer and purer the wilder and stormier their homes . . . Here, too, is the familiar robin, tripping on the flowery lawns, bravely singing the same cheery song I first heard when a boy in Wisconsin newly arrived from old Scotland. In this fine company, sauntering enchanted, taking no heed of time, I at length entered the gate of the pass and the huge rocks began to close round me in all their mysterious impressiveness.[33]

At this point, however, it is as if a dark cloud has suddenly shut out the sun:

> Just then I was startled by a lot of queer, hairy muffled creatures coming shuffling, shambling, wallowing towards me as if they had no bones in their bodies. Had I discovered them while they were yet a good way off, I should have tried to avoid them. What a picture they made, contrasted with the others I had just been admiring! When I came up to them, I found that they were only a band of Indians from Mono on their way to Yosemite for a load of acorns. They were wrapped in blankets made of the skins of sage-rabbits. The dirt on some of the faces seemed almost old enough to have a geological significance . . . How glad I was to to get away from the grey, grim crowd and see them vanish down the trail![34]

John Muir's attitudes to North American native peoples are those of a period when a Kansas newspaper could describe Indians as 'a set of miserable, dirty, louse-infected, gut-eating skunks'. And he is maybe not to be condemned too harshly for his failure, in this respect at least, to step outside the mental confines of his time. But the condescending way that Muir wrote about Yosemite's original inhabitants is, for all that, most revealing. It is suggestive of the problem which so many environmentalists have always had in accommodating the claims of people who happen to live in places which the same environmentalists deem special.[35]

It was relatively straightforward, as James Fenimore Cooper had shown, to idealise the Indian in the abstract; to conceive of him as a noble savage whose way of life had somehow served to dignify the American landscape. It was much harder to cope with nineteenth-century Indians as they actually existed. Thus Henry David Thoreau, for all that he spent so much time imagining a pristine Massachussetts inhabited only by America's first nations, saw little merit in the native peoples he actually met in Maine. These real-life Indians, Thoreau commented, were 'sinister and slouching fellows' who made only a 'coarse and imperfect use . . . of nature'. Other romantically inclined whites were to be similarly disparaging about the many native Americans who most uncharitably refused to conform to Ossian-influenced stereotypes. Hence the steadily developing notion of the nineteenth-century Indian as a degenerate; a person who had fallen badly from his primeval state of grace; a person who could thus be dismissed as just one more potential pollutant of those wilderness areas which American governments were persuaded to safeguard for posterity by early environmentalists like John Muir.[36]

When, in 1872, Wyoming's highly scenic and geyser-rich Yellowstone Mountains were declared the world's first national park, the relevant legislation provided 'for the preservation . . . of all timber, mineral deposits, natural curiosities or wonders . . . in their natural condition'. Definitely not scheduled for such preservation, however, were the new park's human occupants. Several Indian bands – drawn from the Crow, the Blackfeet and Shoshone peoples – were forcibly expelled from Yellowstone the year the park was designated. And in 1876, despite its tourist trade being already underway, Yellowstone was the scene of fighting between the US cavalry and one more of America's first nations, the Nez Perce. Reflecting on his people's subsequent defeat and slaughter, Chief Joseph of the Nez Perce commented:

I learned . . . that we were few while the white men were many, and that we could not hold our own with them. We were like deer. They were like grizzly bears. We had a small country. Their country was large. We were contented to let things remain as the Great Spirit Chief made them. They were not and would change the rivers and mountains if they did not suit them.[37]

What the Nez Perce chieftain most disliked about our so-called western civilisation, of course, was what America's earliest environmentalists most disliked about it also. John Muir, for instance, was to spend the last years of his life defending his beloved Yosemite Valley from a planned dam which, if it had gone ahead, would have altered 'the rivers and mountains' more fundamentally than Chief Joseph could have envisaged possible. 'These temple destroyers,' Muir wrote of the Californian businessmen and politicians who were promoting the controversial dam with a view to improving San Francisco's water supplies, 'seem to have a perfect contempt for nature and, instead of lifting their eyes to the God of the mountains, lift them to the almighty dollar.' But for all that he was eventually to develop some sympathy for Indians, most notably those whom he encountered while travelling in Alaska in the 1880s and 1890s, it was never to occur to John Muir that a national park, from the perspective of the native peoples who were deprived of their lands to make its creation possible, might appear to disrupt the natural order every bit as much as the damming of a river.[38]

Many years afterwards, when Indian traditions had been extinguished almost as completely as the clan-based society depicted in Scott's *Waverley*, environmentalists at last got round to ransacking nineteenth-century publications for some record of the environmentally significant remarks made by men like Chief Joseph. One source of such comments, as it happens, was a series of articles published in a Montana newspaper in 1877. These articles told the story of the Nez Perce War of the previous year. Most untypically, they told that story from the Nez Perce point of view. And it is of some passing relevance to this book's themes that the author of the articles in question bore an obviously Highland name. He was called Duncan MacDonald. Through his Indian mother, he was related to the leading families of the Nez Perce. Through his Scottish father, a Hudson's Bay Company fur trader, he was descended from men and women who had been killed, some two hundred years earlier, during the massacre of Glencoe.[39]

Just as men like Henry David Thoreau and John Muir found it difficult to incorporate nineteenth-century Indians into their vision of the American wilderness, so the Scottish successors of James MacPherson and Walter Scott found it hard to make room for nineteenth-century Highlanders in their portrayal of the Highlands as the part of Europe where romanticism's ideals had been realised most concretely. Highlanders, admittedly, were at as low an ebb as they had ever been. But despite their having been removed from much of the area which they had formerly occupied, Highlanders had failed to exit from the Highland scene. Nor had they abandoned all hope of regaining some control of their own lives. At one level, of course, this was recognised by everyone. When Highlanders rioted in protest at the clearances, for example, the consequent affrays were duly reported – and in terms, very often, which might have been employed had neither MacPherson nor Scott ever penned a single word. Just as America's Indian wars were invariably put down to Indian untrustworthiness rather than to white encroachment on Indian lands, so riots which had been provoked by evictions were routinely attributed to Highland undependability. The violent and the disaffected Highlander, however, was firmly confined to just one of the parallel universes in which, as mentioned earlier, the Highlands now seemed to exist. In the alternative Highlands – the Highlands as most southerners increasingly wanted, or pretended, the Highlands to be – a very different sort of Highlander was on display.

When King George IV came to Scotland in 1822, the attendant pageantry – organised by none other than Walter Scott – featured plaided retainers who might have stepped straight out of *Waverley*. When Queen Victoria ventured into the Highlands in the later 1840s, a decade during which the crofting population suffered enormously from poverty and hunger, these things were never mentioned in her journal. Victoria could not have been ignorant of the famine relief programmes which had been organised to keep crofting families alive. Nor could she have been unaware of the renewed clearances which were emptying still more Highland glens. But such matters seem to have been excised from her consciousness. Travelling the Highlands in the company of a well-thumbed copy of *The Lady of the Lake*, Britain's queen found the area 'most delightful, most romantic'. The Highlands were characterised by 'quiet', 'retirement', 'wildness', 'liberty' and 'solitude'. Here there were no reminders of humanity's many troubles. 'All seemed to breathe freedom and peace, and to make one forget the world and its sad turmoils.'[40]

Victoria's purchase of Balmoral was to cement a continuing association between the royal family and the Highlands. It was also to usher in the heyday of the deer forest. With imports of overseas wool and mutton now making sheep farming less and less profitable, huge tracts of territory were turned over to field sports. Shooting lodge after shooting lodge was built to accommodate the landed aristocrats and newly monied businessmen who came north each summer with a view to sampling a lifestyle modelled, very often, on largely fictional accounts of how the Highland chieftains of a previous era had organised their homes.

The sporting existence was anything but indolent, of course. To engage successfully in stalking, one nineteenth-century authority insisted, a man had to be 'able to run like an antelope and breathe like the trade winds'. This was to ask rather a lot of the portly Victorians who now found themselves toiling up Highland hillsides in the rain. By surrounding himself with kilted ghillies, keepers and other flunkies, however, the owner or tenant of a sporting estate – his lodge wall covered with the trophies of the chase – could act out a role that had begun as little other than a literary fantasy of what it meant to live in the grand Highland style.[41]

Crofters, by the 1880s, were organising themselves politically with a view to staking their own claim to deer forests – which almost invariably contained the ruins of former townships. But the activities of the Highland Land League and its allies made little more impression on the cosily cocooned world of the sporting estate than the clearances had earlier made on Queen Victoria. Nor were crofting disorders permitted to trespass into the standard fictional depiction of the Highlands – most such depictions owing a good deal more to the works of James MacPherson and Walter Scott than they did to a Scotland where the military had to be regularly deployed to deal with Land League demonstrations.[42]

Robert Louis Stevenson thought about writing a *History of the Highlands* – this history to deal with 'the collapse of the clan system and the causes and growth of existing discontents'. Instead he wrote *Kidnapped* which, though a great novel, is set firmly in the 1750s. Stevenson gives the clan-based Highlands a superb spokesman in Alan Breck whose real-life namesake was believed to have organised the assassination of one of the government officials charged with the task of rooting out surviving Jacobites. But Alan obviously belongs to a dying society. And the Highlands, significantly enough, are usually seen through the Lowland eyes of David Balfour who is both Stevenson's hero and the embodiment of an external social order which, in *Kidnapped* as in *Waverley*, seems most unlikely to do anything other than to shape Gaelic-speaking Highlanders to its own purposes.[43]

If a first-rate writer like Robert Louis Stevenson was unable or unwilling to challenge the way in which the Highlands were now habitually represented, it was most unlikely that lesser novelists would instigate a new departure. And so it proved. Neil Munro, who came from Inveraray, was by no means unaffected by the results of clearance and depopulation:

O sad for me Glen Aora,
  Where I have friends no more,
For lowly lie the rafters,
  And the lintels of the door.
The friends are all departed,
  The hearth-stone's black and cold,
And sturdy grows the nettle
  On the place beloved of old.[44]

But this was to sentimentalise what had been destroyed rather than to envisage the possibility of its being recreated. And it is indicative of Neil Munro's inherent lack of confidence in a worthwhile Highland future that it is only in his resolutely whimsical *Para Handy Tales* that he deals with the Highlands as they existed in his lifetime. Munro's ostensibly serious novels, most notably *The New Road*, were set, like *Kidnapped*, in the eighteenth century. And while the author of *The New Road* is clearly angered by what was done to Highlanders in the wake of Jacobitism's collapse, he tends to be almost as gloomy as James MacPherson about his people's long-term prospects. The eighteenth-century military roads which provide the novel with its title are symbolic of the triumph of the invader:

Whole tribes, that not so long ago were ill to meddle with as any bike of wasps, were now so little to be feared as butterflies; packmen from the Lowlands sometimes travelled through the worst-reputed valleys selling specs and ribbons.[45]

As *Kidnapped* and *The New Road* proved, the Highland novel remained as popular as ever. But its popularity seemed predicated on its not challenging established stereotypes. The Highlands which the generality of people wanted both to visit and to read about – indeed the Highlands which the sporting fraternity attempted actually to create synthetically – was a place whose primary purpose was to gratify the wider world's conceptions of how the Highlands ought to be. The Highlands of the Land League might be debated in parliament and in the editorial columns of the press. But the Highlands of popular fiction, as can readily be observed in the best-selling romances published in the 1870s and 1880s by a Glasgow-born journalist named William Black, had been transformed into a never-never-land where even the climate, so you sense, was expected to get togged up in the meteorological equivalent of full Highland dress.

An early Black novel, *A Princess of Thule*, makes the point perfectly. The hero and the heroine have been carefully manoeuvered on to a Lewis moor from which they are obliged to run by an approaching downpour:

But this race to escape the storm was needless; for they were just getting within sight of Barvas when a surprising change came over the dark and thundrous afternoon. The hurrying masses of cloud in the west parted for a little space, and there was a sudden fitful glimmer of a stormy blue sky. Then a strange, soft, yellow, and vaporous light shot across the Barvas hills, and touched up palely the great slopes, rendering them distant, ethereal and cloud-like. Then a shaft or two of wild light flashed down upon the landscape beside them. The cattle shone red in the brilliant-green pastures. The grey rocks glowed in their setting of moss. The stream going by the Barvas Inn was a streak of gold in its sandy bed. Presently the sky above them broke into great billows of cloud – tempestuous and rounded masses of golden vapour that burned with the wild glare of the sunset. The clear spaces in the sky widened; and from time to time the wind sent ragged bits of saffron cloud across the shining blue. All the world seemed to be on fire; and the very smoke of it – the majestic heaps of vapour that rolled by overhead – burned with a bewildering glare. Then, as the wind still blew hard, and kept veering round again to the north-west, the fiercely lit clouds were driven over one by one, leaving a pale and serene sky to look down on the sinking sun and the sea. The Atlantic caught the yellow glow on its tumbling waves; and a deeper colour stole across the slopes and peaks of the Barvas hills. Whither had gone the storm? There were still some banks of cloud away up in the north-east; and, in the clear green of the evening sky, they had their distant greys and purples faintly tinged with rose.[46]

William Black, you quickly gather from his many books, tended to go in for this sort of passage at those points in a narrative where one of his modern equivalents might indulge in a spot of bodice-ripping. But his orgasmic gales and thunderstorms were cumulatively to make the Highlands seem so other-worldly as to verge almost on the magical. Although some hints to this effect were certainly implicit in their novels and their poetry, writers like Scott had never gone quite so far. But the notion of the Highlands as a place of spiritual, even religious, significance had now got ineradicably into the atmosphere. And it was one which Black's successors were deliberately to foster.

Foremost among these was William Sharp who, in the 1890s, turned out a whole series of novels and essays so unrelentingly dismal both in tone and content as to make James MacPherson seem positively light-hearted. Sharp's writings were thought at the time to be the work of a woman called Fiona MacLeod. And something of their author's altogether bizarre approach to the Highlands is to be discerned in the fact that Sharp, who took a close interest in the occult, believed Fiona to have a real existence as his feminine – or possibly Celtic – persona.

Nowadays Sharp's books are not just unread but unreadable. In the years around 1900, however, he, or she, was widely regarded as one of the high priests, or priestesses, of the literary movement which became known as the Celtic Twilight. Taking its name from an early collection of short stories by the Irish writer and poet, W. B. Yeats, the Twilight was characterised, above all, by its making the Celtic peoples – whether in Ireland or the Highlands – the repositories of a uniquely mystical, if also pessimistic, way of life. Asserting that 'the old Gaelic race is in its twilight indeed', Fiona MacLeod attempted to recreate, indeed to heighten, the despondency which so suffuses MacPherson's Ossian. Nor was she to be deflected from this task by the fact that land reformers, Gaelic revivalists and Irish nationalists were just then beginning to win victories of a kind that would have seemed wholly beyond the Gaelic-speaking world's reach in the post-Culloden period which had given rise to James MacPherson.

Ireland's dreams of independence were 'a perilous illusion', MacLeod insisted. And no amount of crofting legislation could alter 'the pathos' and 'the gloom' which were intrinsic to the Highlands. The Highland 'race', MacLeod concluded, could look forward only to 'a tragic lighting of torches of beauty around its grave'.[47]

None of this would have mattered a great deal had it not served to take to new extremes the utterly fantastic way in which both Highlanders and their natural environment were now commonly regarded. In the 1920s and the 1930s, in particular, author after author churned out book after book in which the Highlands, their landscapes, their wildlife and their people are described in terms wholly disconnected from reality. Most of Scotland's second-hand bookshops are still replete with the products of this curious industry. And even to dip into the multitudinous offerings of the trade's leading practitioners, Mary Ethel Muir Donaldson and Alasdair Alpin MacGregor, is immediately to wonder if they, their publishers and their readers might have been more than slightly off their heads.

Donaldson was sufficiently aware of what was happening around her as to acknowledge that Highlanders, especially island crofters, were among the 'poorest of the poor'. But this, she implied, was of no real significance. What was important about such 'poor islesmen' was their ability to 'exercise' the 'spiritual and natural graces' which had transformed Barra, for example, into an 'island of visions'.[48]

Alasdair Alpin MacGregor, his very name redolent of the Celtic Twilight he propagated so assiduously, was to indulge in even wilder flights of fancy. The Highlands, to MacGregor, were a place where 'you will find yourself at one with the infinite'; a place of 'faery-haunted isles' steeped in the 'magic peacefulness of dreamland'; a place where cattle 'softly wend their way' across 'sleepy moors' and where birds are forever 'dipping their breasts into the roseate hues of morning'; a place of moonlit lochs where 'little gnomes and fays are wont to play'; a place where 'the soothing balm of the night-tide is sweeter far than the kisses of women'.[49]

For reasons that should now be obvious, it is difficult to take MacGregor seriously. It has been all the harder to do so ever since Compton MacKenzie, both in *Whisky Galore* and several other novels, transformed Alasdair Alpin MacGregor into Hector Hamish MacKay, 'the well-known topographer of the Hebrides and author of *Faerie Lands Forlorn*'. Nobody who thus became acquainted with the not-altogether-fictional Hector Hamish MacKay – 'a small man in a kilt with slightly shrivelled but well-weathered knees, a prim Edinburgh accent, and spectacles' – was likely ever again to take Alasdair Alpin MacGregor at face value. And this, of course, was Compton MacKenzie's purpose. To MacKenzie, who was to live for quite some time on Barra, Donaldson, MacGregor and the rest of the Twilightists seemed simply to be distorting truth for their own ends. MacKenzie made this opinion clear in 1936:

> My complaint as a reader, as a critic, as an inhabitant against some of the numerous works published during the last decade about the Western Isles is not so much of their superficiality as of their effort to make the islands and the islanders conform to a sentimental preconception in the minds of their authors.[50]

Alasdair Alpin MacGregor, not unnaturally, felt deeply wounded. And in his Chelsea home he planned what he conceived as his revenge. This was one more book, *The Western Isles*, which appeared in 1949 and which – though still highly complimentary about island scenery – presents Hebrideans in an altogether less appealing light than its author's earlier works. The people of the Western Isles, MacGregor now tells his readers, are as unattractive and reprehensible a set of folk as are to be met with anywhere. Their 'morals in the sexual sense' are 'extremely lax'. There is much 'early and indiscriminate mating'. It follows that 'bastardy' is 'common' and 'interbreeding' even more so – though quite what it is that the two island sexes see in one another is a little bit mysterious in view of MacGregor's account of their respective characters. Island women are 'plain . . . many of them exceedingly so'. Island males are 'indolent', 'dilatory', 'vindictive' and given to 'drunkenness'. To get off the steamer at Compton MacKenzie's Barra, which MacGregor had previously described as next best thing to paradise, is immediately to meet with islanders who 'stand, in furtive groups, against the post office walls and door, chatting, chaffing, smoking, spitting, swearing, blaspheming and not infrequently giving off alcoholic fumes'. This would be slightly more tolerable, MacGregor observes, were islanders not so dirty. As it is, he comments, men and women alike believe a bath to be 'a piece of nonsense'. Many are 'perpetually in a verminous condition'.[51]

To read MacGregor's last book, then, is to be reminded of John Muir's remarks about the Indians he encountered in Yosemite. 'The worst thing about them,' Muir noted of these people, 'is their uncleanliness.' And there is a sense in which Alasdair Alpin MacGregor – as well as attempting to get back at Compton MacKenzie – was venting a parallel disillusionment with another group of human beings who have similarly shown themselves unworthy of their enchanting natural surroundings. Had MacGregor been able to arrange such a thing, you feel, he would have ideally liked the inhabitants of the Western Isles to be treated in much the same way as the Indians who had been driven out of America's national parks. Such expulsions, after all, would have served to preserve the Western Isles for those best able to appreciate them – a category which, as far as Alasdair Alpin MacGregor was concerned, did not include most islanders.[52]

For all its ever more apparent craziness, it does not do to underestimate the influence of the Celtic Twilight. Alasdair Alpin MacGregor's *Over the Sea to Skye*, a volume which also carried the typically Twilightist subtitle, *Ramblings in an Elfin Isle*, was introduced to the public by none other than James Ramsay MacDonald, Britain's first Labour prime minister. To be in Skye and to sit 'by the ingle of an evening', MacDonald assured MacGregor's many fans, was to have an opportunity to 'wander . . . into fairyland'. And so predominant are such sentiments in early-twentieth-century books about the Highlands that it is an enormous pleasure to come across the writings of the man who, more than any other single individual, can be credited with having begun to rescue the area from its numerous romanticisers.[53]

This man was Seton Gordon. Born in Aboyne, on Deeside, in 1886, Seton Gordon was, above all other things, a naturalist. To read his work is to find Highland hills described more matter-of-factly than they had been since Duncan Ban MacIntyre composed his poem in honour of Ben Dorain:

It is during the first days of August that we make a visit to the hills. The heat wave has broken and the weather is unsettled, though giving promise of better things to come. For some days past a mild breeze from the south has been blowing, and under its genial influence the remaining fields of snow are rapidly diminishing. It is early morning as we leave the shelter where we have been staying overnight. The sun has just risen, and shines brightly on the high ground to the westward, though the pass is as yet in twilight. Thunder showers the night before have cleared off the haze, and the mountains around us stand out with wonderful sharpness in the early morning light. During the hours of darkness a herd of stags have come down to the riverside, and as we open the door of our shelter we find them grazing some 100 yards from us. Evidently they are taken by suprise, for at first they show no inclination to move, but having realised that their arch-enemy, man, is in such close proximity, they set off at a mad rush, and do not pause until the river is crossed and they have climbed some distance up the hillside opposite.

Our way leads up a steep corrie, down which rushes a swift mountain burn, and in the soft sunlight every blade of grass stands out a vivid green. The corrie is rich in plantlife, and we come across several white-flowered specimens of the cross-leaved heath (*Erica tetralix*). The cow-wheat (*Melampyrum montanum*) still shows its delicate blossoms in favoured situations, and we meet with at least two Alpine forms of the staghorn moss. We surprise a fox on an early morning prowl, and the marauder crosses our path with easy stride; his tail is held erect, and this gives him a somewhat unusual appearance. The top of the corrie reached, we have a gradual ascent until a height of some 3,600 feet is reached, when we call a halt and wait for some time on a slope covered with scree, where the snow bunting has his home. In the earlier part of the summer the male bird is in almost continuous song from 1 a.m. until late afternoon, but now the nesting season is over he is silent, and though we watch the nesting site carefully, we are unable to see any traces of the birds.[54]

Like Frank Fraser Darling, who was to follow in his footsteps, Seton Gordon can be criticised for having failed to observe nature with a properly scientific detachment. And he was never to break completely with the romantic tradition. But he was much more inclined than most of his immediate predecessors to take the Highlands as he found them. His interest in Gaelic and piping was the interest of a man who genuinely wanted to understand Highland culture. And he was much more inclined to discern only material disadvantage in those island townships which writers like Fiona MacLeod and Mary Ethel Muir Donaldson had thought awash with Celtic spirituality. Writing of Skye in 1937, Gordon commented:

Life is still hard in the isles. Even at the present day many people have no road to their houses: the sick, the old and the infirm are carried or supported perhaps a distance of half a mile, perhaps more, to the nearest road. There are townships in Skye which it is impossible to reach in autumn or winter without wading over the ankles in mud or water.[55]

In everything except his much greater willingess to learn from those who lived and worked in mountain country, Seton Gordon bears comparison with John Muir. And Gordon was to influence others just as Muir had done. Adam Watson, who would afterwards become the leading scientific authority on the ecology and wildlife of the Cairngorms, remembers how, at the age of eight, he first came across Seton Gordon's books in a library in Ballater:

My parents had taken me to different parts of Scotland, but suddenly Deeside and the Highlands that I thought I knew were immediately relegated into distant memories of no importance. The fact was I had known them only in a superficial and trivial sense. The Highlands that Seton Gordon wrote about were utterly different, a place of endless beauty and variety, with a wonderful wildlife and fine people . . . From then on I saw Scotland, its wildlife, weather, skies, people and culture, with this different eye.[56]

Several other naturalists and ecologists – among them Desmond Nethersole Thomson and John Morton Boyd – were also to attribute their various involvements with the Highlands to their early exposure to Seton Gordon's writings. Although Gordon had his own predecessors, most notably the Victorian naturalist, J. A. Harvie-Brown, he can consequently be seen to have played a key part in promoting a truly ecological understanding of the Highlands. And as Gordon's ecologist successors got more and more to grips with the region, they began inexorably to undermine the whole basis of the romantic approach to it. The Highland landscape, it began to be suspected, was not at all as natural as had been assumed by the many people who had been so charmed by it. That landscape, for example, had been artificially stripped of its forests. It had also, of course, been artificially stripped of its people. And this was one more message that twentieth-century developments – cultural now as well as scientific – were unrelentingly to hammer home.

CHAPTER FIVE

Without the Heartbreak of the Tale

A week or so following their brief halt at Achadh nan Seileach, Samuel Johnson and James Boswell were in Skye where they stayed for a day or two at Corriechatachain, a couple of miles from Broadford. Here the two travellers were the guests of one of the local gentry whose home, Johnson recalled, was 'very pleasantly situated between two brooks, with one of the highest hills of the island behind it'. This hill is Beinn na Caillich. And looking at its scree-covered slopes from the single-track road which nowadays heads out of Broadford in the direction of Torrin, Kilbride, Kilmarie and Elgol, it is easy to understand why Beinn na Caillich's 'height and steepness' should have dissuaded Johnson from climbing to its summit.[1]

Westwards from Corriechatachain is the valley of Strath Suardal. Here, in a township which has long since vanished, there was born William Ross who was about eleven years of age when Samuel Johnson came this way and who was afterwards to produce some of the eighteenth century's more memorable Gaelic poetry. There is no way of identifying now the precise location of the hill shielings which William Ross describes so lyrically in his verse. But some at least of these shielings – the name given to the upland pastures where cattle were driven each summer – would very probably have been tucked away among the low hills on the south side of Strath Suardal. Because there is a lot of limestone in this quarter, its soils are less acidic than one normally expects in Skye. As can be seen from the footpath which leaves Strath Suardal in the vicinity of the ruined church of Kilchrist, there is consequently good grass to be got here – the sort of grass on which to raise fine cows.[2]

This footpath heads eventually due south, traversing the boggy plateau to the west of Loch Lonachan prior to plunging into the gorge cut by the noisy burn called Allt na Pairte. Here you begin to catch sight of the sea and to get spectacular views of Rum and other islands. Here, too, on turning a sudden corner in the path, you find yourself gazing down on the green fields and ruined homes of Boreraig.

In 1850, just before this part of Skye was cleared, there were more than thirty families living in Boreraig and in the neighbouring township of

Suisnish, some two miles to the west. The district's owner was Lord Macdonald of Sleat whose freespending ways had resulted in debts of £218,000 – then a quite staggering sum. This was clearly something of a problem for Lord Macdonald. It was to be rather more than that for the folk of Boreraig and Suisnish. As a newspaper editorial of the time observed:

> When the lands are heavily mortgaged, the obvious, though harsh, resource is dispossessing the small tenants to make room for a better class . . . and this task generally devolves on south country managers . . . who look only to money returns and cannot sympathise with the peculiar situation and feelings of the Highland population.[3]

The Boreraig and Suisnish people were accordingly evicted. Some, as was afterwards remarked, were 'scattered here and there' across the southern half of Skye. Others were shipped to Australia, their departure being witnessed by Archibald Geikie, a pioneering geologist who happened to be investigating rock formations in the vicinity of Strath Suardal on the day that many of Lord Macdonald's newly dispossessed tenants made their way to Broadford and the waiting emigrant ship. His recollections of the Boreraig and Suisnish evictions, as is clear from Geikie's memoirs, were to stay with him always:

> I had heard some rumours of those intentions, but did not realise they were in process of being carried into effect until, one afternoon, as I was returning from my ramble, a strange wailing sound reached my ears at intervals from the west. On gaining the top of one of the hills on the south side of the valley, I could see a long and motley procession winding along the road that led north from Suisnish. It halted at the point of the road opposite Kilbride, and there the lamentation became loud and long . . . It was a miscellaneous gathering of at least three generations of crofters. There were old men and women, too feeble to walk, who were placed in carts; the younger members of the community on foot were carrying their bundles of clothes and household effects, while the children, with looks of alarm, walked alongside . . . Everyone was in tears . . . When they set forth once more, a cry of grief went up to heaven, the long plaintive wail, like a funeral coronach, was resumed, and after the last of the emigrants had disappeared behind the hill, the sound seemed to re-echo through the whole wide valley . . . in one prolonged note of desolation.[4]

One modern historian of the clearances has called Boreraig 'bleak country'. It is hard to believe, however, that the historian in question has ever been here. Certainly he has not been here on the sort of day when the township – south-facing and sheltered by enclosing hills – is warmed by a summer sun. On such a day, as you sit among its empty houses and look across its meadows in the direction of the sea, Boreraig seems more beautiful than bleak. Nor is it nearly as difficult as is usually the case in such deserted villages to imagine how the place would have been when inhabited. Boreraig, as an archaeologist has commented, 'survives almost as when cleared in the 1850s'. You can readily envisage, therefore, how its various component parts connected with each other:

> The relationship between crofting township, the later sheep folds and enclosures, a standing stone in the centre of the infield, a dun and chapel on the seashore and different phases of settlement inside and outside the head-dyke all point to the dynamics of settlement in the area.[5]

Think about that standing stone, that dun, that chapel. Collectively they demonstrate that people lived in Boreraig for one, two, three, four, or even five, millennia before the place was cleared. People have been missing from this spot, then, for fewer than one hundred and fifty of the last five thousand years. That is why the Boreraig landscape, from a Highland standpoint, seems so terribly unnatural. That is why, as in this poem by Iain Crichton Smith, the clearances can still cause so much anger. Their consequences, after all, are still so very obvious:

> The thistles climb the thatch. Forever
> this sharp scale in our poems,
> as also the waste music of the sea.
>
> The stars shine over Sutherland
> in a cold ceilidh of their own,
> as, in the morning, the silver cane
>
> cropped among corn. We will remember this.
> Though hate is evil we cannot
> but hope your courtier's heels in hell

are burning: that to hear
the thatch sizzling in tanged smoke
your hot ears slowly learn.[6]

Anger of this kind, however, was to take a long time to make its presence felt. The clearances, as well as depopulating so much of the Highlands, went a long way to breaking the spirit of those communities which managed to escape destruction. Crofters did not resist eviction in anything other than a sporadic and uncoordinated fashion. And although Iain MacCodrum, Duncan Ban MacIntyre and other eighteenth-century poets were highly critical of those former chieftains to whom money came to matter more than clanship, worthwhile opposition to evicting landlords was made all the harder to organise by the fact that these landlords, very often, were men whom the Gaelic world had customarily regarded as its leaders and protectors. Had Boreraig's landlord been a foreigner, so to speak, it might have been comparatively easy to mobilise his tenants against him. But the man who was ultimately responsible for Boreraig's clearance, Lord Macdonald, was also the latest representative of a chieftainly dynasty to whom Skye people had owed allegiance since the fourteenth century. This maybe did not mean a lot to Lord Macdonald – whose family had long since ceased to care about their Gaelic heritage. But it was no easy thing for other, still Gaelic-speaking, Highlanders to come to terms with the extent to which their former chiefs were now reneging on traditional obligations.

From the first, of course, the extinction of communities like Boreraig and Achadh nan Seileach caused Highlanders to look on landscape in a wholly novel way. Places which had previously been regarded with the sort of affection which Duncan Ban MacIntyre felt for Ben Dorain were now associated with the melancholy which so infuses this nineteenth-century poem from Morvern:

*As I go up the face of Ben Hiant
my thoughts are very sad;

seeing the mountain a wilderness
with no tillage on its face.

As I look down over the pass
the view I have is very chill.

There is many a poor hut levelled,
a green site on every side . . .

Where the fire and children were
the rushes grow the highest. [7]

Such sentiments could hardly have been more at odds with those expressed, during the same general period, by Wordsworth, Scott, Byron and other exponents of a romanticism which saw nothing but grandeur where many Highlanders discerned only cause for grief. Nor was there anything at all transient about such differences of opinion as to the meaning and significance of Highland landscape. In one form or another they have endured into the present. They underlie the contrast between Hugh MacLennan's response to Kintail and the much more general tendency to think Kintail an altogether splendid place. They are equally evident in two modern approaches to the countryside around Loch Shiel – the area where Alasdair MacMhaighstir Alasdair grew up. To an environmentalist like Mike Tomkies, this countryside, as the title of one of his books puts it, is nothing other than *A Last Wild Place*. But where Tomkies is content to celebrate the Loch Shiel landscape as it now exists, a Highland writer like the late Calum MacLean was much more inclined to mourn the human beings who were previously integral to the Loch Shiel scene:

I have never seen anything so beautiful as Loch Shiel in the sunshine of an early June morning. But the beauty of Loch Shiel makes one sad, for on the wooded slopes can still be seen clear traces of tillage . . . left to be overgrown with grass when the tillers left over a hundred years ago to face an uncertain future and to start life anew beyond the seas.[8]

Mike Tomkies writes well about wildlife. But his failure to grasp the essential artificiality of an environment from which people have been forcibly removed is indicative of a wider failing on the part of the environmental movement as a whole. Although environmentalist approaches to the Highlands, as the following chapter will acknowledge, are at last starting to take account of Highland susceptibilities, environmentalist thinking about the area remains shot through with notions which owe much more to romanticism and to the Celtic Twilight than they do to any genuine understanding of how the Highlands came to be the way they are. So much has been made by so many for so long about the haunting beauty of our empty glens and our unpopulated lochsides that it seems little short of heretical to suggest that human communities should be established in these places once again. But a willingness to contemplate just such resettlement, so this book argues, will be a necessary element in any general rapprochement between environmentalists and the many Highlanders who have felt strongly, for a hundred years or more, that the consequences of the clearances both can, and must, be utterly reversed.

A vital step in the direction of Highland betterment was taken by the Highland Land League which, by finally making it impossible for crofters to be evicted, brought the clearances to an end. But the Crofters Act of 1886, the Land League's main achievement, was deficient in one key respect. It made no provision for restoring to the crofting population the many areas from which crofters had already been expelled. Hence the extent to which the Highlands continued to be convulsed, into the 1920s and beyond, by land raids mounted by crofting communities attempting to stake their claims to the sheep farms and deer forests from which earlier generations had been evicted. Nothing of this, it goes almost without saying, was reflected in the work of writers of the Celtic Twilight school. But the Celtic Twilight, it had become clear by the 1920s, was not forever to have things all its own way. An alternative view of the Highlands was at last beginning to find literary expression. And this view was one that sought explicitly to promote the regeneration of a culture and a population which a whole succession of hugely influential writers – from the eighteenth century onwards – had assumed to have no future.[9]

He would have found it 'comparatively easy and acceptable', Neil Gunn commented in 1929, to fill his novels with 'the staple fare of kilts, sporrans and romance in island dawns and Celtic twilights'. But Gunn, to begin with anyway, was determined to depict the Highlands as they really were. And his characters consequently interact with their surroundings in a way that must have seemed extraordinarily discomfiting to anyone whose reading had previously consisted of Mary Ethel Muir Donaldson, Alasdair Alpin MacGregor and other writers of that type:

This land was too old. Scarred and silent, it was settling down to decay . . . A huddle of grey houses, straw-thatched, lying to the earth with an aged decrepitude that humped their backs. Seven of them all told. No life stirred urgently, nor cry of child. An old man came to a gable-end and, his shoulders hunched, stood looking at Ewan.

A middle-aged man ploughed slowly in a field . . . Ewan's eyes fell on the houses that now seemed to be huddled for warmth, and all at once he saw them mean and wretched, and understood that they were dying, thin-blooded and miserable.[10]

But the Highland predicament, as far as Gunn was concerned, was neither inevitable nor unalterable. It was the product, as Gunn observed in 1931, of conscious human action:

The people were not only cleared out of the glens, hunted and dragooned or shipped aboard like cattle, but those who remained, after being cowed into a mood of utter subjection, were by the most subtle and insidious means . . . made to despise their language and tradition.[11]

With Neil Gunn, then, this book returns to its opening chapter and, in particular, to Frantz Fanon's conviction that any people wishing to regain control of their own destiny had best begin by retrieving their own past from those who have sought to impugn and devalue it. Highlanders, Gunn admitted, had long since ceased to produce 'music or poetry or anything of the slightest consequence'. But this was because they had been so exploited as to have become 'a really first-class slave race'; watching the Highlands degenerate into 'a sporting preserve'; 'glad of any chance of earning a pound or two from . . . your wealthy outsider'. None of this, Neil Gunn contended in 1945, was necessary. The Highlands need not be so deprived. The area could be revitalised. But such revitalisation would not be brought about by means of economic development alone. Highlanders had to be roused from the torpor and apathy to which evicting landlords had reduced them. They had to be persuaded to take a pride both in themselves and in their heritage. They had to be made aware of the achievements of a Gaelic civilisation which had once brought 'Christianity and learning' to much of Europe:

It is the simplest matter in the world to set down on paper a full scheme for Highland regeneration. We all know the ingredients by this time as we know the words of an old song: crofting, hill sheep farming, sea fisheries, hydro-electric development, afforestation, appropriate light industries, transport and so on. But there is one thing that is always missing, one all-important matter which the paper economists forget, and that is the general lack of belief among the Highland people themselves in the future of their own land as a place where life could be lived interestingly and well.[12]

A lot of this was music to the ears of Christopher Murray Grieve, or Hugh MacDiarmid, who also began to attract attention in the 1920s. Like Gunn, MacDiarmid was heavily embroiled in the politics of Scottish nationalism. Like Gunn, MacDiarmid looked to Ireland – then newly independent – for both political and cultural inspiration. And like Gunn, whom he believed to be leading Scotland 'out of the Celtic Twilight and into the Gaelic sun', MacDiarmid insisted that Highlanders, indeed Scots generally, had to be made to realise just how much Gaels had once accomplished.[13]

The Caithness-born Neil Gunn's father was a Gaelic-speaker. Hugh MacDiarmid, who came from the Borders, had first been exposed to Gaelic when, as a child, he spent his holidays in the Easter Ross household of an uncle whose second wife was as much at home in Gaelic as in English. Both the language and its literature clearly intrigued the young MacDiarmid. Nor was this most eminent of twentieth-century Scottish poets ever to lose interest in Gaelic. Eventually, in fact, MacDiarmid was to become convinced, as he put it, that 'a Scottish Scotland must be a Gaelic Scotland'. Hence his adoption of the Highland name, MacDiarmid. Hence his translations of the poetry of Alasdair MacMhaighstir Alasdair. Hence his typically virulent assaults on the 'trite moralisings', 'mawkish sentimentality', 'supernatural fancies' and 'outrageous banality' which MacDiarmid thought characteristic of writers like Fiona MacLeod and Alasdair Alpin MacGregor. The Highlands and Islands, MacDiarmid observed, were certainly worth knowing. But their fame ought not to rest on the increasingly widespread conviction that the area and its people possessed some sort of direct line to the hereafter:

Not a bit of it! That is the bunkum of the Celtic Twilight. There is nothing more detestable, perhaps, than this Tibetization of the Hebrides – this myth that represents the islanders as all some sort of spiritual sportsmen, specialising in weird and wonderful soul states.[14]

Ever since James MacPherson had first put pen to paper, the Gaelic and the Highland mind had been imagined to be dark, mysterious, brooding, mystic, fey. MacDiarmid's purpose was to overturn all such ideas. That was why he wanted as many people as possible to know something of the Gaelic literature of earlier ages. To be acquainted with this literature, as

MacDiarmid realised, was immediately to be convinced that James MacPherson and the Twilight circle had got the Highlands, and the Celtic world generally, quite wrong. Another modern Scottish poet, William Neill, makes essentially the same point in these words:

> I have read a great deal of poetry in the Celtic tongues. Formal stanzas, clear images and a lack of obscurity are the characteristics of its best exemplars; Celtic mistiness is an invention of non-Celts and bad romantic novelists. It is this 'bright' poetry which is to my taste and I hope it has influenced my own work.[15]

A good deal of Neill's 'own work' – although he was born in Ayrshire and although he writes also in Scots and in English – is in Gaelic. But the style and ethos of the older poetry to which Neill refers have equally influenced the thinking of a poet like Norman MacCaig – for all that English has been his sole linguistic medium. In an interview touching on his family connections with the Highlands, the Edinburgh-born MacCaig once commented:

> Celtic art is not at all the romantic, not to say sentimental, thing of popular belief. Its extreme formality is to be seen in all the forms it takes – in its carvings and sculptures, its personal ornaments, its poetry and its music. Think of pibroch![16]

Similar observations have been made by several of the twentieth-century scholars, such as Kuno Meyer and Kenneth Jackson, who translated into English the very ancient Gaelic nature poetry quoted in a previous chapter. 'The Celtic literatures,' Jackson wrote in his preface to a series of translations on which that chapter drew substantially, 'are about as little given to mysticism or sentimentality as it is possible to be; their most outstanding characteristic is rather their astonishing power of imagination.' These are MacCaig's views exactly. And Jackson's comments, interestingly enough, might readily be applied to Norman MacCaig's own poetry:

> A bird's voice chinks and tinkles
> Alone in the gaunt reedbed –
> Tiny silversmith
> Working late in the evening.

I sit and listen. The rooftop
With a quill of smoke stuck in it
   Wavers against the sky
In the dreamy heat of summer.

Flowers' closing time: bee lurches
Across the hayfield, singing
   And feeling its drunken way
Around the air's invisible corners.[17]

There is a sense in these lines of something reaching back, across the centuries, to the hermit-poets of very long ago. And that same sense of a modern poet being in touch with the remotest of his predecessors is still more evident in Sorley MacLean's great evocation of the woods on his native Raasay:

  *Straight trunks of the pine
     on the flexed hill-slope:
     green, heraldic helmets,
     green unpressed sea:
     strong, light, wind-headed,
     untoiling, unseeking,
     the giddy, great wood,
     russet, green, two plaitings.

Floor of bracken and birch
     in the high green room:
     the roof and the floor
     heavily coloured, serene:
     tiny cups of the primrose,
     yellow petal on green,
     and the straight pillars of the room,
     the noble restless pines . . .

The great wood in motion,
     fresh in its spirit;
     the high green wood,
     in a many-coloured waulking;
     the wood and my senses
     in a white-footed rapture;
     the wood in blossom
     with a fleeting renewal.

The sunlit wood
   joyful and sportive,
   the many-winded wood,
   the glittering-jewel found by chance;
   the shady wood
   peaceful and unflurried,
   the humming wood
   of songs and ditties. [18]

Sorley MacLean, born at Osgaig in Raasay in 1911, and easily the most significant Gaelic poet of recent times, had much in common with the rather older MacDiarmid – whose poetry MacLean has always valued very highly. Like MacDiarmid, MacLean is deeply scornful both of the Celtic Twilight and its romantic antecedents. Also like MacDiarmid, MacLean looks for inspiration to the eighteenth-century Gaelic poets – most notably, in MacLean's case, to William Ross and Duncan Ban MacIntyre – whose works were generally ignored by the very large number of people who preferred to think of the Highlands in the way that Scott, Wordsworth and the romantics thought about them. For all such romantics, as is evident from a comment which he made in the mid-1930s, the young MacLean had nothing but contempt. MacLean was speaking about Duncan Ban MacIntyre's *Moladh Beinn Dhobhrain*, the poem with which this book began. He said of it:

Exquisitely subtle in technique, it is in content, I believe, the greatest example of naturalistic realism in the poetry of Europe . . . In my opinion, MacIntyre's objective naturalist realism is likely to be considered far more permanently significant than the mixture of sentimentalism, pure illusion and ruminating subjectivity . . . which constitutes Wordsworth's poetry.[19]

Sorley MacLean was also to discern in Hugh MacDiarmid's early lyrics 'a sensitivity to certain impressions from external nature' which MacLean, as a Gaelic poet striving to write about landscape in an authentically Gaelic manner, also thought superior to anything in Wordsworth. Such comments – despite the fact that the more mature MacLean was to retract the statement in which he compared the great English romantic poet so adversely to Duncan Ban MacIntyre – provide a highly informative insight into the major literary effort being made, by the 1930s, to develop a new understanding of Scotland's natural environment. This understanding – as generated by writers like Neil Gunn, Hugh MacDiarmid and Sorley

MacLean – was inevitably a twentieth-century one. But it also contained important elements of the way that nature and landscape had been understood, especially by Gaelic poets, in the era prior to MacPherson, Scott and their disciples so successfully transforming the Highlands into one of romanticism's best-known icons.[20]

His natural surroundings consequently mattered very much to Hugh MacDiarmid:

> My earliest impressions are of an almost tropical luxuriance of nature – of great forests, of honey-scented heather hills, and moorlands infinitely rich in little-appreciated beauties of flowering, of animal and insect life, of strange and subtle relationships of water and light.[21]

Much the same is true of Sorley MacLean. Landscape, he has stressed in interview after interview, was one of the key creative influences on his work. And this is instantly apparent in the poem MacLean called *An t-Eilean*, meaning Skye, the island:

> *O great Island, Island of my love,
>   many a night of them I fancied
>   the great ocean itself restless
>   agitated with love of you
>   as you lay on the sea,
>   great beautiful bird of Scotland,
>   your supremely beautiful wings bent
>   about many-nooked Loch Bracadale,
>   your beautiful wings prostrate on the sea
>   from the Wild Stallion to the Aird of Sleat,
>   your joyous wings spread
>   about Loch Snizort and the world.
>
> O great Island, my Island, my love
>   many a night I lay stretched
>   by your side in that slumber
>   when the mist of twilight swathed you.
>   My love every leaflet of heather on you
>   from Rudha Hunish to Loch Slapin,
>   from Stron Bhiornaill to the Garsven,
>   every tarn, stream and burn a joy
>   from Romisdale to Brae Eynort,

and even if I came in sight of Paradise
what price its moon without Blaven?[22]

Here landscape is personalised, even eroticised, as it is also in Norman
MacCaig's poem, *A Man in Assynt*:

Glaciers, grinding West, gouged out
these valleys, rasping the brown sandstone,
and left, on the hard rock below – the
ruffled foreland –
this frieze of mountains, filed
on the blue air – Stac Polly,
Cul Beag, Cul Mor, Suilven,
Canisp – a frieze and
a litany.

Who owns this landscape?
Has owning anything to do with love?
For it and I have a love affair, so nearly human
we even have quarrels. –
When I intrude too confidently
it rebuffs me with a wind like a hand
or puts in my way
a quaking bog or a loch
where no loch should be. Or I turn stonily
away, refusing to notice
the rouged rocks, the mascara
under a dripping ledge, even
the tossed, the stony limbs waiting.

I can't pretend
it gets sick for me in my absence,
though I get sick for it. Yet I love it
with special gratitude, since
it sends me no letters, is never
jealous and, expecting nothing
from me, gets nothing but
cigarette packets and footprints.

Who owns this landscape? –
The millionaire who bought it or
the poacher staggering downhill in the early morning
with a deer on his back?

Who possesses this landscape? –
The man who bought it or
I who am possessed by it?[23]

To read *A Man in Assynt* is immediately to be reminded of Hugh MacLennan's reaction to Kintail. For MacCaig, unlike the Gaelic poets of an earlier time, cannot simply treat landscape as a given fact, a simply present entity. He is ineradicably aware, as Hugh MacLennan was aware, as every Highlander has been aware since the early nineteenth century, of the extent to which community and landscape have been severed by the complex of forces, the sequence of events, we call the Highland Clearances:

Or has it come to this,
that this dying landscape belongs
to the dead, the crofters and fighters
and fishermen whose larochs
sink into the bracken
by Loch Assynt and Loch Crocach? –
to men trampled under the hoofs of sheep
and driven by deer to
the ends of the earth – to men whose loyalty
was so great it accepted their own betrayal
by their own chiefs and whose descendants now
are kept in their place
by English businessmen and the indifference
of a remote and ignorant government.[24]

The clearances loom large, then, for Norman MacCaig. For Sorley MacLean – writing always in Gaelic and, as a result of his Raasay upbringing, rather closer than the Edinburgh-born MacCaig to family memories of eviction – the clearances loom larger still. So intermingled were his surroundings with his community's often tragic past, in fact, that it was clearly difficult for MacLean to separate the one from the other:

My symbols almost automatically became the landscape of my physical environment. But, of course, that was always blended with what I knew of the history of my people.[25]

An especially inescapable fact of that history was the clearance of the greater part of Raasay in the 1850s. It was with the implications of this clearance that Sorley MacLean was to wrestle in a poem he entitled simply *Hallaig* – the name of one of the twelve Raasay townships which were then emptied of their people. Assessing the significance of *Hallaig*, John MacInnes, perhaps the most perceptive analyst of MacLean's poetry and certainly the analyst most conscious of the historical influences operating on that poetry, has commented:

Hallaig is a twentieth-century poem and contains images of its time. Setting these aside, I have a feeling that it is also a poem that would have been understood a thousand years ago and more.[26]

What would certainly have been understood by the Gaels of many centuries back, whether in Scotland or in Ireland, is the emphasis in MacLean's work on the link between people and locality. Community and place have always been believed by Gaelic-speakers to be integral to each other. That is one reason why the destruction of villages like Hallaig, Boreraig and Achadh nan Seileach had such traumatic repercussions. By no means the least powerful aspect of MacLean's *Hallaig*, therefore, is the way the poem encapsulates the terrible hurt involved in the breaking of the bond between Hallaig's human occupants and the little piece of ground to which these same folk, and so many of their ancestors, had for so long belonged. The point is well made by a modern Irish Gael, Brendan Devlin, in the course of a reflection on MacLean's unusually intimate relationship with the island environment in which so many of his poems are set:

This sense of landscape and attachment to place is closely bound up with human relations, not merely with personal memories of friends and their company . . . but with a profound awareness of the community extended not only in place but also in time; an awareness of all those who lived and strove and were buried in the earth, not as remote figures in a history-book but as part of one's own flesh and blood.[27]

Just as a living community is made the more attractive by its possessing a collective consciousness of its own continuity, so a place which has been cleared seems, from a Highland perspective at all events, to have about it something of the dreariness which Hugh MacLennan sensed so strongly in Kintail. The romantic mind, as the previous chapter argued, might sometimes have been thrilled by a depopulated landscape's tragic associations. The Highland mind, however, is much more likely to find the self-same landscape merely saddening and depressing. That is why Loch Shiel's surroundings seemed so dispiriting to Calum MacLean. That is why Neil Gunn invariably felt dejected when visiting the once thickly peopled Strath of Kildonan:

> For not only does environment affect human development, but human development in turn affects environment. In a happy, thriving community the very land, to our senses, takes on a certain pleasant friendliness. Children feel this particularly and, in after life, have an enhanced memory of sunlight and flowering growths. On the other hand, in Kildonan there is today a shadow, a chill, of which any sensitive mind would, I am convinced, be vaguely aware, though possessing no knowledge of the clearances. We are affected strangely by any place from which the tide of life has ebbed.[28]

Hugh MacDiarmid, for his part, compared the almost audible silence of a depopulated glen to 'the stillness of foetal death' – an extinguished community, as his image suggests, having something of a still-born infant's 'unevolved' potential. Death resonates through MacLean's *Hallaig* also; for the poem is, in its way, a lament, a cry of heartfelt anguish for what has been so wantonly, so casually, destroyed. As Iain Crichton Smith has observed, however, there is much more to *Hallaig* than that:

> Sometimes in certain texts in literature we sense that the poet has reached levels of intuition that go beyond the intelligence and the reasoning mind, that he has made contact with his theme in a very direct way. I have myself sensed this often in Shakespeare and in some Greek poetry. We find it, I believe, very finely in *Hallaig*. In this poem it is as if MacLean felt and sensed quite clearly the desolation, the sadness, the terrible emptiness of the Highlands, its ghosts and presences, in an absolute intuitional music.[29]

In *Hallaig*, as in so many of the older Gaelic poems cited earlier, trees are very much in evidence. But these trees are symbols now as well as simple objects of affection. The township's former community, its 'ghosts and presences', have been transformed and transmuted into a wood. And it is this touch, perhaps, which gives to *Hallaig* its strangest, most unanticipated, quality. Iain Crichton Smith again:

> In this poem there is not only desolation, the loneliness of the Highlands, but also a deep central joy, as if there is also immortality.[30]

This book returns in due course to MacLean's transcendent optimism. But first to an extract from *Hallaig*, 'this most beautiful, mysterious and intriguing poem', as Iain Crichton Smith has called it:

> *The window is nailed and boarded
> through which I saw the West
> and my love is at the Burn of Hallaig,
> a birch tree, and she has always been
>
> between Inver and Milk Hollow,
> here and there about Baile-chuirn:
> she is a birch, a hazel,
> a straight, slender young rowan.
>
> In Screapadal of my people
> where Norman and Big Hector were,
> their daughters and their sons are a wood
> going up beside the stream.
>
> Proud tonight the pine cocks
> crowing on the top of Cnoc an Ra,
> straight their backs in the moonlight –
> they are not the wood I love.
>
> I will wait for the birch wood
> until it comes up from the cairn,
> until the whole ridge from Beinn na Lice
> will be under its shade.

If it does not, I will go down to Hallaig,
to the sabbath of the dead,
where the people are frequenting,
every single generation gone.

They are still in Hallaig,
MacLeans and MacLeods,
all who were there in the time of Mac Gille Chaluim
the dead have been seen alive.

The men lying on the green
at the end of every house that was,
the girls a wood of birches,
straight their backs, bent their heads.

Between the Leac and Fearns
the road is under mild moss
and the girls in silent bands
go to Clachan as in the beginning,

and return from Clachan
from Suisnish and the land of the living;
each one young and high-stepping,
without the heartbreak of the tale.[31]

When looking on a Highland scene – on Boreraig, on Achadh nan Seileach or on Hallaig itself – you find yourself imagining very often, the more so maybe if you are a Highlander, how that scene might be today if what took place in the nineteenth century had not done so. You find yourself, in other words, trying to envisage the Highlands as they would be without the heartbreak of the tale. And it is in this sense, one suspects, that *Hallaig* is inextricably bound up with the cultural setting – possibly even with the language – in which it was conceived. Certainly this was Seamus Heaney's conviction when, in Dublin's Abbey Theatre, this leading Irish poet first read aloud the English translation of *Hallaig*, as quoted above, and then listened, in mounting awe, to Sorley MacLean recite his own poem in Gaelic:

This had the force of revelation: the mesmeric, heightened tone; the weathered voice coming in close from a far place; the swarm of the vowels; the surrender to the otherness of the poem; above all the sense of bardic dignity that was entirely without self-parade but was instead the effect of proud self-abnegation, as much a submission as a claim to heritage.[32]

It is as a result of his ability thus to connect with our past that Sorley MacLean, more than any other twentieth-century figure, has been able so forcefully to express, on behalf of Highlanders generally, the feelings so strongly evoked by those landscapes where, as Hugh MacLennan observed, you feel that everyone who ever mattered is dead and gone. MacLean's own family, as it happens, had links, just like MacLennan's, with Kintail. But it was Mull, a place depopulated more than most in the course of the nineteenth century, which, on his going to teach in Tobermory in 1938, affected Sorley MacLean especially deeply:

> I think Mull had much to do with my poetry: its physical beauty, so different from Skye's, with the terrible imprint of the clearances everywhere on it, made it almost intolerable for a Gael.[33]

Mull's unpeopled terrain, MacLean remarked on another occasion, 'nearly drove me mad'. Sutherland's equally empty straths, you gather from Norman MacCaig's response to an interviewer who asked about this other landscape-obsessed poet's relationship with the part of the Highlands which features so largely in his output, are quite capable of producing a very similar effect:

> Sutherland, the county, the whole of it, was most shamefully treated in the clearances. And it's a beautiful, beautiful countryside. But it's also very sad, because there are hardly any people in the place. And you keep coming across ruins of what used to be crofts, in the most unlikely places, from a time when the population was much bigger than it now is. So it's a sad landscape in that way. You can walk for miles and miles and miles and never see a house, let alone a person. It's got that sadness in it, and you can't help being afflicted by that history in that landscape, because there it is under your eyes.[34]

A key element in this sadness – and one which is especially evident to those of us who have inherited the merest smattering of the language – is to be found in the fact that the snuffing out of community has led, inexorably and inevitably, to the snuffing out of a great deal of Gaelic also. The effect of this has been to break the previously intimate connection between the natural environment of the Highlands, on the one hand, and the Highland population's everyday speech, on the other:

> *Words rise out of the country. They are around us. In every month of the year we are surrounded by words.[35]

These lines are Iain Crichton Smith's. Later in this same poem, he observes:

> *He who loses his language loses his world. The Highlander who loses his language loses his world.

This loss, as far as landscape is concerned, is both literal and symbolic; literal in that it is impossible for anyone who is not fluent in the language to appreciate the highly descriptive way in which particular localities were often named by their Gaelic-speaking occupants; symbolic in that the snapping of the linguistic link between people and place is a metaphor for the much more all-encompassing collapse of Gaelic civilisation. William Neill – in lines which embody a translingual pun and which can be fully appreciated, therefore, only by a reader understanding both Gaelic and English – makes the latter point exactly:

> When Irongray grew out of *Earran Reidh*
> the culture could not stand on level ground.[36]

A comment made by a character in Fionn MacColla's 1932 novel, *The Albannach*, is equally suggestive:

> Now in our own Gaelic a man can't tell his name itself without every man will know his whole history and his people's before him; and the name of every place will be a picture of what will be there, so that a man will almost know a place on its first seeing by its likeness to the name that will be on it. Say Achadh nam beith to a Gaelic man and he will be seeing in his mind a level place and the birch trees growing here and there, and they white and slender. Say Achadh nan siantan and he will be seeing a little plain between great mountains and the rain driving down on it. But will a man of you tell me what Achbay or Achnasheen will mean in the Beurla [English], or what kind of place is in Lowestoft or Dover?[37]

The anglicisation of Gaelic placenames – the turning of *Achadh nan Siantan* into Achnasheen or the much more offensive transformation of *Aonach Mor* into Nevis Range – can thus be seen as a type of linguistic imperialism. Indeed the practice is explicitly portrayed in just this light – though from an Irish rather than a Highland standpoint – in Brendan Friel's play, *Translations*, which deals with the activities of Ordnance Survey mapmakers sent from Britain to Ireland in the 1820s. 'My job,' one of these mapmakers remarks to one of Friel's Irish characters, 'is to translate the quaint, archaic tongue you people persist in speaking into the king's good English.'[38]

The Scottish Highlands, fortunately, were treated less offhandedly by the Ordnance Survey than was Ireland. But Highland placenames, as a result of the contraction of the area where Gaelic is still spoken, have become steadily less comprehensible all the same. That is one reason why such placenames run, in an almost talismanic fashion, through so much modern Gaelic poetry. It is as if the minority who understand their meaning are endeavouring, by constant repetition of these names, to conserve what would otherwise be lost. And Gaelic-influenced English poetry, by no means coincidentally, is equally given to what one Irish writer has dubbed 'topophilia'. Sometimes, as by William Neill and Norman MacCaig, Gaelic placenames are translated literally into English – emerging into this new language as 'the Black Loch' and 'the Glen of Rushes', 'the Loch of the Wolf's Pass' and 'the Loch of the Green Corrie'. At other times, even in English poetry, placenames are untranslated. But whether in English or in Gaelic, they constitute a kind of litany; a telling of linguistic beads for those communities which have vanished so completely from the earth.[39]

This book does not contend, it should be made clear at this stage, that there is anything intrinsically invalid about those perspectives on the Highlands which differ from its own. No condemnation is to be attached to the innumerable tourists who, never having heard of either Hugh MacLennan or Achadh nan Seileach, are content to treat Kintail as nothing more than an uncomplicatedly beautiful piece of scenery. Nor are the hundreds of climbers whose cars fill Glen Shiel's lay-bys every Saturday and Sunday committing any crime when they experience on Kintail's high tops that soaring of the spirit which a whole series of twentieth-century lovers of Highland hills, from Seton Gordon to Mike Tomkies, have so emotively described. Nobody – other than those of our native Calvinists to whom a sunny day is a suspiciously sensual pleasure to be 'paid for' by some ensuing climatic calamity – should ever feel guilty about enjoying the Scottish Highlands.

But a powerful sense of Glen Shiel, of Boreraig, of Hallaig and a thousand other such locations being places where everyone who ever mattered is dead and gone is a meaningful response to Highland landscape also. It is one, or so this book asserts, which requires to be taken much more seriously outside the Highlands if environmentalists – whether individually or collectively – are ever to be at one with Highlanders on how the Highlands should be treated in the future. And there is something else that needs to get more emphasis in this context; something which is evident in the concluding lines of Norman MacCaig's fine poem, *A Man in Assynt.*

Greenshank, adder, wildcat, guillemot, seatrout,
fox and falcon – the list winds through
all the crooks and crannies of this landscape, all
the subtleties and shifts of its waters and
the prevarications of its air –
while roofs fall in, walls crumble, gables
die last of all, and man becomes,
in this most beautiful corner of the land,
one of the rare animals.

Up there, the scraping light
whittles the cloud edges till, like thin bone,
they're bright with their own opaque selves. Down here,
a skinny rosebush is an eccentric jug
of air. They make me,
somewhere between them,
a visiting eye,
an unrequited passion,
watching the tide glittering backward and making
its huge withdrawal from beaches
and kilted rocks. And the mind
behind the eye, within the passion,
remembers with certainty that the tide will return
and thinks, with hope, that that other ebb,
that sad withdrawal of people, may, too,
reverse itself and flood
the bays and the sheltered glens
with new generations replenishing the land

with its richest of riches and coming, at last,
into their own again.[40]

There is an echo here of the great bard of the nineteenth-century
Highland Land League, Mary MacPherson, *Mairi Mhor nan Oran*. In one
of her songs – set, significantly enough to the tune of a much earlier
composition in which Alasdair MacMhaighstir Alasdair, writing in the
bitterness of Jacobitism's defeat, envisages Charles Edward Stuart coming
back from exile to lead the Gaels at last to triumph – Mary looks far
beyond the crofting community's battles for security of tenure. She
imagines a time when both the physical and the mental impact of eviction
and depopulation will have been utterly expunged. She visualises how her
native Skye, and the rest of the Highlands, will appear when the empty
glens have finally been reclaimed:

> *And when I am under boards
> my words will be as a prophecy,
>
> and there will return the stock of the tenantry
> who were driven over the sea.
>
> And the beggars of gentry
> will be routed as they, the crofters, were;
>
> deer and sheep will be wheeled away
> and the glens will be tilled;
>
> a time of sowing and of reaping
> and a time of reward for the robbers;
>
> and the cold ruined stances of houses
> will be built up by our kinsmen. [41]

To anyone determined to deal only with the 'facts' of Highland history, to
anyone concerning himself or herself only with the seeming 'realities' of
contemporary Highland life, this must seem a wholly fanciful, indeed
illusory, aspiration. But it is one that is held strongly by many
Highlanders for all that. This was convincingly demonstrated, during the
1970s, by the rapturous reception given in village halls and community
centres, right across the northern half of Scotland, to John McGrath's
musical play, *The Cheviot, the Stag and the Black, Black Oil.* Towards the

143

end of McGrath's drama, which takes the form of a ceilidh, Mary MacPherson's vision – articulated in the play in her own words – is made to seem both a legitimate and an attainable political objective:

> *Remember your hardships and keep up your struggle.
> The wheel will turn for you
> By the strength of your hands and the hardness of your fists.
> Your cattle will be on the plains,
> Everyone in the land will have a place,
> And the exploiter will be driven out.[42]

Not for nothing has Edward Said noted of the very similarly expressed ambitions of the world's more directly colonised peoples:

> One of the first tasks of the culture of resistance was to reclaim, rename and reinhabit the land. And with that came a whole set of further assertions, recoveries and identifications, all of them quite literally grounded on this poetically projected base. The search for authenticity, for a more congenial national origin than that provided by colonial history, for a new pantheon of heroes and (occasionally) heroines, myths and religions – these, too, are made possible by a sense of the land reappropriated by its people. And along with these nationalistic adumbrations of the decolonised identity, there goes an almost magically inspired, quasi-alchemical redevelopment of the native language.[43]

Edward Said, as his tone suggests, sees manifold dangers in such projects. So does this book. That is why the following chapter, although it strongly advocates the repopulation of the Highlands, suggests that such repopulation, if it is to help put right the long-term damage inflicted by the clearances, will have to be much less exclusively Highland in character than *Mairi Mhor nan Oran* might have wished. The present chapter's task is more straightforward. It is to emphasise – by way of introducing this book's concluding arguments – that, in many parts of the Highlands, it is only through the restoration of a permanent human presence that our artificially depopulated landscapes can be returned to their natural condition.

It was 'futile to imagine that the common people are sensible to the peculiar charms of a mountainous and romantic country', a visitor to the Highlands commented in 1820:

If the Highlander would show you a fine prospect, he does not lead you to the torrent and the romantic rocky-glen, to the storm-beaten precipice of the cloud-capped mountain. It is to the strath covered with hamlets and cultivations, or to the extended tract of fertile lowlands, where the luxuriance of vegetation and wood depends on the exertion of human labour.[44]

Many such fine prospects and hamlet-covered straths have long since been denuded of their people. But the wholly unoccupied tracts of territory which have resulted seem, to some at least of their visitors, never quite to have recovered from the ejection of the folk who formerly inhabited them. 'I'm never sure whether it's imagination or something less easily explained,' the modern writer, Derek Cooper, has remarked in the introduction to one of his several books about the Highlands, 'but there are times in some emptied glen when I can almost feel the physical presence of the dispossessed.' Nor is there anything unique about Derek Cooper's feelings. Frank Fraser Darling more than once experienced very similar sensations when exploring the hills of Wester Ross:

I have lain sometimes on the western slopes of Beinn a' Chaisgein Beag . . . which are rich and pleasant and where, doubtless, man's animals have grazed in past times. The burns fall to the waters of the Fionn Loch, gleaming as white as its name in the June sun, and there are traces of the dwellings of men. I have heard the singing of women's voices and the laughter of children in this place. Perhaps the play of wind and falling waters made these sounds – I neither know nor care – I was content to listen to the beauty of the moment.[45]

Just two or three years before Frank Fraser Darling got there, Wester Ross was made the setting of Fionn MacColla's novel, *The Albannach* – MacColla, whose real name was Tom MacDonald, having been a teacher for some time in Gairloch. In the course of his book's closing chapter, MacColla brings Murdo Anderson, the novel's hero, to a place rather like the one which Fraser Darling was subsequently to describe:

On a sudden he became very sad because of the people of the glen. He saw it there as it had been, a little world in itself, savouring its own joys, tholing its own peculiar sorrows. There had been old people in it, old men and women with a lifetime's memories . . . There had been young men and lasses, and they at the courting on summer evenings in the woods of lapping water. There had been little children running about the grassy braes and knolls, shouting to each other in their play . . . But that day was no more. Instead was the light on the loch face, the moss-grown mounds among the braes, and silence.

For some reason he kept coming back to the thought of the children . . . Suddenly it seemed to him that *there* if you want it is an ordering for the world. How else should the world be ordered but that little children should run barelegged on the grassy knolls shouting out of the gladness of their hearts? What else is there that should take first place to that in the ruling of man's affairs? What else in the name of God?[46]

Mere sentiment? Perhaps. But it as well, before peremptorily dismissing Fionn MacColla's fiction, to be aware of a story told by Angus Macleod, a Lewisman who, in the mid-1980s, became the principal founder of the Scottish Crofters Union. Angus's story deals with the part of Lewis to which he belongs. The area is known as Pairc and Angus is an expert on its history, its genealogy and tradition. He can tell you, should you make the time, of clearance after clearance – some three dozen Pairc communities having been destroyed to make way for a single sheep farm. Angus tells, in particular, of the clearance of Steinreway on the north shore of Loch Shell. This clearance took place in 1857 and Angus, himself an old man now, first heard about it from other old men who, as boys, had been among its victims.

Steinreway, as it happens, was one of the numerous localities which, some twenty years into the twentieth century, were 'raided' by ex-servicemen who, on their return from the Great War, were looking to get the 'homes for heroes' which they had been promised by their country's politicians. Many such raids were successful. But the raid on Steinreway, which took place in 1921, was not. Again the township had to be abandoned by its occupants. And except for a few hours in 1991, Steinreway has since remained every bit as unpopulated as Boreraig, Hallaig or Achadh nan Seileach.

So what of these few hours? Well, Pairc possesses a flourishing local history society. And the society, with Angus Macleod's enthusiastic participation, organised – on a July Saturday in the year in question – a day trip to Steinreway. A lot of local people – men, women and children – took part in the excursion. Some walked to Steinreway across the hill which separates the former township from the end of the Pairc road. Others travelled there by sea. And though the day was much enjoyed, it undoubtedly contained, as Angus Macleod observes, its sadder moments also:

> When we were there on the 'day out', it was a nice, warm summer's day and the children were playing on a green, sloping hill on the eastern side of the old village. As I watched the dozen or two young, noisy, boisterous children playing on the hill, I could not help reflecting on the community that had lived there peacefully for generations. Since I am familiar with the names of all the families who were there in 1857, and with the names of all the families who were there in 1921 as well, I saw in my mind's eye how Steinreway should be. A vibrant crofting community with its own carefree children. What a mad world landlordism imposed on our Highland people! What tragedy, what hardship![47]

For Angus Macleod, then, Fionn MacColla's imagery was transiently made real that summer day in Steinreway. It is the following chapter's key contention that much the same should be made to happen – permanently this time – in many other parts of the Scottish Highlands.

CHAPTER SIX

The Highlands are a Devastated Countryside

No matter how well you get to know the Scottish Highlands, no matter how often you have glimpsed a particular scene, this tremendously varied area seems forever to retain its power to impose itself, all of a sudden, on your mind. Perhaps you have stepped out on to the deck of the Stornoway–Ullapool ferry in the bitter cold of a winter's morning and found yourself watching the dawn break over range after range of snow-covered mountains. Perhaps you are sitting by Loch Indaal in Islay on the sort of summer's afternoon that makes white sands whiter, green fields greener and blue seas bluer than you would have thought was possible. Maybe you are simply driving through Strathnaver, Strathdon or Glen Lyon when a particular combination of cloud and light throws into sharp relief some set of features which, despite your having often passed that way, you have never previously noticed. At moments of this sort, and it is quite remarkable how they stay with you, it seems almost unbelievable that Highland landscapes are anything other than exactly as they ought to be.

But if you want to understand the Highlands – instead of simply looking at them – you have to start by accepting that very little hereabouts is as nature intended. And this can be unsettling. 'One of the perils of an ecological education,' an American conservationist once commented, 'is that one lives alone in a world of wounds. Much of the damage inflicted on land is quite invisible to laymen.' That conservationist, Aldo Leopold, was writing in the 1940s. And there is no doubt that far more people are aware today than were aware then of the extent to which the earth has been harmed by humanity's activities. Most of us, however, still find it very difficult to accept that there is no escape – not even in so attractive a location as the Highlands – from the frequently pernicious consequences of our own collective conduct.[1]

We can readily understand, and be outraged by, the more obvious manifestations of pollution and destructiveness: the spilling of oil around Shetland or Alaska; the felling of tropical rainforest; the dumping of poisonous waste. What is much harder to comprehend is the altogether more insidious way we have altered those localities where nothing of that kind is going on. But by modifying – albeit involuntarily – the chemical composition of the air we have begun to change the weather and to destroy the upper atmosphere gases which have long protected life on earth from the full force of solar radiation. Nowhere is immune from the effects of these far-reaching transformations. The storm which rages today across the Antarctic plateau, by far the remotest corner of our planet, may be a wholly natural phenomenon. But it may equally be a result of climatic changes caused by our civilisation's output of carbon dioxide. And even if that polar storm should, in fact, owe absolutely nothing to humanity's tampering with nature, it is unnecessary to leave Antarctica in order to discover a still more compelling instance of the environmental cataclysms we can now so easily bring about. The yawning hole in the ozone layer high above the world's most isolated continent is a perpetual reminder of the extraordinary universality of our influence on our surroundings.

The Scottish Highlands are as susceptible to this type of environmental injury as anywhere else. Thus emissions from distant power stations, by making Highland rain acidic, have had an adverse impact on freshwater life in Highland lochs and streams. But the Highlands also bear much more longstanding scars. These scars have resulted from processes very similar to those which Aldo Leopold described in the case of the American south-west:

> This region, when grazed by livestock, reverted through a series of more and more worthless grasses, shrubs and weeds to a condition of unstable equilibrium. Each recession of plant types bred erosion; each increment to erosion bred a further recession of plants. The result today is a progressive and mutual deterioration, not only of plants and soils, but of the animal community subsisting thereon... So subtle has been its progress that few residents of the region are aware of it. It is quite invisible to the tourist who finds this wrecked landscape colourful and charming.[2]

The tourist finds the typically treeless Highland glen equally charming. The tourist probably considers such a glen to be in its natural condition. But the tourist, as Frank Fraser Darling pointed out some half a century back, is wrong. The Highlands, Fraser Darling observed, had been stripped of their original vegetation every bit as comprehensively as New Mexico. And the consequences, as described by this Highland-based ecologist whose thinking was very much influenced by Aldo Leopold, were just as disastrous for the Highlands as they were for those faraway landscapes to the south of Albuquerque:

The Highlands, as a geologic and physiographic region, are unable to withstand deforestation and maintain productiveness and fertility. Their history has been one of steadily accelerating deforestation until the great mass of the forests was gone, and thereafter of forms of land usage which prevented regeneration of tree growth and reduced the land to the crude values and expressions of its solid geological composition. In short, the Highlands are a devastated countryside . . . Devastation has not quite reached its uttermost lengths, but it is quite certain that present trends in land use will lead to it, and the country will then be rather less productive than Baffin Land.[3]

Frank Fraser Darling acknowledged that people might actually like the Highlands in the state to which such environmental degradation had brought them. In the mass of romantic literature inspired by the area's landscapes, after all, there is not the slightest indication of any awareness that these landscapes were, in a real sense, man-made. A Gaelic poet like Duncan Ban MacIntyre might have lamented the land use changes which had resulted in the obliteration of so many Highland woods – 'the thickets that were fruitful' having 'withered as though plucked up' and many 'shoots', 'wands' and 'young saplings' having disappeared entirely. But Walter Scott and his successors had shared none of these concerns. The sheer starkness of the archetypal Highland landscape had seemed, to the romantics, both the essence of its appeal and the very emblem of this landscape's supposed lack of artificiality.[4]

Frank Fraser Darling duly recognised that, if maltreatment of the Highland environment was to be ended, it would first be necessary to convince the wider British public that the Highlands, despite the closeness of the area's links with the romantic cult of nature, were not actually in a natural condition. The 'jaded townsman', Fraser Darling commented, inevitably held a high regard for what this same jaded townsman liked to think was 'wilderness'. The jaded townsman might even be prepared to contribute to the cost of keeping the Highlands in the mostly treeless, and increasingly eroded, condition in which he found them:

But if the jaded townsman attains to an ecological knowledge and appreciation he will not necessarily wish his wilderness to be the desolation caused by the devastation of land by his own species . . . Man-made devastation is no environment for psychological health in a people as a whole.[5]

To get some sense of the Highlands as they were prior to their having been transformed into what Frank Fraser Darling memorably called 'a wet desert', you are best advised to visit some of the area's few remaining fragments of native forest. One of these, the oakwood at Ariundle, was mentioned in an earlier chapter. Others include the pinewoods of Glen Tanar, Rothiemurchus, Abernethy and Glen Affric. 'Even to walk through the larger of them,' remarked the authors of a pioneering scientific study of these woods, 'gives one a better idea of what a primeval forest was like than can be got from any other woodland scene in Britain . . . To stand in them is to feel the past.' It is also to appreciate something of what it is that has been lost.[6]

In the course of the four or five millennia following the melting – some 10,000 years ago – of the last of Scotland's Ice Age glaciers, the Highlands were colonised by a whole range of tree species. Birch arrived, then hazel, elm, oak, scots pine, ash, alder, rowan, willow, aspen, holly and several others. The resulting forest cover was never absolutely total, of course. Bogs and marshes on the one side, and high hilltops on the other, were always free of trees. But woodland was enormously more extensive than it has been in more recent centuries all the same. And it provided shelter for a whole succession of animals which have long since vanished – the Highland wildwood containing giant elk, wild ox, reindeer, brown bear, wild boar, lemming, wolves, northern lynx and beaver as well as the still-surviving red deer, fox, badger, pine marten, stoat and weasel.

Not least among the early animal colonists of the Highlands, however, was man. And man, as has been characteristic of our species for much longer than we have been resident in Scotland, promptly set about the modification of the natural environment in ways which were utterly beyond the scope of any of his competitors. The earliest known human settlement in post-glacial Scotland was established, about 8,000 years ago, at Kinloch on the island of Rum. And Rum's natural woodland – which had itself begun developing not terribly long before – was promptly subjected to felling, clearance and other interference.[7]

Far from being intended to remove trees entirely, a good deal of this interference was probably undertaken with a view to enabling Rum's first settlers to engage in the sustainable harvesting of timber products by means of coppicing hazel, willow, alder and those other varieties which lend themselves to this particular technique. Management of that kind poses no threat to the survival of woodland as such. Indeed the more that is discovered about the history and composition of those equatorial and other forests which have traditionally been assumed to be in something approximating to a pristine state, the more it becomes evident that they, too, have been manipulated extensively by their human inhabitants. In the course of their account of the Amazonian rainforest, for example, Susanna Hecht and Alexander Cockburn comment:

> The impact of human activity on the biogeography and structure of plant and animal communities in the tropics has been given short shrift by many biologists and agronomists, but the fact is that there are vast tracts of forest created by man. Those of the babassu palm cover hundreds of thousands of acres . . . Such palm forests, initially viewed as natural, are now clearly discerned and documented as the consequence of human action. Large areas along the rivers that again appear to be natural . . . are the consequence of careful choices. Indeed much of the the Amazon's forests may very well reflect the intercessions of man.[8]

Just as the latest research findings have resulted in a setting aside of earlier notions of Brazil's native peoples having had merely a hunter-gatherer relationship with their forest environment, so our concepts of how woodland has developed historically in the Scottish Highlands almost certainly require to make more allowance than they generally do for management regimes that reach back at least as far, and probably a lot further, than the timber-conserving formulae of the earliest Gaelic law tracts. In fact, the survival into modern times of woods like those at Ariundle and Rothiemurchus may – somewhat paradoxically – owe rather more to the intensity of their exploitation than to their having been left alone. Because such woods were an especially valuable resource, or so it now seems likely, they were subjected to controls of a kind which prevented the wholesale depredation which so many other Highland forests have indubitably suffered at various points in the past. Although the woods you see today at Ariundle and Rothiemurchus are certainly ancient, in the sense that tree has very probably followed tree in such localities for several millennia, these woods exist because human beings – over very many centuries – took steps to nurture and protect them. The pity is that so small a number of our woodlands were thought worthy of such treatment.

Frank Fraser Darling inclined to the view that the Highlands lost their forests comparatively recently. It is more and more evident, however, that woodland has been in retreat in northern Scotland for a long, long time. Some part of that retreat has been due to naturally occurring climate change. But a good deal has been due to human action. And it is not just trees which have given way to people in the Highlands. A great many bird and mammal species have also been eliminated. The lynx was probably wiped out by neolithic hunters whose most complex weapons were flint-tipped spears and arrows. The brown bear was made extinct in the tenth century, the reindeer in the twelfth century, the elk and the wild ox in the fourteenth century, the beaver in the sixteenth century, the wild boar in the seventeenth century and the wolf in the eighteenth century. The pine marten just escaped eradication. The crane, the bittern, the great auk, the sea eagle, the goshawk and the osprey were, sadly, not so fortunate.[9]

But if the ecological degradation of the Highlands began in the more or less distant past, there is equally no doubt – as Frank Fraser Darling so clearly discerned – that such degradation was enormously speeded up by developments which date from the century following the Battle of Culloden. One has only to glance at the memoirs of the nineteenth-century Highland landlord, Osgood MacKenzie, to grasp something of the carnage associated with the rise of the sporting estate and, more specifically, with the war waged by the owners of such estates on what they termed 'vermin'. Included in this category, MacKenzie wrote, were 'all kinds of beasts and birds' – 'a good many of which,' he added without irony, 'are now extinct.' Hare carcases were baited with strychnine in order to eliminate kites. An 'average of forty or fifty skins of marten' were brought in by MacKenzie's keepers every year. Badgers were turned into fireside rugs. And the total of 1,900 living creatures which Osgood MacKenzie killed personally in one twelve-month period was made up of '1,314 grouse, 33 black game, 49 partridges, 110 golden plover, 35 wild ducks, 53 snipe, 91 blue rock-pigeons, 184 hares, without mentioning geese, teal, ptarmigan and roe'.[10]

Still more devastating ecologically were the effects of the introduction of sheep-farming to the Highlands in the years around 1800. The region's pre-clearance agriculture had been based on a combination of cattle and cropping. The higher ground was lightly grazed each summer when each township's cows were driven to hill shielings of the type which William Ross depicted in his poetry. The better, lower-lying land was well manured and highly cultivated. These traditional techniques – as is demonstrated by the contraction of forest cover and the loss of several animal species during the period prior to Culloden – were not without their own adverse impact on the Highland environment. But they nevertheless resulted in an accumulated store of fertility on which sheep farmers drew quite recklessly. No small part of the massive profits generated by Highland sheep-farming during the first three-quarters of the nineteenth century thus resulted from the 'mining' of agricultural resources created over many generations. By the 1870s, however, these resources were beginning to be exhausted. The formerly productive fields of townships which had earlier been cleared were now vanishing under bracken. And because sheep graze much more selectively than cattle, hill pastures, too, were deteriorating as higher quality grasses were literally eaten out of existence – to be replaced by coarser, less nutritious, types.[11]

Not for nothing did John Muir, noting the identical effect of introducing sheep to the Californian Sierra, dismiss the species as so many 'hoofed locusts'. But for all that Highland sheep-farming crashed financially in the 1880s, when the effects of the mounting ecological crisis were combined with the equally disruptive consequences of much lower-cost competition from newly opened up countries like Australia, there was to be no reversion to anything approximating to the more sustainable land uses of the past. 'I found myself going dead against the political and administrative trends and against the pseudo-scientific opinion of the agricultural advisers,' Frank Fraser Darling commented when recalling his failure to persuade the responsible authorities to encourage a return to cattle husbandry. Nor was anyone else to be more successful. For most of the twentieth century, therefore, Highland sheep-farming – despite its having been hopelessly unprofitable in anything other than the most cushioned circumstances for more than a hundred years – has been kept going by means of public subsidy. And in those places where sheep production was actually given up in the pre-subsidy decades immediately preceding the First World War, it was mostly replaced by sporting preserves where deer numbers have long since soared to levels which ensure both that the available herbage continues to be overgrazed and that native trees – if they survive at all – continue to be unable to regenerate themselves because of browsing pressure on their seedlings.[12]

In a pamphlet published in 1994, the Highland naturalist and conservationist, John Lister-Kaye, summed up the consequent catastrophe:

I can walk you across many a dry moor for mile upon mile where the cropped and twiggy heather never comes above your ankles – moors where thousands of grouse were shot every year for the first thirty years of this century. You will be lucky to see more than a handful of red grouse now, but you will see many deer and many sheep.

I recently returned to the spot where I shot my first stag in 1963. The memory is vivid to me, the excitement still tingles. My diary records the deep heather in which the stalker and I lay after the gralloch, waiting for the ponyman, pulling on my hip flask in the hazy September afternoon sun. The place is now an ocean of coarse purple moor grass, molinia, one of the least nutritious upland grasses, with only an occasional burr of stunted heather spotting the yellow-green hill.

When I came to live in Strathglass in the northern central Highlands in 1968, each spring the glens around my home echoed with the bubbling calls of curlew. The rough pastures along the river flashed with gyrating, mewing lapwings staking out their tussocky nesting grounds. High above the woods, deep in the hill beside wet yellow flushes, redshank, greenshank, golden plover and dunlin nested. On a June walk I could be certain of finding them and hearing their thin moorland calls. And as I made for home through the shadowy pine and the birchwoods so I could always put up a capercaillie or a trio of black grouse which would darkly wing away into the gloaming.

It is not so now. The capercaillie have all gone and the black game are so rare a sight that I stop to make sure I have seen aright. The sound of curlews is missing from many a spring morning and I have to drive several miles to find the nearest nesting lapwings. Gone are the blue mountain hares from these parts, and the wigeon which used to nest on the rushy river flats. The salmon in the Glass and the Beauly have also declined alarmingly. The boys who fish the two miles of bank I used to own tell me that there are no big brown trout there any more. But there are thousands of red deer and thousands of hill sheep – so many, in fact, that I am forced to conclude that there is an incontrovertible connection – that we have been getting things badly wrong for a long time.[13]

At the end of the twentieth century, then, the romantic ideal of the Highlands – that ideal which derives ultimately from the writings of James MacPherson, Walter Scott and all their many imitators – seems more and more bankrupt with every year that passes. Highlanders, as the previous chapter demonstrated, remain deeply conscious of the fact that the unpopulated glens which so many visitors have found so captivating are also monuments to the deliberate eradication of hundreds, even thousands, of human communities. Ecologists, as the present chapter has tried to show, are becoming equally conscious that these same glens are the end product of environmental degradation on a very lavish scale. The longstanding notion that the Highlands are some kind of demi-paradise is consequently one that needs now to be declared dead and buried as a prelude to working up a strategy for the area's rehabilitation.

The Highlands, as this chapter began by acknowledging, retain a good deal of their natural beauty. And the Highlands, for all the environmental damage done to them, could still be restored to something approximating to their original condition. Our native trees are by no means extinct. Neither are many of our birds and mammals. We possess extensive areas of natural grassland on the Hebridean machairs; still more extensive areas of blanket bog in Sutherland and Caithness; large tracts of heather moor; impressive mountains; seas which, for all the modern fishing industry's efforts to do to the ocean what sheep farms and deer forests have already done to the land, remain among the most productive in the world. The materials with which to repair and regenerate the Highland environment are readily available. Indeed just such restoration and regeneration is at last beginning to get under way.

Writing in the 1940s, the decade which also saw Frank Fraser Darling's studies of the Highlands reach their culmination, Naomi Mitchison, an Argyll novelist, commented:

> The cultural problem of Highlands and Lowlands and what might become of their fusion was never taken seriously between the eighteenth century, which broke the Highland pattern of development, and now when tentative regionalism and a scunner at the culture of cities has begun to open possibilities even for the remote islands. By and large, the Highlands have suffered two centuries of being looked down upon, oppressed, killed off and at the same time sentimentally exploited. It may be too late now to take them seriously. But I believe – and think – not.[14]

Mitchison's optimism has been justified by subsequent developments. The modern Highlands, to be sure, have not been without their equivalents of Patrick Sellar. John McGrath's Andy McChuckemup – whose ambition it was to have 'a drive-in clachan on every hill-top where formerly there was hee-haw but scenery' – has clearly had his real-life counterparts. So has McGrath's oilman, Texas Jim, another of the characters in *The Cheviot, the Stag and the Black, Black Oil*:

> All you folks are off your head,
> I'm getting rich from your sea bed.
>
> I'll go home when I see fit,
> All I'll leave is a heap of shit.[15]

But those who still see the Highlands as Patrick Sellar saw them – a place to be exploited regardless of the consequences – now quickly find themselves encountering obstacles of a kind which were never placed in Sellar's way. Outside the more directly affected communities, scarcely a voice was raised in criticism of the policies which resulted in clearance and eviction. But when, in the 1980s, the parts of Sutherland which Sellar long ago denuded of their people were threatened by a further change in land use, a most effective campaign was promptly mounted in this area's defence. And that campaign was national, even international, in its scope.

What was at stake was the future of the so-called flow country – the largest expanse of blanket peatland in all of Europe and a locality which supports a veritable wealth of birds as well as a whole range of most distinctive plant formations. The flow country – a place of shallow lochs, wide vistas and huge skies – was steadily being drained and ploughed by forestry companies whose managers were purchasing estate after estate in order to turn more and more land over to lodgepole pine and sitka spruce. The likelihood of such afforestation yielding worthwhile timber was, to say the least, not great – the terrain which was so rapidly going under trees being both exposed and infertile. But plantation forestry of the flow country type was driven by forces which owed almost nothing to silvicultural considerations. Successive British governments, in an attempt to boost the country's timber output, had made extraordinarily generous tax concessions available to forestry investors. These concessions made planting of the Sutherland sort a very worthwhile financial speculation for individuals in the higher tax brackets. And the question of whether or not their trees would ever reach maturity was as immaterial to those individuals as was the fact that they were profiting financially from the destruction of a globally scarce environmental resource.[16]

What is enduringly important about the flow country story, however, is that it ended in a substantial victory for the environmental movement. Under concerted attack from the Royal Society for the Protection of Birds and other well-supported conservation groups, both the forestry industry and the government were obliged to abandon policies which would have resulted in much of the flow country going under row after row of North American conifers. The controversial tax concessions were ended. Statutory conservation designations were gradually applied to much of the area which had previously been scheduled for commercial afforestation. The RSPB even bought its own way into Sutherland.

Nor was the environmental movement, by the 1980s and the 1990s, content merely with mounting successful defences of those parts of the Highlands which happened to be under threat from new forms of exploitation. It was certainly well worth while, from an environmentalist perspective, to have halted – or, at the very least, massively impeded – the advance of forestry across the flow country; just as it had been equally worth while, a few years earlier, to have stopped the construction of chairlifts and ski-tows in the northern corries of the Cairngorms. But it would clearly be even better, as environmentalists readily acknowledge, if the British government and its various agencies could be made to take cognisance of what Frank Fraser Darling called 'the bald unpalatable fact' that the wider Highland landscape – if the consequences of the earlier hurts done to the region are ever to be made good – requires to be treated in a wholly innovative manner.[17]

Today this is starting to happen. Forestry policy, to take the most obvious example of the quite startling changes which have occurred in the last few years, now places a great deal of stress on the need to expand the area under native trees – especially, but by no means exclusively, scots pine. Several well-funded programmes have been put in place to encourage crofters, farmers and landowners to involve themselves in both the regeneration and the re-establishment of woodlands of a sort which, not so long ago, the Highlands seemed destined to lose completely. Already enough has been accomplished to ensure that, by the close of the twenty-first century, pine and oak and birch will be more plentiful in northern Scotland than they have been for several hundred years.

Much remains to be done, of course. If native woodland is to reappear beyond the comparatively restricted and well-fenced corners where it is currently being re-established, the numbers of both sheep and deer will require to be enormously reduced across whole tracts of territory – probably by curtailing agricultural subsidies to sheep producers and by simultaneously enforcing wholesale culls of deer. This might seem rather drastic. But the ecological benefits of such a course – as has been recognised by practically every scientific commentator on the Highlands from Frank Fraser Darling onwards – would be immediately apparent. Tree-covered slopes would resist erosion in ways which treeless ones do not. Both soil fertility and a much healthier vegetation mix would gradually return to the many districts which have been so comprehensively wrecked by persistent overgrazing. Even Highland rivers – large numbers of which, as John Lister-Kaye observes, are now increasingly bereft of trout and other fish – would experience a marked increase in their biological productivity as leaves and other debris once more provided the nutrients needed to sustain the full range of acquatic life.

A Highland future planned on lines like these is one to which environmentalists would nowadays unhesitatingly subscribe. Others are understandably more dubious. A number of influential interest groups – among them locally resident crofters and farmers as well as absentee owners of sporting estates and equally absentee land speculators of the Andy McChuckemup type – are still far from convinced that policy for the Highlands requires a radical reshaping. This is one reason why environmental organisations – most notably the RSPB, the John Muir Trust and the National Trust for Scotland – have embarked on land-purchase policies, designed to provide them with their own extensive landholdings in the Highlands.

Their ownership of several hundred thousand acres in the region will clearly allow environmentalists to heal some of the ecological wounds which the Highlands have so conspicuously suffered. Whether such developments will help make good the wrongs which have been done to Highlanders – as opposed to the Highland environment – is a matter yet to be determined, however. And as this book's introduction commented, the omens so far have been less than favourable – both Highlanders and environmentalists having engaged in a good deal of mutual name-calling, not to say vilification. But this need not continue. And should both parties eventually adopt a more tolerant manner in their dealings with each other, as this book suggests they should, that would be a development of some significance. For if Highlanders and environmentalists can come to an agreement as to how the Highlands should be organised and managed, they will have sent a very encouraging signal to the many other parts of the world where the environmental movement regularly finds itself at odds with locally resident communities.

When it was decided in the 1950s and the 1960s to establish a national park in the Ngorongoro crater area of Tanzania, it was also decided to exclude from the crater those Masai communities who – their traditional economy being very similar to that of the Highlanders who once drove their cattle into the hills each summer – had always moved their herds on to Ngorongoro's grasslands at particular seasons of the year. The consequences of their being denied access to Ngorongoro have been just as disastrous for many twentieth-century Masai as the loss of their hill grazings was for nineteenth-century victims of the Highland Clearances. 'The majority of families in a community of previously well-off pastoralists are falling destitute at the hands of conservation,' an international conference at Arusha, Tanzania, was told in 1988. Of the 280 employees of the Ngorongoro conservation area, only seven had been recruited locally. And the only way in which a Masai herdsman might

BLABHEINN FROM TORRIN, ISLE OF SKYE (CAILEAN MACLEAN)

Previous page: BEN TIANAVAIG FROM BRAES, ISLE OF SKYE
(CAILEAN MACLEAN)

LOCH BEE, SOUTH UIST (CAILEAN MACLEAN)

LOCH GARRY AND THE ROUGH BOUNDS (CAILEAN MACLEAN)

WATER LILIES, SOUTH UIST (CAILEAN MACLEAN)

HAYMAKING IN SOUTH UIST (CAILEAN MACLEAN)

NETTING SALMON, SKEABOST, ISLE OF SKYE (CAILEAN MACLEAN)

LOCH QUOICH AND THE HILLS OF KNOYDART (CAILEAN MACLEAN)

BIRCH TREE (CAILEAN MACLEAN)

SCOTS PINES (CAILEAN MACLEAN)

legitimately enter Ngorongoro was on one of the buses which carry the thousands of tourists who come to this part of East Africa in the hope of seeing something of its wildlife.

No wonder, then, that the Masai and their sympathisers should have become increasingly embittered:

> The African crater came to an end when the Masai, who had enriched its life were banished from it. Now that has been succeeded by a European crater, empty of man as an inhabitant, but seething with man as a day-tripper . . . Nothing could be more forced than the pretence that Ngorongoro is in some way preserved from human influence. The magnificent display of unspoiled nature is as artificial as a safari park in the grounds of an English stately home.[18]

Speaking at one more international conference, this one convened to consider the plight of the indigenous peoples of continents like Africa and Latin America, Moringue Parkipuny, himself a Masai, warned that policies of the Ngorongoro sort would eventually prove utterly counter-productive from an environmentalist point of view. His people, Parkipuny said, were 'turning against wild animals because now they have been brought up to realise that the main cause of their sufferings is wild animals. They say that it is better that these wild animals disappear.' [19]

Although the process is a slow one, environmentalists are becoming aware of the need to grapple with the underlying causes of such forcefully expressed grievances. In his opening address to the Fourth World Congress on National Parks and Protected Areas in Caracas in 1992, Shridath Ramphal, president of the International Union for the Conservation of Nature, commented:

> We must find ways to ensure that protected areas provide more benefits to local people. This cannot mean locking up resources for the sole benefit of tourists from distant lands or scientists pursuing elusive ecological truths. Quite simply, if local people do not support protected areas, then protected areas cannot last . . . Protected areas cannot co-exist for very long with communities that are hostile to them.[20]

Removing the causes of such hostility, however, will be no simple task. In the course of the 120 years since the establishment of the world's first national park at Yellowstone, some 7,000 additional areas in about 130 different countries have been subjected to legally enforcible designations of the Yellowstone variety. No less than five per cent of the entire world's land surface is consequently affected by measures which are intended to safeguard the natural environment of the places to which they apply. And although the environmental case for constituting such protected areas may seem obvious enough, it is by no means clear that they have been properly integrated into the human societies on which they inevitably impinge. By far the most depressing feature of a remarkably high proportion of the world's protected areas is the extent to which the authorities responsible for their creation have managed to alienate and antagonise the peoples who traditionally occupied those lands which have now been set aside for nature conservation purposes. In this respect at least, as is noted by a 1993 survey of the problems highlighted by both Moringue Parkipuny and Shridath Ramphal, not much has changed since the United States government expelled Yellowstone's original inhabitants:

> Many . . . protected areas overlap the homelands of indigenous people. Regrettably, many were also created without consultation with the communities that lived in or near them . . . Ironically, it was these people who were for millennia the custodians of the earth, not always, but usually, caring for it so well that it had maintained its natural ecosystems in an unspoiled state. Frequently, when protected areas were established, indigenous and local residents were moved out, often to the detriment of the land itself.[21]

The American author of these remarks, Elizabeth Kemf, goes on to comment that indigenous peoples, far from posing a threat to places of especially high environmental value, can make their own constructive contribution to conserving localities which, after all, they know more intimately than anyone else. Addressing an audience of conservationists in 1988, Chief Paulinho Paiakan of Brazil's Kayapo people delivered much the same message in the context of the then developing campaign to safeguard the Amazonian rainforest:

> The forest is one big thing; it has people, animals and plants. There is no point in saving the forest if the people and animals who live in it are killed or driven away. The groups trying to save the race of animals cannot win if the people trying to save the forest lose; the people trying to save the Indians cannot win if either of the others lose; the Indians cannot win without the support of these groups; but the groups cannot win without the help of the Indians who know the forest and the animals and can tell what is happening to

them. No one of us is strong enough to win alone; together we can be strong enough to win.[22]

Although the Scottish Highlands, as stressed in this book's first chapter, were once a test-bed for forms of exploitation and oppression not at all dissimilar to those still being suffered by tribal peoples in Amazonia, it would be absurd to suggest that the north of Scotland is nowadays in the same position as the rainforest regions of Brazil. The Highlands, however, are also 'one big thing'; a place where close co-operation between environmentalists and the locally resident population ought ideally to be much more in evidence than it has been; a place where the scope for such co-operation, so this book argues, is potentially immense.

An essential preliminary to the development of more collaborative attitudes on the part both of environmentalists and Highlanders will involve the taking on board, by both sides, of the fact that the Highlands are, as Frank Fraser Darling put it, a devastated countryside. Some unwillingness to accept this truth is only to be expected on the part of Highlanders. There follows from it, after all, the inescapable conclusion that many deeply entrenched land use practices – on crofter common grazings, on hill farms and on deer forests – ought to be altered fundamentally. Environmentalists, however, have their difficulties with Fraser Darling's findings also.

Conservation organisations nowadays take for granted that the Highlands are degraded ecologically. They are consequently committed, as this chapter has stressed, to enhancing the region's biodiversity; to restoring its woodlands; to assisting with the reintroduction of those birds and mammals which, in the Highlands anyway, have long been extinct. The osprey and the sea eagle have already been reinstated. The crane, the beaver, even the wolf, could well be brought back in the future. But there is one species which environmentalists seem curiously reluctant to have re-established in the numerous Highland localities from which this species was expelled in the course of the nineteenth century. The species in question is man.

Environmentalists are disinclined to contemplate the resettlement of places like Boreraig or Achadh nan Seileach for a whole variety of reasons. The ecological devastation which such environmentalists are seeking to make good has resulted, after all, from human action. And it is perfectly understandable that a conservationist struggling to restore extensive pinewoods to the almost totally depopulated Knoydart peninsula, for example, should be a little less than enthusiastic about the possible reappearance there of a substantial human population – on the grounds that such a population, or so the conservationist might fear, would tend to make excessive demands on an environment which, because of earlier abuse, is dreadfully susceptible to further damage.

This is a quite legitimate anxiety. But it is by no means the sole explanation for the relatively lowly role allocated to *homo sapiens* in environmentalist strategies for those parts of the Highlands most affected by the clearances. Environmentalist suspicion of human beings is bound up also with ideas which the concept of the Highlands as a devastated landscape should have long since served to undermine, indeed discredit. Today's environmentalists have inherited from their nineteenth-century predecessors – not least Henry David Thoreau and John Muir – the notion that the perfect landscape is one bereft of people. This notion, as a previous chapter demonstrated, derives in part from those writers who so effectively romanticised the depopulated landscapes of the Highlands. But since the landscapes which were thus held up as little short of ideal are now known to have actually been horrifically degraded, it is at least an arguable proposition that environmentalists and conservationists ought to be questioning philosophical assumptions which were founded on very basic misunderstandings of the character of the landscapes from which they were derived. If it makes sense to re-instate scots pines to settings from which scots pines are today known to have been artificially stripped, might it not be equally acceptable – bearing in mind that human beings have been part of the total Highland ecosystem for just about as long as pine trees – to restore people to some at least of the many glens from which human beings were removed by men like Patrick Sellar? Is it not the case that clearance and eviction were every bit as disruptive of the settled order as those processes which resulted in so much ecological devastation? Is there not as good an argument for the social rehabilitation of our glens as for their ecological restoration?

Speaking at one of the sessions of a local authority enquiry into the probable environmental consequences of covering the Sutherland flow country with non-native conifers, a Rogart postman and crofter, John MacDonald, said:

> I want to make clear my own view that no trees should ever be planted on much of the flow country. That landscape is a precious, living thing. But all around it there are empty places where our people used to live. I see no reason why they shouldn't be able to live there again.[23]

Might John MacDonald's outlook be adopted by environmentalist organisations? One hopeful omen was the appearance in 1992 of a report which was itself a harbinger of something of a rapprochement between nature conservationists and Highlanders – this report, *Crofting and the Environment: A New Approach*, being a joint production by the Royal Society for the Protection of Birds and the Scottish Crofters Union. In a section headed, not insignificantly, 'The Wilderness Fallacy', the RSPB–SCU report comments:

> Many parts of the Highlands . . . have been described, from time to time, as wilderness. This is unscientific. Almost every landscape in northern Scotland bears the mark of human influence. Many of the most unpopulated localities were once thickly peopled – their populations having been expelled forcibly by the landlords responsible for the Highland Clearances. Crofters still aspire to win back these lost lands. There is no environmental reason why a measure of resettlement should not occur. Indeed there would be every reason to welcome reforms which made it possible to combine an element of resettlement with, for example, woodland regeneration and other measures designed to rehabilitate habitats which have been seriously degraded in the period since the clearances.[24]

The foreword to this RSPB–SCU report emphasises both the 'outstanding natural environment' of crofting areas and their 'distinct culture'. In fact, the one is stated by the report to be as deserving of survival as the other. That is important; for, as this book has emphasised repeatedly, the environmental movement has found it much harder to accept the need for diversity in the cultural sphere than in the biological one. That is why environmentalists acquiesced so readily in – indeed even advocated – the exclusion of the Shoshone from Yellowstone and the Masai from Ngorongoro. That is why relations between environmentalists and whole human populations – in Asia, the Americas, Africa and, for that matter, the Scottish Highlands – have so often been extremely bad.

When Africans and others accuse European and North American environmentalists of racism, as has happened fairly frequently in recent years, the environmentalists in question get understandably aggrieved. But their accusers have a point. The approach which many environmentalists have adopted to numerous minority cultures, even in the second half of the twentieth century, has frequently been no more enlightened or sympathetic than was John Muir's attitude to the Indians he encountered in Yosemite. And this is all the stranger in view of the fact that the case against the curtailment of cultural variety is virtually identical to the case against the diminution of global biodiversity.

Just as the earth is impoverished by the wanton destruction of animal and plant species, so humanity, as a spokesman for one of America's first nations has observed, is impoverished by the loss of any of its cultures:

> What sets worlds in motion is the interplay of differences, their attractions and repulsions. Life is plurality, death is uniformity. By suppressing differences and peculiarities, by eliminating different civilisations and cultures, progress weakens life and favours death. The idea of a stable civilisation for everyone, implicit in the cult of progress and technique, impoverishes and mutilates us. Every view of the world that becomes extinct, every culture that disappears, diminishes a possibility of life.[25]

Why, to adapt the terminology which Naomi Mitchison employed some half-a-century ago, do the Scottish Highlands matter? What is it about them that we ought to be conserving for the benefit of future generations? Our natural environment, our scenery, our wildlife will properly loom large in any reasoned answer to these questions. But other aspects of our heritage should surely feature in our thinking also – not least our Gaelic language and the wealth of human feeling and experience which this language, just like every other language spoken on the planet, encapsulates in ways that are, to some extent, unique.

Once there were corncrakes to be found nesting in practically every part of Britain. Now just a handful of pairs nest each summer on the croftlands of the Uists, Barra, Tiree and one or two more islands. Once Gaelic was spoken in almost every part of Scotland. Now it, too, is confined very largely to the Hebrides.

As a result of pressures from nature conservationists, on the one side, and Highland language campaigners, on the other, considerable efforts are being expended currently to ensure that neither the corncrake nor Gaelic become extinct. Because of the bureaucratic way in which we organise our national affairs, however, policy for the corncrake tends to be kept in one hermetically sealed compartment of our public life, while policy for Gaelic is kept in another. Perhaps this situation is unalterable. But suppose that it is not. Suppose that it is possible to break down the barriers which separate one area of policy from another – those barriers which place the environment in one box, Gaelic in another, crofting in a third, and hill farming, forestry, economic development, tourism, education and transport in further boxes still. Suppose that we were to knock the different boxes into one. Suppose that we were to integrate our various environmental, agricultural, social, cultural, linguistic and other objectives into a single strategy for the future of the Scottish Highlands. And suppose, finally, that we were to be successful. We should then have made a very worthwhile contribution to solving the ever more insistent question of how to sustain life on earth.

Iain Cattanach, the hero of Neil Gunn's novel, *The Drinking Well*, comes home to the Highlands from Edinburgh. He is a young man who, for a variety of reasons, has given up a legal career. He is full of ideas as to how the land which had earlier been cleared can once again be populated. But his response to the way these ideas are received by Mary, the young woman whom he loves, is both interesting and revealing. She exclaims:

> O Iain, wouldn't it be lovely if you got things going, and all the young fellows, and the girls, too, were in it, happiness and work, and your fiddle going and dancing! And one day – it would be the people's glen.[26]

It is as if Mary's naïvely enthusiastic interpretation of his own – initially secretive – ambitions makes Iain suddenly conscious of their inherent improbability. At any rate, he answers her with one word only: 'Dreams!'

But in life as well as in fiction there are dreams which do come true. In 1937, while sailing in the Minch, Neil Gunn visited Portnalong beside Loch Harport on the western coast of Skye. This area had been cleared completely in the nineteenth century when its landlord, MacLeod of Dunvegan, had got rid of many hundreds of people in order to make way for what eventually amounted to a 60,000-acre sheep farm. But in 1919 the farm had been bought by a government agency, the Board of Agriculture for Scotland, and the Portnalong part of it was afterwards resettled by crofting families who were brought here from Harris for that purpose. These were the people whom Neil Gunn met while in Portnalong. And they were, as he acknowledged, by no means living easily:

> But however one may argue or discuss the merits of the present settlement, there can be no doubt of the happy contrast in which it stands to the same land under the dominion of the old lairds . . . As

we wandered in the hilly lands about Portnalong, towards Carbost on the one hand and Fiskavaig on the other, we came on the new houses everywhere . . . and their bright faces seemed like the mind of a folk who throve for untold centuries, and would thrive for centuries more, if the greed and egoism of the landed or plutocratic designers of our worldly affairs gave them half a chance.[27]

The Portnalong resettlement scheme was one of a whole series of officially sponsored initiatives which, in the course of the twentieth century's first three decades, resulted in the creation of several thousand new crofts on land from which crofters had earlier been evicted. Prior to its reoccupation, much of this land – most of it in islands like Skye and the Uists – had been every bit as depopulated as localities like Boreraig still are. And environmentalist apprehensions as to the likely consequences of renewed resettlement schemes in places of that sort ought to be somewhat mitigated by the fact that the hundreds of thousands of acres which were restored to crofting occupancy between 1900 and 1930 – as can be seen by glancing at a map of Environmentally Sensitive Areas and Sites of Special Scientific Interest – are nowadays reckoned to include some of the most valuable wildlife habitats in the entire British Isles.

As a result of families moving in once more to Portnalong and neighbouring localities, the population of the Skye parish of Bracadale soared by some 52 per cent between 1921 and 1931. This upward momentum was not to be maintained, however. Irrespective of whether they lived on new holdings or old, crofters needed to supplement their agricultural earnings with income derived from some other source. And since the economy both of Skye and of the wider Highlands was far from buoyant throughout the first half of the twentieth century, the necessary non-agricultural earnings were simply not available. Young people, in particular, were obliged to move elsewhere in search of work. In the 1920s, as in every other decade from the 1840s to the 1960s, Skye's overall population consequently fell – plunging from some 23,000 to some 7,000 in the course of 130 years.

Had such trends continued, as was generally thought likely until very recently, all talk of renewed ventures of the Portnalong variety would today be wholly academic. What is making just such ventures steadily more probable, however, is the fact that the population of places like Skye is now expanding at an almost unprecedented rate. The last quarter of a century has seen Skye's population increase by some 40 per cent to around 10,000. And the wider Skye and Lochalsh District – which, incidentally, includes Glen Shiel – experienced a 15 per cent rise in its population during the

1980s alone. This rate of increase – which occurred at a time when Scotland as a whole was losing population and which was exceeded in all of Scotland only by two local government districts on the outskirts of the oil-boom city of Aberdeen – is indicative of the extent to which the Highlands are beginning to be transformed demographically. With many parts of the mainland Highlands – including the west coast – experiencing only slightly less dramatic upsurges in total population, and with continuing depopulation increasingly confined to Lewis, Harris and the Uists, the case for re-establishing a human presence in places which were previously populated is one that will gradually become quite irresistible.

So who exactly will constitute the new Highland communities of the twenty-first century? If present trends continue – given that about one-sixth of Skye's current population was born in England and that a considerable proportion of the remainder come from more or less distant parts of Scotland – very few such communities will consist of native Highlanders. And there are those, of course, who discern in this fact – and its possible cultural consequences – the imminent demise of the Gaelic-speaking civilisation established in the Scottish Highlands at the time of St Columba.

One Skye-born poet, Catriona Montgomery, has imagined herself returning to her native township of Roag in the year 2000. And she certainly does not like what she finds there:

*When the hoodiecrow
  takes the eye out of the last sheep,
  I will be peeping in at your windows.
  They will be there,
  playing cards,
  drinking Beaujolais,
  a poodle prancing about their feet.
  The warm smell of the milk will have left the byres,
  and they will be full of hard cold pottery for the tourists;
  the sound of tackety boots like ghosts walking on moors,
  the crofts green and unproductive
  without spade-breaking.

When the hoodiecrow takes
the eye out of the last sheep,
I will be eavesdropping at your windows,
listening to the breezes sighing
and the harsh English voices clashing with the wind.[28]

ON THE OTHER SIDE OF SORROW

Some small part of any Highlander's mind is likely to have some sympathy with Catriona Mongomery's sentiments. And yet these sentiments deserve, in the end, to be rejected as exclusivist, reactionary and inadmissibly pessimistic: exclusivist because Montgomery appears to believe that Gaelic culture cannot belong to anyone but those who are, by descent and upbringing, Gaels; reactionary because Montgomery's poem explicitly associates that culture with milk in the byre, tackety boots and other symbols of a past now every bit as irretrievable, for better or worse, as the world of Colum Cille; pessimistic because the poem assumes that neither the Gael nor the incomer are interested in, or capable of, reaching out to one another. It would be foolish to deny that in-migration of the Skye type has produced tensions of the kind one sees reflected in Catriona Montgomery's verse. But it would be equally foolish to insist that the people now moving into the Highlands from other parts of Britain are not, in any circumstances, to be tolerated and encouraged. Down that road there will be found only still more strife and bitterness of the sort which, if the cultural and other consequences of earlier oppression are ever to be got over, everybody involved in trying to shape the Highland future must, one way or another, put aside in favour of something more constructive.

These latter reflections may be thought to sit a little bit uneasily in a book which began by stressing the importance of our Highland culture and by citing Frantz Fanon in support of its thesis that, only after recapturing some sense of their distinctive identity, will Highlanders be psychologically equipped to take on the task of creating something better from the wreckage of the past. But there is no point in regenerating our culture if we are simply going to use that culture to fuel the flames of racial intolerance and antipathy. The fact that Highlanders have been on the receiving end of just such prejudice in previous centuries does not in any way justify our becoming racists in our turn. Indeed, if we do so, we shall have paid our earlier oppressors the ultimate compliment of adopting their bigoted, aggressive, jingoistic outlook on the world.

Towards the end of *Culture and Imperialism*, a book already mentioned more than once, Edward Said comments:

No one today is purely one thing. Labels like Indian, or woman, or Muslim or American are no more than starting-points which, if followed into actual experience for only a moment, are quickly left behind. Imperialism consolidated the mixture of cultures and identities on a global scale. But its worst and most paradoxical gift was to allow people to believe that they were only, mainly, exclusively, white, or black, or Western, or Oriental. Yet just as human beings make their own history, they also make their cultural and ethnic identities. No one can deny the persisting continuities of long traditions, sustained habitations, national languages, and cultural geographies, but there seems no reason except fear and prejudice to keep insisting on their separateness and distinctiveness, as if that was all human life was about.[29]

In relation to this book's central themes, that is a thought-provoking passage. It might arguably be interpreted in such a way as to negate the present chapter's contention that cultural diversity, like biodiversity, ought to be seen as automatically worthy of preservation. It might equally be understood, however, as posing a question of huge contemporary significance: how can a particular group of human beings safeguard their own uniqueness in ways that incorporate rather than exclude, welcome rather than reject, offer friendship rather than hostility?

In an especially memorable poem, *The Norsemen Coming Ashore at Ness*, Derick Thomson writes:

> *When the galley touched the shore,
>   when they hauled her up
>   on the sand at Port,
>   though the sea was blue,
>   and the sand white,
>   though flowers grew
>   on both banks of the burn,
>   and green grass in the ditches,
>   though the sun shone
>   on the buckles of their shields,
>   on their helmets,
>   and there was a grey-green haze of barley on the fields,
>   though that was how things were,
>   and the roar of the waves was behind them,
>   the solan plunging out of space,
>   and foam on the warm milk of the sea,
>   they were afraid.
>
> But they went up into the land,
>   and got houses,
>   and women,
>   and families,

and they cut the barley,
and sowed the barley,
took birds from the rock ledges,
and fish from the sea,
gave names to rocks and children,
and filled the barns,
and their homesickness went away.[30]

It might be considered a little perverse to present the Vikings, of all people, as an example of a group who were assimilated successfully into Highland society. But Thomson's poem is a reminder that just such assimilation did occur. Ness, like much of the rest of Lewis, is a place where men, women and children of Norse ancestry have been speaking Gaelic for hundreds of years. And other illustrations of the same sort of process can readily be provided. There are Gaelic-speaking families in the modern Highlands with Borders names like Eliot and Kerr and Lockhart, for example. These families are descended, like the author of this book, from men who came north at the time of the clearances to work as shepherds on Highland sheep farms.

Can those of us living today in the Scottish Highlands – those of us who came here last week, as it were, as well as those of us who could, in principle at least, trace our descent from the Gaelic-speaking folk who came from Ireland to Argyll some fifteen centuries ago – shape our own cultural identity in the way that Edward Said suggests is possible? Can we turn our backs completely on what Said calls the 'appalling tribalism' which, right across the modern world, 'is fracturing societies, separating peoples, promoting greed, bloody conflict and uninteresting assertions of minor ethnic or group particularity'? Can we define the term 'Highlander' in such a way that the issue of a person's ancestry becomes of much less importance than the fact that such a person lives in, works in, is committed to, this quite amazing tract of territory? And can we do all these things while still ensuring that Gaelic does not quickly join the list of many hundreds, even thousands, of languages which have become, or are about to become, extinct?[31]

A visit to one of the fifty or so Gaelic-medium units which have recently been developed in Highland primary schools, and which now cater for well over a thousand pupils, provides some cause for optimism on these counts. To sit in a corner of Catriona MacIntyre's classroom in Acharacle Primary School, for instance, listening to the enthusiastic exchanges going on in Gaelic between Catriona and a group of newly fluent seven-year-olds, very many of them possessing obviously non-

Highland surnames, is immediately to be convinced that there remains some life in what Alasdair MacMhaighstir Alasdair correctly claimed as Scotland's oldest spoken language.

A mile or so beyond Acharacle Primary School you cross the bridge which takes you into Moidart. Two or three miles beyond that is the turn-off for Dalilea where Alasdair MacMhaighstir Alasdair grew up. And if you leave your car at Dalilea and take the track which runs along Loch Shiel's north shore, you find yourself, at the end of half an hour, within a hundred or so yards of Eilean Fhionain. This island's name is that of the Columban monk who established his church here at least a thousand years before Alasdair MacMhaighstir Alasdair was born. As many as fifty generations of Gaelic-speaking Moidart people have been buried in this tiny patch of earth. And you would need to have an extraordinarily hard heart if, on standing by the lochside, and looking across to Alasdair MacMhaighstir Alasdair's 'Eilean Fhionain of the saplings', you did not feel that the culture to which Alasdair belonged has made its case to be considered an integral element of the Highland scene.[32]

The Highlands will never again be exactly as they once were. Nor is it necessarily desirable that they should. There can be no question, for example, of attempting to replicate in new or expanded Highland settlements the social conditions of earlier ages. The families who set up home in such settlements ought certainly to be entitled to look to the land and the sea for some proportion of their livelihoods. But such families ought also to have access to the various modern technologies – especially those having to do with computing and telecommunications – which increasingly make it possible to provide, even in relatively remote locations, commercial and entrepreneurial opportunities of the sort which were previously confined to urban areas.

This book, then, is not in the business of advocating a return to subsistence agriculture. Nor is it intended to endorse the transformation of the Highlands into some sort of cross between a national park and an open-air folk museum. To go down that road would simply be to evade the challenge which this magnificent piece of territory poses to anyone prepared to think seriously about its future. Central to that challenge is the need to demonstrate that the environmental rehabilitation of the Scottish Highlands can be achieved by means which simultaneously bring about the restoration of people to some at least of the many localities where both human communities and the Gaelic culture associated with these communities were long ago destroyed.

The Highlands, if such a course were to be embarked upon, would be very different from the Highlands of today. Much of the area would be more thickly populated than has been the case in recent times. It would be more thickly wooded also – with timber and timber products being of greater economic importance, in all probability, than either sheep or deer. And since it is difficult to envisage changes of this sort occurring under the auspices of a landownership system which has been identified so strongly with so many of the wholly negative developments of the last two centuries, movement in this direction will require to be accompanied, or preceded, by reforms which give Highland communities a worthwhile say in the management of land and other natural resources.

No matter what happens eventually to presently deserted spots like Boreraig, it is worth underlining in this context, much of the Highlands will remain unpopulated. The region's higher hills, its more inaccessible glens and its more isolated islands will be available in the future – as they were available in the distant past – to those individuals who like to be able to escape occasionally from the company of other human beings. All that will have happened is that places which were once inhabited will be inhabited again. And if this can be accomplished in ways which also promote the regeneration of one of Europe's older and more distinctive human cultures, so much the better.

None of this might come about, of course. Boreraig may remain forever ruinous. Trees may never reappear on the numerous bare hillsides where they once grew in profusion. The much more varied wildlife, together with the much more diverse vegetation, which the Highlands formerly supported may not, in the event, be re-established. And even if people return to those glens and other localities which were so brutally depopulated, these people may well choose to take no interest in either the Gaelic language or the wider cultural heritage to which that language and its literature are the keys.

But the prospect at least exists of a more encouraging outcome to the story which this book has tried to tell. Not every Highlander is blind to the urgent need to implement the measures needed to set our natural environment to rights. Not every environmentalist is unaware of the importance of keeping in existence the endangered human culture which, for some one-and-a-half millennia, has been so closely bound up with that self-same environment. And if this book has managed even to raise the possibility that these two objectives might be pursued in tandem, by the environmental movement and by Highlanders alike, then it will have served its purpose.

In the preface to his collected poetry, Sorley MacLean recalls the origin of his attempt – made more than half a century ago – to gaze, in an altogether more ambitious way than even Mairi Mhor nan Oran had done, far, far beyond the grim realities of what was then the present:

> It was in Mull in 1938 that I conceived the idea of writing a very long poem, 10,000 words or so, on the human condition, radiating from the history of Skye and the West Highlands to Europe and what I knew of the rest of the world.[33]

This poem Sorley called *An Cuilithionn*, The Cuillin. It was never finished. But enough of it has now been published to allow us to grasp something of its maker's purpose. Through the poem there moves a very large cast of characters drawn from many places, many epochs; from the Skye of Mairi Mhor and of earlier eras also; from Spain, from Poland, from Russia and from all those other countries threatened, at the time of the poem's birth, by fascist takeover and conquest; from Africa, from China, from America; from many different zones of struggle between the oppressed and their oppressors. But for all its dwelling on human suffering, and on man's seemingly endless capacity to cause hurt to his fellow human beings, *An Cuilithionn*, like *Hallaig*, is finally redolent with hope. Here are the poem's closing lines:

> *Beyond the lochs of the blood of the children of men,
> beyond the frailty of plain and the labour of the mountain,
> beyond poverty, consumption, fever, agony,
> beyond hardship, wrong, tyranny, distress,
> beyond misery, despair, hatred, treachery,
> beyond guilt and defilement; watchful,
> heroic, the Cuillin is seen
> rising on the other side of sorrow. [34]

In *An Cuilithionn*, then, the clearances and all the other disasters which have befallen Highlanders become – what historically, of course, they truly were – merely one small aspect of a much vaster human trauma. And the Cuillin themselves, in all that mountain range's sharply pinnacled solidity, are transformed, by Sorley MacLean, into an emblem of salvation. Since the poem was written by a man who was, at the time of its composition anyway, a Marxist, this salvation might be construed as deriving from Marx's own vision of the classless society which is to be brought into existence by proletarian revolution. But MacLean's imagery is arguably a lot less grounded in political specifics than is suggested by this relatively limited interpretation. Not least because so much of its symbolism is drawn from the landscapes with which this book has been concerned, *An Cuilithionn* is seen here as pointing to the part which the Highlands could play in resolving some of the dilemmas now looming so large internationally.

We have the opportunity today in the Scottish Highlands to turn around those processes which have done so much damage both to this area's people and to its natural environment. All of us with an interest in the Highlands – established residents, incomers, environmentalists and others – could readily resolve to work together for the region's general benefit. We could jointly bring about the repopulation, as well as the ecological restoration, of all the many places where, as Hugh MacLennan commented, you feel that everyone who ever mattered is dead and gone. We could, in other words, undo some of the consequences arising from the horrors of the past.

The Highlands, if we were to attempt these things, would still be beautiful. The Highlands would still offer anyone who wanted it the chance to be alone in some wild corner. But the Highlands would also be a living demonstration that community, culture and nature can, after all, be made compatible with one another. To accomplish this would be no small achievement. It would help bring all humanity a little nearer to the better-ordered world which Sorley's poem glimpses on the other side of sorrow.

NOTES

Introduction: Your Blooms in Agreement like Elegant Music

1. I. C. Smith, *Collected Poems*, Manchester, 1992, 81.
2. T. C. Smout, *The Highlands and the Roots of Green Consciousness, 1750–1990*, Battleby, 1993, 7–8.

Chapter One: Everyone Who Ever Mattered is Dead and Gone

1. S. Johnson, *A Journey to the Western Islands of Scotland*, Penguin Edition, London, 1984, 60–61.
2. Johnson, *Journey to the Western Islands*, 62; J. Boswell, *Journal of a Tour to the Hebrides*, Penguin Edition, London, 1984, 237.
3. Boswell, *Tour to the Hebrides*, 237.
4. Smith, *Collected Poems*, 51; Johnson, *Journey to the Western Islands*, 97.
5. W. Matheson (ed), *The Songs of John MacCodrum*, Edinburgh, 1938, 199–203.
6. M. MacDonell, *The Emigrant Experience: Songs of Highland Emigrants in North America*, Toronto, 1982, 36–37.
7. Johnson, *Journey to the Western Islands*, 59.
8. J. Hunter, *A Dance Called America: The Scottish Highlands, the United States and Canada*, Edinburgh, 1994, 83–87; J. MacRae, 'Parish of Glen Shiel', *Old Statistical Account of Scotland: Ross and Cromarty*, EP Publishing Edition, Wakefield, 1981, XVII, 408. Also, M. MacLean, *The People of Glengarry: Highlanders in Transition, 1745–1820*, Montreal, 1991.
9. I. R. MacKay, 'The Pet Lamb Case', *Transactions of the Gaelic Society of Inverness*, XLVIII, 1972–74, 184–85.
10. *Report of the Royal Commission on the Highlands and Islands*, Parliamentary Publication, London, 1895, 387; J. MacRae, 'The Parish of Glen Shiel', *New Statistical Account of Scotland*, Edinburgh, 1855, XIV, 195.

11. H. MacLennan, *Scotchman's Return and Other Essays*, Toronto, 1960, 1–2. Also, Hunter, *Dance Called America*, 146–48.
12. MacLennan, *Scotchman's Return*, 7.
13. T. D. MacLulich, *Hugh MacLennan*, Boston, 1983, 3. For examples of MacLennan's attempts to provide Highlanders with a Canadian destiny, see H. MacLennan, *Barometer Rising*, New Canadian Library Edition, Toronto, 1969.
14. C. W. Nicholson, *Poem, Purpose and Place*, Edinburgh, 1992, 121.
15. See especially, E. W. Said, *Culture and Imperialism*, London, 1993.
16. T. M. Devine, 'Landlordism and Highland Emigration' in T. M. Devine (ed), *Scottish Emigration and Scottish Society*, Edinburgh, 1993, 84–103. Also, T. M. Devine, *The Great Highland Famine*, Edinburgh, 1988; T. M. Devine, *Clanship to Crofters War: The Social Transformation of the Scottish Highlands*, Manchester, 1994. Professor Devine, it is fair to point out, considers that the present author's approach to Highland history 'has not been generally accepted within the mainstream of historical scholarship'. (Devine, *Scottish Emigration*, 85.)
17. J. McGrath, *The Cheviot, the Stag and the Black, Black Oil*, Revised Edition, Isle of Skye, 1975, 21.
18. R. Nicholson, *Scotland: The Later Middle Ages*, Mercat Press Edition, Edinburgh, 1989, 206.
19. Nicholson, *Scotland*, 205; R. Crawford, *Devolving English Literature*, Oxford, 1992, 16; W. C. MacKenzie, *History of the Outer Hebrides*, Mercat Press Edition, Edinburgh, 1974, 174–96.
20. J. Prebble, *Glencoe*, Penguin Edition, London, 1968, 19; C. W. J. Withers, *Gaelic Scotland: The Transformation of a Culture Region*, London, 1988, 82; A. J. Youngson, *After the Forty–Five: The Economic Impact on the Scottish Highlands*, Edinburgh, 1973, 45; P. Womack, *Improvement and Romance: Constructing the Myth of the Highlands*, London, 1989, 4; B. Lenman, *The Jacobite Clans of the Great Glen, 1650–1784*, London, 1984, 26; B. Lenman, *The Jacobite Risings in Britain, 1689–1746*, London, 1980, 262.
21. J. Prebble, *Culloden*, Penguin Edition, London, 1967, 181; T. Royle, *The Mainstream Companion to Scottish Literature*, Edinburgh, 1993, 246.
22. A. Calder, *Revolutionary Empire: The Rise of the English–Speaking Empires from the Fifteenth Century to the 1780s*, London, 1981, 36; E. Richards, *A History of the Highland Clearances, Volume Two: Emigration, Protest, Reasons*, London, 1985, 392–408.
23. Said, *Culture and Imperialism*, 8.

24. D. Corkery, *The Hidden Ireland*, Gill and MacMillan Edition, Dublin, 1967, 9.
25. V. E. Durkacz, *The Decline of the Celtic Languages*, Edinburgh, 1983, 5; Withers, *Transformation of a Culture Region*, 114, 334; A. Martin, *Kintyre: The Hidden Past*, Edinburgh, 1984, 29–30.
26. Said, *Culture and Imperialism*, 269–70.
27. N. Gunn, *Highland River*, Canongate Classics Edition, Edinburgh, 1991, 21.
28. J. Hunter, 'The Gaelic Connection: The Highlands, Ireland and Nationalism, 1873–1922', *Scottish Historical Review*, LIV, 1975, 183.
29. Hunter, 'Gaelic Connection', 183; J. Hunter, *For the People's Cause: From the Writings of John Murdoch*, Edinburgh, 1986, 28.
30. Several of these points are elaborated in: L. P. Curtis, *Anglo–Saxons and Celts: A Study of Anti–Irish Prejudice in Victorian England*, Bridgeport, 1968; L. P. Curtis, *Apes and Angels: The Irishman in Victorian Caricature*, Newton Abbott, 1971; V. G. Kiernan, *The Lords of Human Kind*, New York, 1986.
31. C. Whyte (ed), *An Aghaidh na Siorraidheachd: In the Face of Eternity: Eight Gaelic Poets*, Edinburgh, 1991, 129.
32. A. MacNeacail (ed), *A Writers Ceilidh for Neil Gunn*, Nairn, 1991, 27.
33. A. P. Campbell, *The Greatest Gift*, Isle of Skye, 1992, 77.
34. F. Fanon, *The Wretched of the Earth*, Penguin Edition, London, 1967. An attempt to apply Fanon's thinking to Scottish circumstances can be found in: C. Beveridge and R. Turnbull, *The Eclipse of Scottish Culture*, Edinburgh, 1989.
35. Fanon, *Wretched of the Earth*, 172.
36. Fanon, *Wretched of the Earth*, 168–69.
37. F. Wilmer, *The Indigenous Voice in World Politics*, London, 1993, 125.

Chapter Two: The Glory of Great Hills is Unspoiled

1. L. Laing and J. Laing, *The Picts and the Scots*, Stroud, 1993, 55–56; M. Dillon and N. Chadwick, *The Celtic Realms*, London, 1967, 178–79. See also, M. Robson, *Rona: The Distant Island*, Stornoway, 1991; D. Lavelle, *The Skellig Story*, Dublin, 1993.
2. N. M. Gunn, *Off in a Boat*, Richard Drew Publishing Edition, Glasgow, 1988, 116–17.
3. G. Bruce and F. Rennie, *The Land Out There: A Scottish Land Anthology*, 331; I. Bell, *Robert Louis Stevenson: Dreams of Exile*, Edinburgh, 1992, 67.

4. J. M. Boyd, *Fraser Darling's Islands*, Edinburgh, 1986, 13.
5. F. F. Darling, *A Naturalist on Rona*, Oxford, 1939, 38; B. Cunliffe, *The Celtic World*, London, 1992, 190.
6. M. H. Nicolson, *Mountain Gloom and Mountain Glory: The Development of the Aesthetics of the Infinite*, Ithaca, 1959, 39–40; R. Nash, *Wilderness and the American Mind*, Third Edition, Yale, 1982, 9–10.
7. Nash, *Wilderness and the American Mind*, 1, 12; K. Thomas, *Man and the Natural World: Changing Attitudes in England, 1500–1800*, Penguin Edition, London, 1984, 14–24, 192–95. See also, M. Alexander (ed), *Beowulf*, Penguin Edition, London, 1973; D. Worster, *Nature's Economy: A History of Ecological Ideas*, Second Edition, Cambridge, 1994; P. Marshall, *Nature's Web: An Exploration of Ecological Thinking*, London, 1992. For the classic biblical statement of man's dominion over nature see, *Genesis*, I, 26.
8. K. H. Jackson (ed), *A Celtic Miscellany*, Penguin Edition, London, 1971, 72.
9. F. F. Darling, *Island Years*, Pan Books Edition, London, 1973, 29–30.
10. Jackson, *Celtic Miscellany*, 70. For other examples, see, D. Greene and F. O'Connor (eds), *A Golden Treasury of Irish Poetry AD 600 to 1200*, London, 1967; K. Meyer, *Ancient Irish Poetry*, Constable Edition, London, 1994.
11. Smith, *Collected Poems*, 45. Also, K. H. Jackson, *Studies in Early Celtic Nature Poetry*, Cambridge, 1935.
12. Meyer, *Ancient Irish Poetry*, xii.
13. I. Mosley (ed), *The Green Book of Poetry*, Kirstead, 1994, 44; H. C. Chang, *Chinese Literature: Nature Poetry*, 58–66. See also, Marshall, *Nature's Web*.
14. M. Richter, *Medieval Ireland: The Enduring Tradition*, London, 1988, 1–2. It should be noted that 'medieval' is used by Richter in the continental sense of 'post–classical'.
15. Dillon and Chadwick, *Celtic Realms*, 176–78; Laing and Laing, *Picts and Scots*, 44–45, 50–52; P. O'Dwyer, *Celi De: Spiritual Reform in Ireland, 750–900*, Dublin, 1981, 62; Cunliffe, *Celtic World*, 176.
16. Laing and Laing, *Picts and Scots*, 49; Dillon and Chadwick, *Celtic Realms*, 188–91; Richter, *Medieval Ireland*, 189; Cunliffe, *Celtic World*, 161, 188–95; P. Brown, *The Book of Kells*, London, 1980, 17–31; R. Welch, *Changing States: Transformations in Modern Irish Writing*, London, 1993, 12.
17. K. Clark, *Civilisation*, Penguin Edition, London, 1982.
18. Brown, *Book of Kells*, 83.

19. H. MacDiarmid, *Selected Poems*, Penguin Edition, London, 1994.

20. This aspect of MacDiarmid's thinking is examined in more detail in Chapter Five.

21. For the contribution of the Gaels to Scotland's political development, see, J. Bannerman, 'The Scots of Dalriada', in, G. Menzies (ed), *Who are the Scots?*, London, 1971, 66–79; M.O. Anderson, 'Dalriada and the Creation of the Kingdom of the Scots', in, D. Whitelock, R. McKitterick and D. Dumville (eds), *Ireland in Early Medieval Europe*, Cambridge, 1982, 106–32. See also, A. P. Smyth, *Warlords and Holy Men: Scotland, AD80–1000*, London, 1984.

22. *Matthew*, IV, 2.

23. P. F. Anson, *The Call of the Desert: The Solitary Life in the Christian Church*, London, 1964, 1–54; A. M. Allchin, *Solitude and Communion: Papers on the Hermit Life*, Oxford, 1977, 2–3; Nash, *Wilderness and the American Mind*, 16–18; Cunliffe, *Celtic World*, 173–74.

24. R. Flower, *The Irish Tradition*, Oxford, 1947, 55; Jackson, *Celtic Nature Poetry*, 97–99.

25. B. Devall, *Simple in Means, Rich in Ends: Practising Deep Ecology*, 74; Marshall, *Nature's Web*, 404–07. See also, R. Attfield, *Environmental Philosophy: Principles and Prospects*, Aldershot, 1994. The term 'deep ecology' was coined by a Norwegian philosopher, Arne Naess, in 1972.

26. O'Dwyer, *Celi De*, 191; Devall, *Simple in Means*, 47.

27. H. D. Thoreau, *Walden*, Everyman Edition, London, 1992, 99.

28. Jackson, *Celtic Nature Poetry*, 3, 5, 11; Dillon, *Celtic Realms*, 233.

29. I. Finlay, *Columba*, London, 1979, 45–46; Flower, *Irish Tradition*, 42; O'Dwyer, *Celi De*, 184–91. See also, K. H. Jackson, *The Oldest Irish Tradition: A Window on the Iron Age*, Cambridge, 1964.

30. I. C. Smith, 'The Future of Gaelic Literature', *Transactions of the Gaelic Society of Inverness*, XLIII, 1960–63, 172.

31. A. MacLean, *Night Falls on Ardnamurchan: The Twilight of a Crofting Family*, London, 1984, 170.

32. G. Maxwell, *Raven Seek Thy Brother*, London, 1968, 67.

33. D. Botting, *Gavin Maxwell: A Life*, London, 1993, 32.

34. G. Maxwell, *Ring of Bright Water*, Isis Edition, Oxford, 1991, 29.

35. Jackson, *Celtic Nature Poetry*, 100.

36. I. Bradley, *God is Green: Christianity and the Environment*, London, 1990, 12–13; Jackson, *Celtic Nature Poetry*, 101–03; O'Dwyer, *Celi De*, 190–91; Flower, *Irish Tradition*, 61–62; Finlay, *Columba*, 23–24.

37. F. F. Darling, *Wild Country*, Cambridge, 1938, 5.

38. Jackson, *Celtic Miscellany*, 177.

39. For a recent, if somewhat overstated, account of the ecological devastation caused by pre–industrial societies, see, J. Diamond, *The Rise and Fall of the Third Chimpanzee*, Vintage Edition, London, 1992.

40. Laing and Laing, *Picts and Scots*, 57–58; E. MacNeill, *Early Irish Laws and Institutions*, Dublin, 1935, 41; Richter, *Medieval Ireland*, 17–19; T. W. Moody and F. X. Martin (eds), *The Course of Irish History*, Revised Edition, Dublin, 1984, 48–56. See also, A. Dobson, *Green Political Thought*, London, 1990; E. F. Schumacher, *Small is Beautiful*, Abacus Edition, London, 1974.

41. J. Bannerman, 'The Scots of Dalriada', in, G. Menzies, *Who are the Scots?*, London, 1971, 72.

42. Cunliffe, *Celtic World*, 106.

43. Cunliffe, *Celtic World*, 106–07; Dillon and Chadwick, *Celtic Realms*, 92–97; Jackson, *Oldest Irish Tradition*, 32–25.

44. H. Fife, *Warriors and Guardians: Native Highland Trees*, Glendaruel, 1994, 15.

45. Cunliffe, *Celtic World*, 69, 88–89; Dillon and Chadwick, *Celtic Realms*, 138; Finlay, *Columba*, 31.

46. Jackson, *Celtic Nature Poetry*, 11–12. Also, H. McSkimming, *The Trees of the Celtic Alphabet*, Brodick, 1992.

47. E. Neeson, *A History of Irish Forestry*, Dublin, 1991, 27–28; MacNeill, *Celtic Ireland*, Dublin, 1921, 167–69.

48. F. Kelly, 'The Old Irish Tree List', *Celtica*, XI, 107–23.

49. F. Kelly, *A Guide to Early Irish Law*, Dublin, 1988, 113; J. Bannerman, 'The Lordship of the Isles', in, J. M. Brown (ed), *Scottish Society in the Fifteenth Century*, London, 1977, 220–21.

50. Kelly, *Guide to Early Irish Law*, 100–08; MacNeill, *Celtic Ireland*, 167–69.

51. I. F. Grant, *Highland Folk Ways*, London, 1961, 7.

52. J. Hunter, *The Making of the Crofting Community*, Edinburgh, 1976, 156. Also, D. Hart–Davis, *Monarchs of the Glen: A History of Deer Stalking in the Scottish Highlands*, London, 1978, 43–57.

53. Hunter, *Crofting Community*, 156.

54. Hunter, *People's Cause*, 21.

55. Hunter, *Crofting Community*, 157. Also, Grant, *Folk Ways*, 7–8; R. A. Dodgshon, *Land and Society in Early Scotland*, Oxford, 1981, 109–14; I. Whyte, *Agriculture and Society in Seventeenth Century Scotland*, Edinburgh, 1979, 30–31.

56. *Report of the Commissioners of Enquiry into the Condition of the*

Crofters and Cottars in the Highlands and Islands of Scotland, 5 volumes, Parliamentary Publication, London, 1884, I, 8.

57. For the full text of the Letterewe Accord, see, Scottish Natural Heritage, *Enjoying the Outdoors: A Programme for Action*, Battleby, 1994, 47.

58. Jackson, *Celtic Miscellany*, 72; D. Meek, 'The Gaelic Ballads of Scotland: Creativity and Adaption', in, H. Gaskill (ed), *Ossian Revisited*, Edinburgh, 1991, 24–25.

Chapter Three: The Hind is in the Forest as She Ought to Be

1. D. S. Thomson, *Gaelic Poetry in the Eighteenth Century: A Bilingual Anthology*, Aberdeen, 1993, 22–25; H. Cheape, 'Woodlands on the Clanranald Estates', in, T. C. Smout (ed), *Scotland Since Prehistory: Natural Change and Human Impact*, Aberdeen, 1993, 60.

2. R. Black, *Alasdair MacMhaighstir Alasdair: The Ardnamurchan Years*, Isle of Coll, 1986, 3–9; J. L. Campbell (ed), *Highland Songs of the Forty–Five*, Revised Edition, Edinburgh, 1984, 33–41; I. Grimble, *The World of Rob Donn*, Edinburgh, 1979, 30–31.

3. Smith, *Collected Poems*, 341.

4. F. MacColla, *The Albannach*, Reprographia Edition, Edinburgh, 1971, 72–73.

5. W. Gillies, 'The Prince and the Gaels', in, L. Scott–Moncrieff (ed), *The Forty–Five: To Gather an Image Whole*, Edinburgh, 1988, 55–59. Also, Campbell, *Songs of the Forty–Five*.

6. Thomson, *Poetry in the Eighteenth Century*, 24–25.

7. Black, *Alasdair MacMhaighstir Alasdair*, 33; D. S. Thomson, *An Introduction to Gaelic Poetry*, London, 1974, 160–61. Also, H. H. Campbell, *James Thomson*, Boston, 1979; K. Simpson, *The Protean Scot: The Crisis of Identity in Eighteenth Century Scottish Literature*, Aberdeen, 1988.

8. R. Watson, *The Literature of Scotland*, London, 1984, 197; K. Wittig, *The Scottish Tradition in Literature*, Edinburgh, 1958, 192; D. S. Thomson, 'Gaelic Poetry in the Eighteenth Century: The Breaking of the Mould', in, A. Hook (ed), *The History of Scottish Literature: Two, 1660–1800*, Aberdeen, 1987, 180–83.

9. W. J. Watson (ed), *Scottish Verse from the Book of the Dean of Lismore*, Edinburgh, 1937, 92–93.

10. A. Carmichael, *Carmina Gadelica*, 6 Volumes, Edinburgh, 1928–71, I, xxiii–xxiv; Jackson, *Oldest Irish Tradition*, 9–10; I. F. Grant and H.

Cheape, *Periods in Highland History*, London, 1987, 25–28.

11. R. Black, 'The Genius of Cathal MacMhuirich', *Transactions of the Gaelic Society of Inverness*, L, 1976–78, 348–58; Bannerman, 'Lordship of the Isles', 232–35; D. S. Thomson, 'Gaelic Learned Orders and Literati in Medieval Scotland', *Scottish Studies*, 12, 1964, 57–58.

12. M. O'Riordan, *The Gaelic Mind and the Collapse of the Gaelic World*, Cork, 1990, 3–4; D. S. Thomson, 'The Seventeenth Century Crucible of Scottish Gaelic Poetry', *Studia Celtica*, XXVI–XXVII, 1991–92, 155–62; W. Gillies, 'Gaelic: The Classical Tradition', in, R. D. S. Jack (ed), *The History of Scottish Literature: One, Origins to 1660*, Aberdeen, 1988, 246–254.

13. O. Bergin, *Irish Bardic Poetry*, Dublin, 1970, 5–7; Thomson, 'Gaelic Poetry in the Eighteenth Century', 175; Corkery, *Hidden Ireland*, 68–94; Gillies, 'The Classical Tradition', 247.

14. F. J. Stafford, *The Sublime Savage: A Study of James MacPherson and the Poems of Ossian*, Edinburgh, 1988, 122. Also, D. S. Thomson, 'The MacMhuirich Bardic Family', *Transactions of the Gaelic Society of Inverness*, XLIII, 1960–63, 276–304.

15. W. Neill, *Straight Lines*, Belfast, 1992, 29.

16. Hunter, *Dance Called America*, 106.

17. A. MacLeod (ed), *The Songs of Duncan Ban MacIntyre*, Edinburgh, 1952, 346–47.

18. For ecologists on sheep, see, F. F. Darling, *West Highland Survey: An Essay in Human Ecology*, Oxford, 1955; J. Lister–Kaye, *Ill Fares the Land: A Sustainable Land Ethic for the Sporting Estates of the Highlands and Islands of Scotland*, Isle of Skye, 1994.

19. Thomson, *Introduction to Gaelic Poetry*, 67.

20. Thomson, *Introduction to Gaelic Poetry*, 110.

21. Gillies, 'Gaelic: The Classical Tradition', 254; J. MacInnes, 'The Panegyric Code in Gaelic Poetry and its Historical Background', *Transactions of the Gaelic Society of Inverness*, XLVIII, 1972–74, 457–58.

22. J. Purser, *Scotland's Music*, Edinburgh, 1992, 23; Carmichael, *Carmina Gadelica*, V, 368–73.

23. I. C. Smith, *Selected Poems, 1955–1980*, Loanhead, 1981, 90.

24. Smith, *Collected Poems*, 77–80; I. C. Smith, *Towards the Human: Selected Essays*, Edinburgh, 1986, 133.

25. MacLeod, *Songs of Duncan Ban MacIntyre*, xvii–xliv.

26. Smith, *Towards the Human*, 134–35.

27. N. MacCaig, *Collected Poems: A New Edition*, London, 1993, 251.

28. MacLeod, *Songs of Duncan Ban MacIntyre*, 204–07.
29. MacLeod, *Songs of Duncan Ban MacIntyre*, xvii–xliv; A. J. Youngson, *The Making of Classical Edinburgh*, Edinburgh, 1966, 239–40.

Chapter Four: Oh for the Crags that are Wild and Majestic

1. Stafford, *Sublime Savage*, 6–20.
2. J. MacQueen (ed), *Poems of Ossian*, 2 Volumes, Edinburgh, 1971, II, 386.
3. MacQueen, *Poems of Ossian*, II, 197–98.
4. MacQueen, *Poems of Ossian*, II, 390.
5. For varied views on MacPherson's sources, see, M. Chapman, *The Gaelic Vision in Scottish Culture*, London, 1978; D. S. Thomson, *The Gaelic Sources of MacPherson's Ossian*, Edinburgh, 1953; D. Meek, 'The Gaelic Ballads of Scotland: Creativity and Adaption', in, Gaskill, *Ossian Revisited*, 19–48; H. Trevor-Roper, 'The Highland Tradition of Scotland', in, E. Hobsbawm and T. Ranger (eds), *The Invention of Tradition*, Cambridge, 1983, 15–41; J. MacKillop, *Fionn MacCumhaill: Celtic Myth in English Literature*, Syracuse, 1986.
6. P. France, 'Primitivism and Enlightenment: Rousseau and the Scots', *Yearbook of English Studies*, 15, 1986, 64–79; Simpson, *Protean Scot*, 42–55.
7. MacQueen, *Poems of Ossian*, I, 105–06.
8. D. Daiches, *The Paradox of Scottish Culture: The Eighteenth Century Experience*, London, 1964, 88; France, 'Primitivism and Englightenment', 77–78; A. Hook, 'Scotland and Romanticism: The International Scene', in, Hook, *History of Scottish Literature*, 316–17.
9. Stafford, *Sublime Savage*, 1–2, 163–80; MacQueen, *Poems of Ossian*, Introduction; Hook, 'Scotland and Romanticism', 313–15; P. J. Degategno, *James MacPherson*, Boston, 1989, 112–34.
10. W. Scott, *Poetical Works*, London, 1894, 208; E. Muir, *Scott and Scotland*, London, 1936, 11; G. Friden, *James Fenimore Cooper and Ossian*, Cambridge, Mass., 1949, 19.
11. W. Scott, *Poetical Works*, London, 1894, 210; T. Royle, *The Mainstream Companion to Scottish Literature*, Edinburgh, 1993, 175.
12. W. Scott, *Waverley*, Penguin Edition, London, 1972, 135.
13. Scott, *Waverley*, 131.
14. Scott, 'Preface of 1830', in Scott, *Poetical Works*, 274.
15. MacQueen, *Poems of Ossian*, II, 30–34.
16. W. Scott, 'Preface of 1830', in, Scott, *Poetical Works*, 274; Watson,

Literature of Scotland, 253.
17. Scott, *Waverley,* 333.
18. D. Daiches, *Sir Walter Scott and His World,* London, 1971, 82.
19. D. Cooper, *The Road to the Isles: Travellers in the Hebrides, 1770–1914,* London, 1979, 47.
20. Devine, *Clanship to Crofters War,* 97.
21. L. Stott, *Robert Louis Stevenson and the Highlands and Islands of Scotland,* Aberfoyle, 1992, 64.
22. Johnson, *Journey to the Western Islands,* 60; Nicolson, *Mountain Gloom and Mountain Glory,* 2; Prebble, *Culloden,* 177; Grant and Cheape, *Periods of Highland History,* 213.
23. T. Scott (ed), *The Penguin Book of Scottish Verse,* London, 1970, 272; Nash, *Wilderness and the American Mind,* 3.
24. W. Wordsworth, *The Works of William Wordsworth,* Wordsworth Poetry Library Edition, Ware, 1994, 289; Thomas, *Man and Nature,* 261.
25. Wordsworth, *Works,* 289.
26. J. F. Cooper, *The Last of the Mohicans,* Panther Edition, London, 1970, 289; Friden, *James Fenimore Cooper and Ossian,* 10–53; R. Crawford, *Devolving English Literature,* Oxford, 1992, 127–28, 182–90; Degategno, *James MacPherson,* 130–31.
27. Cooper, *Last of the Mohicans,* 35.
28. Nash, *Wilderness and the American Mind,* 23–24, 75–78.
29. Nash, *Wilderness and the American Mind,* 84.
30. H. D. Thoreau, *A Week on the Concord and Merrimack Rivers,* Princeton, 1983, 343–46, 366–67.
31. J. Muir, *The Story of My Boyhood and Youth,* Canongate Classics Edition, Edinburgh, 1987, 1; S. Fox, *John Muir and his Legacy: The American Conservation Movement,* Boston, 1981, 76, 82; Nash, *Wilderness and the American Mind,* 125–28.
32. J. Muir, *My First Summer in the Sierra,* Canongate Classics Edition, Edinburgh, 1988, 28, 39.
33. Muir, *First Summer in the Sierra,* 131–32.
34. Muir, *First Summer in the Sierra,* 132.
35. Wilmer, *Indigenous Voice in World Politics,* xii, 11.
36. Nash, *Wilderness and the American Mind,* 91–92.
37. Nash, *Wilderness and the American Mind,* 108; E. Kemf, *The Law of the Mother: Protecting Indigenous Peoples in Protected Areas,* San Francisco, 1993, 5–6; Hunter, *Dance Called America,* 242.
38. Nash, *Wilderness and the American Mind,* 161–81. Also, J. Muir, *Travels in Alaska,* Sierra Club Edition, San Francisco, 1988.

39. Hunter, *Dance Called America*, 240–44.

40. D. Duff (ed), *Queen Victoria's Highland Journals*, Exeter, 1983, 6–9, 32, 43–47, 74, 148. Also, J. Prebble, *The King's Jaunt: George IV in Scotland*, Fontana Edition, London, 1989.

41. J. Hunter, 'Sheep and Deer: Highland Sheep Farming, 1850–1900', *Northern Scotland*, I, 199–222; Hart–Davis, *Monarchs of the Glen*; W. Orr, *Deer Forests, Landlords and Crofters*, Edinburgh, 1982; M. Wigan, *The Highland Estate: Preserving an Environment*, Shrewsbury, 1991.

42. For a full account of the Highland Land League, see, Hunter, *Making of the Crofting Community*.

43. Stott, *Robert Louis Stevenson and the Highlands*, 103. Also, R. L. Stevenson, *Kidnapped*, Puffin Classics Edition, London, 1983.

44. N. Munro, *The Poetry of Neil Munro*, Edinburgh, 1931, 23.

45. N. Munro, *The New Road*, London, 1930, 23.

46. W. Black, *A Princess of Thule*, 116–17. Also, W. Reid, *William Black: Novelist*, London, 1902.

47. F. MacLeod, *The Winged Destiny: Studies in the Spiritual History of the Gael*, London, 1910, 178–79, 225. Also, F. Alaya, *William Sharp: Fiona MacLeod*, Cambridge, Mass., 1970; M. G. H. Pittock, *Spectrum of Decadence: The Literature of the 1890s*, London, 1993.

48. M. E. M. Donaldson, *Islesmen of Bride*, Paisley, 1922, 7, 83.

49. A. A. MacGregor, *Behold the Hebrides*, London, 1925, 27, 58; A. A. MacGregor, *Summer Days Among the Western Isles*, London, 1929, 151, 156, 262.

50. C. MacKenzie, 'Catholic Barra', in, J. L. Campbell, *The Book of Barra*, London, 1936, 1; C. MacKenzie, *Whisky Galore*, London, 1947, 9; C. MacKenzie, *The Rival Monster*, London, 1952, 78.

51. A. A. MacGregor, *The Western Isles*, London, 1949, 214–52.

52. Muir, *First Summer in the Sierra*, 136.

53. J. R. MacDonald, 'Foreword', in, A. A. MacGregor, *Over the Sea to Skye*, London, 1926, ix.

54. S. Gordon, *The Charm of the Hills*, London, 1912, 1–2.

55. S. Gordon, *Afoot in the Hebrides*, London, 1950, viii.

56. A. Watson, 'Foreword', in, S. Gordon, *The Immortal Isles*, Melven Press Edition, Perth, 1979, xii.

Chapter Five: Without the Heartbreak of the Tale

1. Johnson, *Journey to the Western Islands*, 70–71.
2. A. Nicolson, *History of Skye*, Second Edition, Isle of Skye, 1994, 231–37. Also, G. Calder (ed), *Gaelic Songs by William Ross*, Edinburgh, 1937.
3. E. Richards, *A History of the Highland Clearances, Volume One: Agrarian Transformation and the Evictions, 1746–1886*, London, 1982, 421–23.
4. D. Cooper, *Skye*, London, 1990, 195–96; *Report of the Royal Commission on the Highlands and Islands*, Parliamentary Publication, London, 1995, 164.
5. D. Mackay, 'Scottish Rural Highland Settlement: Preserving a People's Past', in, R. Hingley (ed), *Medieval or Later Rural Settlement in Scotland*, Historic Scotland, Edinburgh, 1993, 48.
6. Smith, *Collected Poems*, 52.
7. S. MacLean, *Ris a'Bhruthaich*, Stornoway, 1985, 58–59.
8. C. I. MacLean, *The Highlands*, Mainstream Edition, Edinburgh, 1990, 118. Also, M. Tomkies, *A Last Wild Place*, London, 1984.
9. For fuller accounts of these episodes, see, Hunter, *Making of the Crofting Community*; J. Hunter, *The Claim of Crofting: The Scottish Highlands and Islands, 1930–1990*, Edinburgh, 1992.
10. N. M. Gunn, *The Lost Glen*, Richard Drew Publishing Edition, Glasgow, 1985, 58–59; R. Price, *The Fabulous Matter of Fact: The Poetics of Neil M. Gunn*, Edinburgh, 1991, 22.
11. A. McCleery (ed), *Landscape and Light: Essays by Neil M. Gunn*, Aberdeen, 1987, 168.
12. McCleery, *Landscape and Light*, 158; Gunn, *Lost Glen*, 282–83; N. M. Gunn, *The Grey Coast*, Jonathan Cape Edition, London, 1972, 76.
13. MacDiarmid, *Selected Poems*, 254; McCleery, *Landscape and Light*, 14, 284; Pride, *Fabulous Matter of Fact*, 57. Also, R. J. Finlay, *Independent and Free: Scottish Politics and the Origins of the Scottish National Party, 1918–1945*, Edinburgh, 1994.
14. H. MacDiarmid, *Lucky Poet*, Berkeley, 1972, 299; H. MacDiarmid, *The Islands of Scotland*, London, 1939, vii; A. Bold, *MacDiarmid*, Paladin Edition, London, 1990, 158–59, 286–97; N. K. Gish, *Hugh MacDiarmid: The Man and his Work*, London, 1984, 10, 22; Pride, *Fabulous Matter of Fact*, 42.
15. W. Neill, *Wild Places: Poems in Three Leids*, Barr, 1985, 6.
16. J. MacInnes, 'MacCaig and Gaeldom', in, J. Hendry and R. Ross (eds), *Norman MacCaig: Critical Essays*, Edinburgh, 1990, 31.

17. MacCaig, *Collected Poems*, 111; Jackson, *Celtic Miscellany*, 20.
18. S. MacLean, *From Wood to Ridge: Collected Poems in Gaelic and English*, Manchester, 1989, 170–73.
19. MacLean, *Ris a'Bhruthaich*, 33–34; S. MacLean, 'MacDiarmid, 1933–1944', in, P. H. Scott and A. C. Davis (eds), *The Age of MacDiarmid*, Edinburgh, 1980, 15–21.
20. MacLean, 'MacDiarmid, 1933–1944', 16.
21. MacDiarmid, *Lucky Poet*, 219.
22. MacLean, *From Wood to Ridge*, 56–59.
23. MacCaig, *Collected Poems*, 224–225.
24. MacCaig, *Collected Poems*, 226.
25. D. A. MacDonald, 'Some Aspects of Family and Background', in, R. J. Ross and J. Hendry (eds), *Sorley MacLean: Critical Essays*, Edinburgh, 1986, 220.
26. J. MacInnes, 'Language, Metre and Diction in the Poetry of Sorley MacLean', in, Ross and Hendry, *Sorley MacLean*, 149. Also, J. MacInnes, 'Sorley MacLean's *Hallaig*: A Note', *Calgacus*, 2, 1975; J. MacInnes, 'A Radically Traditional Voice: Sorley MacLean and the Evangelical Background', *Cencrastus*, 7, 1981.
27. B. Devlin, 'In Spite of Sea and Centuries', in Ross and Hendry, *Sorley MacLean*, 86.
28. McCleery, *Landscape and Light*, 32.
29. Smith, *Towards the Human*, 130–31; MacDiarmid, *Selected Poems*, 209.
30. Smith, *Towards the Human*, 131.
31. MacLean, *From Wood to Ridge*, 226–231.
32. S. Heaney, 'Introduction', in, Ross and Hendry, *Sorley MacLean*, 2.
33. MacLean, *Ris a'Bhruthaich*, 12.
34. C. Nicholson, *Poem, Purpose and Place: Shaping Identity in Contemporary Scottish Verse*, Edinburgh, 1992, 54; J. Hendry, 'Sorley MacLean: The Man and his Work', in, Ross and Hendry, *Sorley MacLean*, 20.
35. Smith, *Collected Poems*, 102–07.
36. Neill, *Wild Places*, 10. *Earran Reidh*, the Gaelic original of the phrase which was anglicised or scotticised to Irongray, can be translated, Neill points out, as 'level ground'. For a more general appreciation of the descriptive force of Gaelic placenames, see, A. Watson and E. Allan, *The Placenames of Upper Deeside*, Aberdeen, 1984.
37. MacColla, *The Albannach*, 70–71.
38. B. Friel, *Translations*, London, 1981, 29.
39. J. W. Foster, *Colonial Consequences: Essays in Irish Literature and*

Culture, Dublin, 1991, 31; W. Neill, *Blossom, Berry, Fall*, St Andrews, 1986; MacCaig, *Collected Poems*, 123.
40. MacCaig, *Collected Poems*, 230–31.
41. MacLean, *Ris a'Bhruthaich*, 74.
42. McGrath, *The Cheviot*, 33.
43. Said, *Culture and Imperialism*, 273.
44. Withers, *Gaelic Scotland*, 70.
45. Boyd, *Fraser Darling's Islands*, 46; Cooper, *Road to the Isles*, 4.
46. MacColla, *The Albannach*, 284.
47. Personal communication from Angus Macleod to the author, 16 August 1994; J. Hunter, *The Scottish Highlands: A People and their Place*, Edinburgh, 1992, 181–82.

Chapter Six: The Highlands are a Devastated Countryside

1. A. Leopold, *A Sand County Almanac: With Essays on Conservation from Round River*, Ballantine Books Edition, New York, 1970, 197.
2. Leopold, *Sand County Almanac*, 242.
3. F. F. Darling, *West Highland Survey: An Essay in Human Ecology*, Oxford, 1955, 192.
4. MacLeod, *Songs of Duncan Ban MacIntyre*, 178–79.
5. Darling, *West Highland Survey*, 192–93.
6. F. F. Darling, *Pelican in the Wilderness*, London, 1956, 353; H. M. Steven and A. Carlisle, *The Native Pinewoods of Scotland*, Edinburgh, 1959, v.
7. K. J. Edwards, 'Human Impact on the Prehistoric Environment', in, Smout, *Scotland Since Prehistory*, 17–19.
8. S. Hecht and A. Cockburn, *The Fate of the Forest: Developers, Destroyers and Defenders of the Amazon*, Penguin Edition, London, 1990, 35.
9. F. F. Darling, 'History of the Scottish Forests', as reprinted in, *Reforesting Scotland*, 7, 1992, 25–27; B. Murray, 'The High Tops', in, F. Holliday (ed), *Wildlife of Scotland*, London, 1979, 19; T. C. Smout, 'Trees as Historic Landscapes', *Scottish Forestry*, 48, 1994, 244–52.
10. O. MacKenzie, *A Hundred Years in the Highlands*, National Trust Edition, Edinburgh, 1988, 63–64, 101–05. Also, Smout, *Highlands and the Roots of Green Conciousness*, 11–12.
11. Hunter, 'Sheep and Deer', 203–04.
12. Fox, *John Muir and his Legacy*, 8; Darling, *Pelican in the Wilderness*, 20.

13. Lister–Kaye, *Ill Fares the Land*, 1–2.
14. N. Mitchison, *The Bull Calves*, London, 1947, 465.
15. McGrath, *The Cheviot, the Stag and the Black, Black Oil*, 23, 28.
16. Royal Society for the Protection of Birds, *Forestry in the Flows of Caithness and Sutherland*, Sandy, 1987; S. C. Tomkins, *The Theft of the Hills: Afforestation in Scotland*, London, 1986.
17. Darling, *West Highland Survey*, viii.
18. F. Pearce, *Green Warriors: The People and Politics Behind the Environmental Revolution*, London, 1991, 79–80.
19. Pearce, *Green Warriors*, 80–81.
20. Cairngorms Working Party, *Commonsense and Sustainability: A Partnership for the Cairngorms*, Edinburgh, 1992, 70.
21. Kemf, *Law of the Mother*, 5.
22. Hecht and Cockburn, *Fate of the Forest*, 217; Pearce, *Green Warriors*, 132–51.
23. F. Rennie, 'A Feeling for the Land', in Bruce and Rennie, *The Land Out There*, 298.
24. Scottish Crofters Union and Royal Society for the Protection of Birds, *Crofting and the Environment: A New Approach*, Isle of Skye, 1992, 15.
25. Wilmer, *Indigenous Voice in World Politics*, 1.
26. N. Gunn, *The Drinking Well*, Souvenir Press Edition, London, 1978, 461.
27. Gunn, *Off in a Boat*, 94–95. Also, L. Leneman, *Fit for Heroes: Land Settlement in Scotland after World War I*, Aberdeen, 1989, 136–48.
28. M. Davitt and I. MacDhomhnaill (eds), *Sruth an Maoile: Modern Gaelic Poetry from Scotland and Ireland*, Edinburgh, 1993, 226–27.
29. Said, *Culture and Imperialism*, 407–08.
30. D. Thomson, *Creachadh na Clarsach: Plundering the Harp: Collected Poems, 1940–1980*, Edinburgh, 1982, 160–61.
31. Said, *Culture and Imperialism*, 21.
32. Black, *Alasdair MacMhaighstir Alasdair*, 5.
33. MacLean, *Wood to Ridge*, xvi.
34. MacLean, *Wood to Ridge*, 130–31.

BIBLIOGRAPHY

Adams, R. J., *Papers on Sutherland Estate Management, 1802–1816,* 2 volumes, Scottish History Society, Edinburgh, 1972.

Adams, W. M., *Nature's Place: Conservation Sites and Countryside Change,* London, 1986.

Aitken, A. J., MacDiarmid, M. P., and Thomson, D. S. (eds), *Bards and Makars: Scottish Language and Literature: Medieval and Renaissance,* Glasgow, 1977.

Aitken, A. J., and MacArthur, Tom (eds), *Languages of Scotland,* Edinburgh, 1979.

Alaya, Flavia, *William Sharp: Fiona MacLeod,* Cambridge, Mass., 1970.

Alexander, Michael (ed), *Beowulf,* Penguin Edition, London, 1973.

Allchin, A. M., *Solitude and Communion: Papers on the Hermit Life,* Oxford, 1977.

Allen, David E., *The Naturalist in Britain: A Social History,* London, 1976.

Amnesty International, *Human Rights Violations Against Indigenous Peoples: The Americas,* London, 1992.

Anderson, Benedict, *Imagined Communities: Reflections on the Origins and Spread of Nationalism,* London, 1983.

Anderson, Mark L, *A History of Scottish Forestry,* 2 volumes, London, 1967.

Anson, Peter F., *The Call of the Desert: The Solitary Life in the Christian Church,* London, 1964.

Ash, Marinell, *The Strange Death of Scottish History,* Edinburgh, 1980.

Attfield, Robin, *Environmental Philosophy: Principles and Prospects,* Aldershot, 1994.

Baker, Frederick, and Thomas, J. (eds), *Writing the Past in the Present,* Lampeter, 1990.

Balfour, Roderick A. C., 'The Highland and Island Emigration Society', *Transactions of the Gaelic Society of Inverness,* LVII, 1990–92.

Bamford, Christopher, and Marsh, William P. (eds), *Celtic Christianity: Ecology and Holiness,* Edinburgh, 1986.

Barber, John, *Innsegall: The Western Isles*, Edinburgh, n.d.

Barrow, G. W. S., *The Kingdom of the Scots: Government, Church and Society from the Eleventh to the Fourteenth Century*, London, 1973.

Bartlett, Robert, *The Making of Europe: Conquest, Colonisation and Cultural Change, 950–1350*, London, 1993.

Bate, Jonathan, *Romantic Ecology: Wordsworth and the Environmental Tradition*, London, 1991.

Baxter, John M., and Usher, Michael B. (eds), *The Islands of Scotland: A Living Marine Heritage*, HMSO, Edinburgh, 1994.

Bell, Ian, *Robert Louis Stevenson: Dreams of Exile*, Edinburgh, 1992.

Bergin, Osborn, *Irish Bardic Poetry*, Dublin, 1970.

Berlitz, Charles, *Native Tongues*, London, 1983.

Beveridge, Craig and Turnbull, Ronald, *The Eclipse of Scottish Culture*, Edinburgh, 1989.

Bil, Albert, *The Shieling, 1600–1840*, Edinburgh, 1990.

Binchy, D. A., 'The Linguistic and Historical Value of the Irish Law Tracts', in, *Proceedings of the British Academy*, XXIX, 1943.

Binchy, D. A., *Corpus Iuris Hibernici*, 6 volumes, Dublin, 1978.

Black, Ronald, 'The Genius of Cathal MacMhuirich', *Transactions of the Gaelic Society of Inverness*, L, 1976–78.

Black, Ronald, *MacMhaighstir Alasdair: The Ardnamurchan Years*, Isle of Coll, 1986.

Black, William, *A Princess of Thule*, London, 1892.

Blunden, John, and Curry, Nigel, *A Future for Our Countryside*, Oxford, 1988.

Bode, Carl (ed), *The Portable Thoreau*, Penguin Edition, London, 1979.

Bold, Alan, *Modern Scottish Literature*, London, 1983.

Bold, Alan, *MacDiarmid*, Paladin Edition, London, 1990.

Boswell, James, *Journal of a Tour to the Hebrides*, Penguin Edition, London, 1984.

Botting, Douglas, *Gavin Maxwell: A Life*, London, 1993.

Boyd, J. Morton, *Fraser Darling's Islands*, Edinburgh, 1986.

Boyd, J. Morton, and Boyd, Ian L., *The Hebrides: A Natural History*, London, 1990.

Bradley, Ian, *God is Green: Christianity and the Environment*, London, 1990.

Bramwell, Anna, *Ecology in the Twentieth Century: A History*, London, 1989.

Brown, Jennifer M. (ed), *Scottish Society in the Fifteenth Century*, London, 1977.

Brown, P. Hume, *Early Travellers in Scotland*, Edinburgh, 1981.

Brown, Peter, *The Book of Kells*, London, 1980.

Bruce, George and Rennie, Frank, *The Land Out There: A Scottish Land Anthology*, Aberdeen, 1991.

Bunce, R. G. H., and Jeffers, J. N. R. (eds), *Native Pinewoods of Scotland*, Cambridge, 1977.

Butler, Marilyn, *Romantics, Rebels and Reactionaries: English Literature and its Background, 1760–1830*, Oxford, 1981.

Caird, James B., 'Gaelic Elements in the Work of Neil Gunn', *Studies in Scottish Literature*, XV, 1980.

Cairngorms Working Party, *Commonsense and Sustainability: A Partnership for the Cairngorms*, Edinburgh, 1992.

Calder, Angus, *Revolutionary Empire: The Rise of the English–Speaking Empires from the Fifteenth Century to the 1780s*, London, 1981.

Calder, George (ed), *Gaelic Songs by William Ross*, Edinburgh, 1937.

Callander, Robin F., *A Pattern of Landownership in Scotland*, Finzean, 1987.

Cameron, Elspeth (ed), *The Other Side of Hugh MacLennan: Selected Essays Old and New*, Toronto, 1978.

Cameron, Elspeth, *Hugh MacLennan: A Writer's Life*, Toronto, 1981.

Cameron, John, *Celtic Law*, Edinburgh, 1937.

Campbell, Angus P., *The Greatest Gift*, Isle of Skye, 1992.

Campbell, Angus P., *One Road*, Isle of Skye, 1994.

Campbell, Hilbert H., *James Thomson*, Boston, 1979.

Campbell, Ian (ed), *Nineteenth Century Scottish Fiction*, Manchester, 1979.

Campbell, John L., *The Book of Barra*, London, 1936.

Campbell, John L. (ed), *Highland Songs of the Forty–Five*, Revised Edition, Scottish Gaelic Texts Society, Edinburgh, 1984.

Campbell, John L., *Canna: The Story of a Hebridean Island*, Third Edition, Edinburgh, 1994.

Campbell, R. H., and Skinner, A. S., *The Origins and Nature of the Scottish Enlightenment*, Edinburgh, 1982.

Cargill, Kenneth (ed), *Scotland 2000: Eight Views on the State of the Nation*, Glasgow, 1987.

Carmichael, Alexander, *Carmina Gadelica*, 6 volumes, Edinburgh, 1928–1971.

Chadwick, Nora, *The Celts*, Pelican Edition, London, 1971.

Chambers, Robert, *Rural Development: Putting the Last First*, Harlow, 1983.

Chang, H. C., *Chinese Literature: Nature Poetry*, Edinburgh, 1977.

Chapman, Malcolm, *The Gaelic Vision in Scottish Culture*, London, 1978.

Chapman, Malcolm, *The Celts: The Construction of a Myth*, London, 1992.

Clark, Kenneth, *Civilisation*, Penguin Edition, London, 1982.

Clunies–Ross, Tracey, and Hildyard, Nicholas, *The Politics of Industrial Agriculture*, London, 1992.

Colchester, Marcus and Lohmann, Larry (eds), *The Struggle for the Land and the Fate of the Forests*, London, 1993.

Colley, Linda, *Britons: Forging the Nation, 1707–1837*, London, 1992.

Comunn na Gaidhlig, *Gaelic 2000: A Strategy for Gaelic Development*, Inverness, 1994.

Conservation Consortium, *Mar Lodge Estate: A New Future*, Edinburgh, 1993.

Cooper, Derek, *Road to the Isles: Travellers in the Hebrides, 1770–1914*, London, 1979.

Cooper, Derek, *Skye*, London, 1990.

Cooper, James Fenimore, *The Last of the Mohicans*, Panther Edition, London, 1970.

Corkery, Daniel, *The Hidden Ireland*, Gill and MacMillan Edition, Dublin, 1967.

Cormack, Mike, 'Programming for Cultural Defence: The Expansion of Gaelic Television', *Scottish Affairs*, 6, 1994.

Cosgrove, Denis E., *Social Formation and Symbolic Landscape*, London, 1984.

Cosgrove, Denis E., and Daniels, Stephen (eds), *The Iconography of Landscape*, Cambridge, 1988.

Countryside Commission for Scotland, *The Mountain Areas of Scotland: Conservation and Management*, Battleby, 1990.

Craig, Cairns (ed), *The History of Scottish Literature: Four, Twentieth Century*, Aberdeen, 1987.

Craig, David, *Scottish Literature and the Scottish People, 1680–1930*, London, 1961.

Craig, David, *On the Crofters' Trail: In Search of the Clearance Highlanders*, London, 1990.

Crawford, Barbara E., *Scandinavian Scotland*, Leicester, 1987.

Crawford, Robert, *Devolving English Literature*, Oxford, 1992.

Crawford, Robert, *Identifying Poets: Self and Territory in Twentieth Century Poetry*, Edinburgh, 1993.

Crosby, Alfred W., *Ecological Imperialism: The Biological Expansion of Europe*, Canto Edition, Cambridge, 1993.

Crumley, Jim, *A High and Lonely Place*, London, 1991.

Cunliffe, Barry, *The Celtic World*, London, 1992.

Curry–Lindahl, K., Watson, Adam, and Watson, R. Drennan, *The Future of the Cairngorms*, Aberdeen, 1982.

Curtin, Philip D. (ed), *Imperialism*, London, 1971.

Curtis, L. P., *Anglo–Saxons and Celts: A Study of Anti–Irish Prejudice in Victorian England*, Bridgeport, 1968.

Curtis, L. P., *Apes and Angels: The Irishman in Victorian Caricature*, Newton Abbott, 1971.

Daiches, David, *The Paradox of Scottish Culture: The Eighteenth Century Experience*, London, 1964.

Daiches, David, *Sir Walter Scott and His World*, London, 1971.

Daiches, David, *Robert Louis Stevenson and His World*, London, 1973.

Daiches, David, and Flower, John, *Literary Landscapes of the British Isles*, London, 1979.

Darling, Frank F., *A Herd of Red Deer*, Oxford, 1937.

Darling, Frank F., *Wild Country*, Cambridge, 1938.

Darling, Frank F., *A Naturalist on Rona*, Oxford, 1939.

Darling, Frank F., *Island Farm*, London, 1943.

Darling, Frank F., *West Highland Survey: An Essay in Human Ecology*, Oxford, 1955.

Darling, Frank F., *Pelican in the Wilderness*, London, 1956.

Darling, Frank F., *Wilderness and Plenty*, London, 1970.

Darling, Frank F., *Island Years*, Pan Books Edition, London, 1973.

Deane, Seamus, *A Short History of Irish Literature*, London, 1986.

Degategno, Paul J., *James MacPherson*, Boston, 1989.

Delaney, Frank, *The Celts*, London, 1986.

Delaney, Frank, *Legends of the Celts*, Grafton Books Edition, London, 1991.

Devall, Bill, *Simple in Means, Rich in Ends: Practising Deep Ecology*, Green Print Edition, London, 1990.

Devine, Thomas M., *The Great Highland Famine*, Edinburgh, 1988.

Devine, Thomas M. (ed), *Scottish Emigration and Scottish Society*, Edinburgh, 1992.

Devine, Thomas M., *Clanship to Crofters War: The Social Transformation of the Scottish Highlands*, Manchester, 1994.

Devine, Thomas M., and Mitchison, Rosalind, *People and Society in Scotland, Volume 1: 1707–1830*, Edinburgh, 1988.

Diamond, Jared, *The Rise and Fall of the Third Chimpanzee*, Vintage Edition, London, 1992.

Dickson, A., and Treble, J. H., *People and Society in Scotland, Volume 3: 1914–1990*, Edinburgh, 1992.

Dickson, J. H., 'Scottish Woodlands: Their Ancient Past and Precarious Present', *Scottish Forestry*, 47, 1993.

Dillon, Myles, *Early Irish Literature*, Chicago, 1948.

Dillon, Myles, and Chadwick, Nora, *The Celtic Realms*, London, 1967.

Dobson, Andrew, *Green Political Thought*, London, 1990.

Dodgshon, Robert A., *Land and Society in Early Scotland*, Oxford, 1981.

Donaldson, Mary E. M., *The Isles of Flame*, Paisley, 1913.

Donaldson, Mary E. M., *Wanderings in the Western Highlands and Islands*, Paisley, 1921.

Donaldson, Mary E. M., *Islesmen of Bride*, Paisley, 1922.

Donaldson, Mary E. M., *Further Wanderings Mainly in Argyll*, Paisley, 1927.

Donaldson, William, *The Jacobite Song: Political Myth and National Identity*, Aberdeen, 1988.

Drabble, Margaret, *A Writer's Britain: Landscape in Literature*, London, 1979.

Duff, David (ed), *Queen Victoria's Highland Journals*, Exeter, 1983.

Duncan, A. A. M., *Scotland: The Making of the Nation*, Mercat Press Edition, Edinburgh, 1989.

Durkacz, Victor E., *The Decline of the Celtic Languages*, Edinburgh, 1983.

Dwyer, J., Mason, R. A., and Murdoch, A. (eds), *New Perspectives on the Politics and Culture of Early Modern Scotland*, Edinburgh, 1982.

Dyck, Noel (ed), *Indigenous Peoples and the Nation State*, St Johns, 1985.

Eagle, Raymond, *Seton Gordon: The Life and Times of a Highland Gentleman*, Moffat, 1991.

Edwards, Nancy, *The Archaeology of Early Medieval Ireland*, London, 1990.

Edwards, Owen D., Evans, G., Rhys, I., and MacDiarmid, Hugh, *Celtic Nationalism*, London, 1968.

Elliott, Robert, and Gare, Arran (eds), *Environmental Philosophy*, Milton Keynes, 1983.

Fanon, Frantz, *The Wretched of the Earth*, Penguin Edition, London, 1967.

Fenton, Alexander, *Scottish Country Life*, Edinburgh, 1976.

Fenton, Alexander, *Country Life in Scotland*, Edinburgh, 1987.

Fife, Hugh, *The Lore of Highland Trees*, Gartocharn, 1987.

Fife, Hugh, *Warriors and Guardians: Native Highland Trees*, Glendaruel, 1994.

Finlay, Ian, *Celtic Art: An Introduction*, London, 1973.

Finlay, Ian, *Columba*, London, 1979.

Finlay, Richard J., *Independent and Free: Scottish Politics and the Origins of the Scottish National Party, 1918–1945*, Edinburgh, 1994.

Flower, Robin, *The Irish Tradition*, Oxford, 1947.

Foster, John W., *Colonial Consequences: Essays in Irish Literature and Culture*, Dublin, 1991.

Fox, Stephen, *John Muir and his Legacy: The American Conservation Movement*, Boston, 1981.

France, Peter, 'Primitivism and Enlightenment: Rousseau and the Scots', *Yearbook of English Studies*, 15, 1985.

Fraser, W. Hamish, and Morris, R. J. (eds), *People and Society in Scotland, Volume 2: 1830–1914*, Edinburgh, 1990.

Friden, Georg, *James Fenimore Cooper and Ossian*, Cambridge, Mass., 1949.

Friel, Brian, *Translations*, London, 1981.

Gaskill, Howard, 'Ossian MacPherson: Towards a Rehabilitation', in, Shafer, E. S. (ed), *Comparative Criticism: An Annual Journal*, Cambridge, 1986.

Gaskill, Howard (ed), *Ossian Revisited*, Edinburgh, 1991.

Gifford, Douglas, *Neil M. Gunn and Lewis Grassic Gibbon*, Edinburgh, 1983.

Gifford, Douglas (ed), *The History of Scottish Literature: Three, Nineteenth Century*, Aberdeen, 1988.

Gilbert, John M., *Hunting and Hunting Reserves in Medieval Scotland*, Edinburgh, 1979.

Gillies, William, 'The Poem in Praise of Ben Dobhrain', *Lines Review*, 63, 1977.

Gillies, William (ed), *Gaelic and Scotland*, Edinburgh, 1989.

Gish, Nancy K., *Hugh MacDiarmid: The Man and his Work*, London, 1984.

Glen, Duncan, *Hugh MacDiarmid and the Scottish Renaissance*, Edinburgh, 1964.

Glen, Duncan (ed), *Selected Essays of Hugh MacDiarmid*, London, 1969.

Goodin, Robert E., *Green Political Theory*, Cambridge, 1992.

Gordon, Seton, *The Charm of the Hills*, London, 1912.

Gordon, Seton, *The Cairngorm Hills of Scotland*, London, 1925.

Gordon, Seton, *Afoot in Wild Places*, London, 1937.

Gordon, Seton, *Afoot in the Hebrides*, London, 1950.

Gordon, Seton, *Highland Days*, London, 1963.

Gordon, Seton, *The Immortal Isles*, Melven Press Edition, Perth, 1979.

Gow, Carol, *Mirror and Marble: The Poetry of Iain Crichton Smith*, Edinburgh, 1992.

Grant, I. F., *Highland Folk Ways*, London, 1961.

Grant, I. F. and Cheape, Hugh, *Periods in Highland History*, London, 1987.

Greene, D., and O'Connor, F. (eds), *A Golden Treasury of Irish Poetry AD600 to 1200*, London, 1967.

Grigor, Murray and Grigor, Barbara, *Scotch Myths*, Edinburgh, 1981.

Grimble, Ian, *The World of Rob Donn*, Edinburgh, 1979.

Grimble, Ian, *Neil M Gunn Memorial Lecture*, Ampthill, 1992.

Gunn, Neil M., *Whisky and Scotland: A Practical and Spiritual Survey*, London, 1935.

Gunn, Neil M., *The Grey Coast*, Jonathan Cape Edition, London, 1972.

Gunn, Neil M., *Butcher's Broom*, Souvenir Press Edition, London, 1977.

Gunn, Neil M., *The Drinking Well*, Souvenir Press Edition, London, 1978.

Gunn, Neil M., *The Lost Glen*, Richard Drew Publishing Edition, Glasgow, 1985.

Gunn, Neil M., *Off in a Boat*, Richard Drew Publishing Edition, Glasgow, 1988.

Gunn, Neil M., *Highland Pack*, Richard Drew Publishing Edition, Glasgow, 1989.

Gunn, Neil M., *Highland River*, Canongate Classics Edition, Edinburgh, 1991.

Gunn, Neil M., *The Man Who Came Back: Short Stories and Essays*, Edinburgh, 1991.

Harding, Walter, *The Days of Henry Thoreau*, New York, 1982.

Harrison, Fraser, *The Living Landscape*, Mandarin Edition, London, 1991.

Hart, Francis R., *The Scottish Novel: A Critical Survey*, London, 1978.

Hart–Davis, Duff, *Monarchs of the Glen: A History of Deer Stalking in the Scottish Highlands*, London, 1978.

Harvie, Christopher, *The Rise of Regional Europe*, London, 1994.

Harvie, Christopher, *Fool's Gold: The Story of North Sea Oil*, London, 1994.

Hay, Deorsa C., *Mochtar is Dughall*, Glasgow, 1982.

Hayne, Barrie, 'Ossian, Scott and Cooper's Indians', *Journal of American Studies*, III, 1969.

Hecht, Susanna, and Cockburn, Alexander, *The Fate of the Forest: Developers, Destroyers and Defenders of the Amazon*, Penguin Edition, London, 1990.

Hechter, Michael, *Internal Colonialism: The Celtic Fringe in British National Development, 1536–1966*, London, 1975.

Henderson, George, *From Durrow to Kells: The Insular Gospel Books, 650–800*, London, 1987.

Henderson, Hamish, *Alias MacAlias: Writings on Songs, Folk and Literature*, Edinburgh, 1992.

Hendry, Joy, and Ross, Raymond (eds), *Norman MacCaig: Critical Essays*, Edinburgh, 1990.

Herbert, Maire, *Iona, Kells and Durrow: The History and Hagiography of the Monastic Familia of Columba*, Oxford, 1988.

Hewison, Robert, *The Heritage Industry*, London, 1987.

Hewitt, David, and Spiller, Michael (eds), *Literature of the North*, Aberdeen, 1983.

Highlands and Islands Enterprise, *A Strategy for Enterprise and the Environment*, Inverness, 1992.

Hingley, Richard (ed), *Medieval or Later Rural Settlement in Scotland*, Historic Scotland, Edinburgh, 1993.

Hobsbawm, Eric, and Ranger, Terence (eds), *The Invention of Tradition*, Cambridge, 1983.

Holliday, Fred (ed), *Wildlife of Scotland*, London, 1979.

Hook, Andrew, *Scotland and America: A Study of Cultural Relations, 1750–1835*, Glasgow, 1975.

Hook, Andrew (ed), *The History of Scottish Literature: Two, 1660–1800*, Aberdeen, 1987.

Hughes, Kathleen, *Celtic Britain in the Early Middle Ages*, Bury St Edmonds, 1980.

Hunter, James, 'Sheep and Deer: Highland Sheep Farming, 1850–1900', *Northern Scotland*, I, 1974.

Hunter, James, 'The Gaelic Connection: The Highlands, Ireland and Nationalism, 1873–1922', *Scottish Historical Review*, LIV, 1975.

Hunter, James, *The Making of the Crofting Community*, Edinburgh, 1976.

Hunter, James, *For the People's Cause: From the Writings of John Murdoch*, Edinburgh, 1986.

Hunter, James, *Skye: The Island*, Edinburgh, 1986.

Hunter, James, *The Claim of Crofting: The Scottish Highlands and*

Islands, 1930–1990, Edinburgh, 1991.

Hunter, James (ed), *North West Scotland: European Heritage Area,* Isle of Skye, 1991.

Hunter, James, *Scottish Highlanders: A People and their Place,* Edinburgh, 1992.

Hunter, James, *A Dance Called America: The Scottish Highlands, the United States and Canada,* Edinburgh, 1994.

Inglis, J. G., 'Days That Are Past', *Scottish Mountaineering Club Journal,* XX, 1934.

Jack, R. D. S. (ed), *The History of Scottish Literature: One, Origins to 1660,* Aberdeen, 1988.

Jackson, Kenneth H., *Studies in Early Celtic Nature Poetry,* Cambridge, 1935.

Jackson, Kenneth H., *The Oldest Irish Tradition: A Window on the Iron Age,* Cambridge, 1964.

Jackson, Kenneth H. (ed), *A Celtic Miscellany,* Penguin Edition, London, 1971.

Jackson, Kenneth H., *The Gaelic Notes in the Book of Deer,* Cambridge, 1972.

Johnson, Samuel, *A Journey to the Western Islands of Scotland,* Penguin Edition, 1984.

Jones, Michael, 'The Elusive Reality of Landscape: Concepts and Approaches in Landscape Research', *Norsk Geografisk Tidsskrift,* 45, 1991.

Jones, Peter, *Indigenous Peoples and Ethnic Minorities,* Edinburgh, 1993.

Kelly, Fergus, 'The Old Irish Tree List', *Celtica,* XI, 1976.

Kelly, Fergus, *A Guide to Early Irish Law,* Dublin, 1988.

Kemf, Elizabeth, *The Law of the Mother: Protecting Indigenous Peoples in Protected Areas,* San Francisco, 1993.

Kiernan, V. G., *The Lords of Human Kind,* New York, 1986.

Kinsella, Thomas, *The Tain,* Oxford, 1969.

Knott, Eleanor, *Irish Classical Poetry,* Dublin, 1957.

Knott, Eleanor, and Murphy, Gerard, *Early Irish Literature,* London, 1966.

Laing, Lloyd, *Celtic Britain,* London, 1979.

Laing, Lloyd, and Laing, Jenny, *The Picts and the Scots,* Stroud, 1993.

Lavelle, Des, *The Skellig Story,* Dublin, 1993.

Leerssen, Joseph T., *Mere Irish and Fíor-Ghael: Studies in the Idea of*

Irish Nationality, Philadelphia, 1986.

Lehane, Brendan, *Early Celtic Christianity*, London, 1994.

Leneman, Leah, *Fit for Heroes: Land Settlement in Scotland after World War I*, Aberdeen, 1989.

Lenman, Bruce, *The Jacobite Risings in Britain, 1689–1746*, London, 1980.

Lenman, Bruce, *The Jacobite Clans of the Great Glen, 1650–1784*, London, 1984.

Leopold, Aldo, *A Sand County Almanac: With Essays on Conservation from Round River*, Ballantine Books Edition, New York, 1970.

Linklater, Andro, *Compton MacKenzie: A Life*, Hogarth Press Edition, London, 1992.

Lister–Kaye, John, *The White Island*, London, 1972.

Lister–Kaye, John, *The Seeing Eye: Notes of a Highland Naturalist*, London, 1980.

Lister–Kaye, John, *Ill Fares the Land: A Sustainable Land Ethic for the Sporting Estates of the Highlands and Islands of Scotland*, Barail, Isle of Skye, 1994.

Lovelock, James, *The Ages of Gaia*, Oxford, 1988.

Mabey, Richard, *The Common Ground*, Arrow Edition, London, 1981.

MacArthur, Colin (ed), *Scotch Reels: Scotland in Cinema and Television*, London, 1982.

MacArthur, E. Mairi, *Iona: The Living Memory of a Crofting Community, 1750–1914*, Edinburgh, 1990.

MacAulay, Donald (ed), *Nua–bhardachd Ghaidhlig: Modern Scottish Gaelic Poems: A Bilingual Anthology*, Canongate Classics Edition, Edinburgh, 1995.

MacCaig, Norman, *Collected Poems: A New Edition*, London, 1993.

McCleery, Alistair (ed), *Landscape and Light: Essays by Neil M Gunn*, Aberdeen, 1987.

MacColla, Fionn, *At the Sign of the Clenched Fist*, Edinburgh, 1967.

MacColla, Fionn, *The Albannach*, Reprographia Edition, Edinburgh, 1971.

MacColla, Fionn, *Too Long in this Condition*, Thurso, 1975.

MacColla, Fionn, *And the Cock Crew*, Souvenir Press Edition, London, 1977.

McCrone, David, *Understanding Scotland: The Sociology of a Stateless Nation*, London, 1992.

MacDiarmid, Hugh, *The Islands of Scotland*, London, 1939.

MacDiarmid, Hugh, *Lucky Poet*, Berkeley, 1972.

MacDiarmid, Hugh, *Selected Poems*, Penguin Edition, London, 1994.

MacDonald, Charles, *Moidart: Or Among the Clanranalds*, Mercat Press Edition, Edinburgh, 1989.

MacDonald, Fiona, *Island Voices*, Canongate Edition, Edinburgh, 1994.

MacDonell, Margaret, *The Emigrant Experience: Songs of Highland Emigrants in North America*, Toronto, 1982.

McGrath, John, *The Cheviot, the Stag and the Black, Black Oil*, Revised Edition, Isle of Skye, 1975.

MacGregor, Alasdair A., *Behold the Hebrides*, London, 1925.

MacGregor, Alasdair A., *Over the Sea to Skye*, London, 1926.

MacGregor, Alasdair A., *Summer Days Among the Western Isles*, London, 1929.

MacGregor, Alasdair A., *The Western Isles*, London, 1949.

MacInnes, John, 'The Oral Tradition in Scottish Gaelic Poetry', *Scottish Studies*, 12, 1968.

MacInnes, John, 'West Highland Sea Power in the Middle Ages', *Transactions of the Gaelic Society of Inverness*, XLVIII, 1972–74.

MacInnes, John, 'Sorley MacLean's *Hallaig*: A Note', *Calgacus*, 2, 1975.

MacInnes, John, 'The Panegyric Code in Gaelic Poetry and its Historical Background', *Transactions of the Gaelic Society of Inverness*, L, 1976–78.

MacInnes, John, 'A Radically Traditional Voice: Sorley MacLean and the Evangelical Background', *Cencrastus*, 7, 1981.

MacKay, D. A., 'The Western Highlands and Islands: A Cultural Backwater', *Scottish Archaeological Review*, 5, 1988.

MacKay, I. R., 'The Pet Lamb Case', *Transactions of the Gaelic Society of Inverness*, XLVIII, 1972–74.

MacKenzie, Compton, *Whisky Galore*, London, 1947.

MacKenzie, Compton, *The Rival Monster*, London, 1952.

MacKenzie, Osgood, *A Hundred Years in the Highlands*, National Trust Edition, Edinburgh, 1988.

MacKenzie, W. C., *History of the Outer Hebrides*, Mercat Press Edition, Edinburgh, 1974.

McKibben, Bill, *The End of Nature*, Penguin Edition, London, 1990.

MacKillop, James, *Fionn MacCumhaill: Celtic Myth in English Literature*, Syracuse, 1986.

MacKinnon, Kenneth, *Language, Education and Social Processes in a Gaelic Community*, London, 1977.

MacKinnon, Kenneth, *Gaelic: A Past and Future Prospect*, Edinburgh, 1991.

MacKinnon, Neil J., 'Strath in Skye: The End of the Nineteenth

Century', *Transactions of the Gaelic Society of Inverness*, LII, 1980–82.

MacLean, Alasdair, *From the Wilderness*, London, 1973.

MacLean, Alasdair, *Night Falls on Ardnamurchan: The Twilight of a Crofting Family*, London, 1984.

MacLean, Calum I., *The Highlands*, Mainstream Edition, Edinburgh, 1990.

MacLean, Donald, *The Spiritual Songs of Dugald Buchanan*, Edinburgh, 1913.

MacLean, Loraine (ed), *The Middle Ages in the Highlands*, Inverness, 1981.

MacLean, Loraine (ed), *The Seventeenth Century in the Highlands*, Inverness, 1986.

MacLean, Magnus, *The Literature of the Highlands*, London, 1926.

MacLean, Malcolm, and Carrell, Christopher (eds), *As an Fhearann: From the Land*, Stornoway, 1986.

MacLean, Sorley, *Ris a'Bhruthaich*, Stornoway, 1985.

MacLean, Sorley, *From Wood to Ridge: Collected Poems in Gaelic and English*, Manchester, 1990.

MacLennan, Hugh, *Barometer Rising*, New Canadian Library Edition, Toronto, 1969.

MacLeod, Angus (ed), *The Songs of Duncan Ban MacIntyre*, Scottish Gaelic Texts Society, Edinburgh, 1952.

MacLeod, Fiona, *Iona*, London, 1910.

MacLeod, Fiona, *The Winged Destiny: Studies in the Spiritual History of the Gael*, London, 1910.

MacLulich, T. D., *Hugh MacLennan*, Boston, 1983.

MacMillan, Duncan, *Symbols of Survival: The Art of Will MacLean*, Edinburgh, 1992.

MacNeacail, Aonghas, *An Seachnadh agus Dain Eile: The Avoiding and Other Poems*, Edinburgh, 1986.

MacNeacail, Aonghas, *Rock and Water*, Edinburgh, 1990.

MacNeacail, Aonghas (ed), *A Writers Ceilidh for Neil Gunn*, Nairn, 1991.

MacNeill, Eoin, *Celtic Ireland*, Dublin, 1921.

MacNeill, Eoin, *Early Irish Laws and Institutions*, Dublin, 1935.

MacNeill, F. Marion, *An Iona Anthology*, Iona Press Edition, Iona, 1990.

McSkimming, Helen, *The Trees of the Celtic Alphabet*, Brodick, 1992.

MacQueen, John (ed), *Poems of Ossian*, 2 volumes, Edinburgh, 1971.

MacQueen, John, *Progress and Poetry*, Edinburgh, 1982.

MacRae, John, 'Parish of Glen Shiel', *The Statistical Account of Scotland*,

EP Publishing Edition, Wakefield, 20 volumes, 1981.

MacRae, John, 'Parish of Glen Shiel', *The New Statistical Account of Scotland*, Edinburgh, 15 volumes, 1855.

MacSween, Ann, *Skye*, Edinburgh, 1990.

Magnusson, Magnus, and White, Graham (eds), *The Nature of Scotland: Landscape, Wildlife and People*, Edinburgh, 1991.

Marsden, John, *The Illustrated Columcille: The Life of St Columba*, London, 1991.

Marshall, Peter, *Nature's Web: An Exploration of Ecological Thinking*, London, 1992.

Martin, Angus, *Kintyre: The Hidden Past*, Edinburgh, 1984.

Martin, Martin, *A Description of the Western Islands of Scotland*, Mercat Press Edition, Edinburgh, 1970.

Martin, Vance, and Inglis, Mary (eds), *Wilderness: The Way Ahead*, Findhorn, 1984.

Mather, Alexander S., 'Protected Areas on the Periphery: Conservation and Controversy in Northern Scotland', *Journal of Rural Studies*, 9, 1993.

Matheson, William (ed), *The Songs of John MacCodrum*, Scottish Gaelic Texts Society, Edinburgh, 1938.

Matheson, William (ed), *An Clarsair Dall: The Songs of Roderick Morrison*, Scottish Gaelic Texts Society, Edinburgh, 1970.

Maxwell, Gavin, *The Rocks Remain*, London, 1963.

Maxwell, Gavin, *Raven Seek Thy Brother*, London, 1968.

Maxwell, Gavin, *Ring of Bright Water*, Isis Edition, Oxford, 1991.

Meek, Donald E., 'Gaelic Poets of the Land Agitation', *Transactions of the Gaelic Society of Inverness*, XLIX, 1974–76.

Meek, Donald E., 'Land and Loyalty: The Gaelic Verse of George Campbell Hay', *Chapman*, 39, 1984.

Meek, Donald E., 'The Gaelic Ballads of Medieval Scotland', *Transactions of the Gaelic Society of Inverness*, LV, 1986–88.

Meek, Ronald L., *Social Science and the Ignoble Savage*, Cambridge, 1976.

Meldrum, Edward (ed), *The Dark Ages in the Highlands*, Inverness, 1971.

Meller, Helen, *Patrick Geddes: Social Evolutionist and City Planner*, London, 1990.

Menzies, Gordon, *Who Are The Scots?*, London, 1971.

Meyer, Kuno, *Ancient Irish Poetry*, Constable Edition, London, 1994.

Millman, Roger, *The Making of the Scottish Landscape*, London, 1975.

Millward, Roy, and Robinson, Adrian, *Upland Britain*, Newton Abbott, 1980.

Mitchison, Naomi, *The Bull Calves*, London, 1947.

Mollison, Denis (ed), *Wilderness with People: The Management of Wild Land*, John Muir Trust, Musselburgh, 1992.

Moody, T. W., and Martin, F. X. (eds), *The Course of Irish History*, Revised Edition, Dublin, 1984.

Morris, David B., *Robert Louis Stevenson and the Scottish Highlanders*, Stirling, 1929.

Mosley, Ivo (ed), *The Green Book of Poetry*, Kirstead, 1994.

Muir, Edwin, *Scott and Scotland*, London, 1936.

Muir, John, *The Mountains of California*, Penguin American Library Edition, New York, 1985.

Muir, John, *The Story of My Boyhood and Youth*, Canongate Classics Edition, Edinburgh, 1987.

Muir, John, *My First Summer in the Sierra*, Canongate Classics Edition, Edinburgh, 1988.

Muir, John, *The Yosemite*, Sierra Club Edition, San Francisco, 1988.

Muir, John, *Travels in Alaska*, Sierra Club Edition, San Francisco, 1988.

Munro, Neil, *The Lost Pibroch and Other Shieling Stories*, London, 1929.

Munro, Neil, *John Splendid*, London, 1929.

Munro, Neil, *The New Road*, London, 1930.

Munro, Neil, *The Poetry of Neil Munro*, Edinburgh, 1931.

Murphy, Gerard, *Early Irish Lyrics: Eighth to Twelfth Century*, Oxford, 1956.

Murray, Isobel, and Tait, Bob, *Ten Modern Scottish Novels*, Aberdeen, 1984.

Murray, W. H., *Highland Landscape: A Survey*, Aberdeen, 1962.

Murray, W. H., *The Islands of Western Scotland*, London, 1973.

Nairn, Tom, *The Break-Up of Britain*, Second Edition, London, 1981.

Nash, Roderick, *Wilderness and the American Mind*, Third Edition, Yale, 1982.

Nash, Roderick, *The Rights of Nature: A History of Environmental Ethics*, Madison, 1989.

Nature Conservancy Council, *Nature Conservation and Afforestation in Britain*, Peterborough, 1986.

Neeson, Eoin, *A History of Irish Forestry*, Dublin, 1991.

Neill, William, *Wild Places: Poems in Three Leids*, Barr, 1985.

Neill, William, *Blossom, Berry, Fall*, St Andrews, 1986.

Neill, William, *Making Tracks*, Edinburgh, 1988.

Neill, William, *Straight Lines*, Belfast, 1992.

Nethersole–Thomson, Desmond, and Watson, Adam, *The Cairngorms*, Perth, 1981.

Newby, Howard, *Green and Pleasant Land: Social Change in Rural England*, Pelican Edition, London, 1980.

Newby, Howard, *Country Life: A Social History of Rural England*, London, 1987.

Newby, Howard, *The Countryside in Question*, London, 1988.

Nicholson, Max, *The New Environmental Age*, Cambridge, 1987.

Nicholson, Ranald, *Scotland: The Later Middle Ages*, Mercat Press Edition, Edinburgh, 1989.

Nicolson, Alexander, *History of Skye*, Second Edition, Isle of Skye, 1994.

Nicolson, Colin, *Poem, Purpose and Place: Shaping Identity in Contemporary Scottish Verse*, Edinburgh, 1992.

Nicolson, Colin (ed), *Iain Crichton Smith: Critical Essays*, Edinburgh, 1992.

Nicolson, Marjorie H., *Mountain Gloom and Mountain Glory: The Development of the Aesthetics of the Infinite*, Ithaca, 1959.

Norton–Taylor, Richard, *Whose Land Is It Anyway?*, Wellingborough, 1982.

O'Baoill, Colm, 'Some Irish Harpers in Scotland', *Transactions of the Gaelic Society of Inverness*, XLVII, 1971–72.

O'Baoill, Colm, 'Scotland in Early Gaelic Literature', *Transactions of the Gaelic Society of Inverness*, XLVIII, 1972–74.

O'Baoill, Colm (ed), *Gair nan Clarsach: The Harps' Cry: An Anthology of Seventeenth Century Gaelic Poetry*, Edinburgh, 1994.

O'Dwyer, Peter, *Celi De: Spiritual Reform in Ireland, 750–900*, Dublin, 1981.

O'Riordan, Michelle, *The Gaelic Mind and the Collapse of the Gaelic World*, Cork, 1990.

Olwig, Kenneth, *Nature's Ideological Landscape*, London, 1984.

Orr, William, *Deer Forests, Landlords and Crofters*, Edinburgh, 1982.

Paor, Maire de, *Early Irish Art*, Dublin, 1979.

Parry, M. L., and Slater, T. R. (eds), *The Making of the Scottish Countryside*, London, 1980.

Paterson, Lindsay, *The Autonomy of Modern Scotland*, Edinburgh, 1994.

Pearce, David, Anil, Markandya, and Barbier, Edward B., *Blueprint for a Green Economy*, Earthscan Publications Edition, London, 1989.

Pearce, David (ed), *Blueprint 2: Greening the World Economy*, London, 1991.

Pearce, Fred, *Green Warriors: The People and the Politics Behind the*

Environmental Revolution, London, 1991.

Pepper, David, *The Roots of Modern Environmentalism*, London, 1986.

Pick, J. B. (ed), *Neil M Gunn: Selected Letters*, Edinburgh, 1987.

Pittock, Murray G. H., *The Invention of Scotland: The Stuart Myth and the Scottish Identity*, London, 1991.

Pittock, Murray G. H., *Spectrum of Decadence: The Literature of the 1890s*, London, 1993.

Porritt, Jonathon, *Seeing Green: The Politics of Ecology Explained*, Oxford, 1984.

Prebble, John, *Culloden*, Penguin Edition, London, 1967.

Prebble, John, *Glencoe*, Penguin Edition, London, 1968.

Prebble, John, *The Highland Clearances*, Penguin Edition, London, 1969.

Prebble, John, *The King's Jaunt: George IV in Scotland*, Fontana Edition, London, 1989.

Price, R. J., *Scotland's Environment During the Last 30,000 Years*, Edinburgh, 1983.

Price, Richard, *The Fabulous Matter of Fact: The Poetics of Neil M Gunn*, Edinburgh, 1991.

Purser, John, *Scotland's Music*, Edinburgh, 1992.

Rackham, Oliver, *Trees and Woodland in the British Landscape*, London, 1976.

Reed, James, *Sir Walter Scott: Landscape and Locality*, London, 1980.

Reforesting Scotland, *Norway and Scotland: A Study in Land Use*, Ullapool, 1994.

Reid, Wemyss, *William Black: Novelist*, London, 1902.

Rennie, Frank W., 'The Electronic Crofter: The Impact of High–Technology Developments in the Highlands and Islands', *Scottish Affairs*, 3, 1993.

Report of the Commissioners of Inquiry into the Condition of the Crofters and Cottars in the Highlands and Islands of Scotland, 5 volumes, Parliamentary Publication, London, 1884.

Report of the Royal Commission on the Highlands and Islands, Parliamentary Publication, London, 1895.

Richards, Eric, *A History of the Highland Clearances, Volume One: Agrarian Transformation and the Evictions, 1746–1886*, London, 1982.

Richards, Eric, *A History of the Highland Clearances, Volume Two: Emigration, Protest, Reasons*, London, 1985.

Richards, Eric, and Clough, Monica, *Cromartie: Highland Life, 1650–1914*, Aberdeen, 1989.

Richter, Michael, *Medieval Ireland: The Enduring Tradition*, London, 1983.

Robson, Michael, *Rona: The Distant Island*, Stornoway, 1991.

Rosie, George, *Hugh Miller: Outrage and Order*, Edinburgh, 1982.

Ross, Anne, *The Pagan Celts*, London, 1986.

Ross, Raymond J., and Hendry, Joy (eds), *Sorley MacLean: Critical Essays*, Edinburgh, 1986.

Royal Society for the Protection of Birds, *Forestry in the Flows of Caithness and Sutherland*, Sandy, 1987.

Royle, Trevor, *The Mainstream Companion to Scottish Literature*, Edinburgh, 1993.

Said, Edward W., *Orientalism*, London, 1978.

Said, Edward W., *Culture and Imperialism*, London, 1993.

Sanger, Keith, and Kinnaird, Alison, *Tree of Strings: A History of the Harp in Scotland*, Shillinghill, 1992.

Schumacher, E. F., *Small is Beautiful*, Abacus Edition, London, 1974.

Scott, Paul H., *Scotland: A Concise Cultural History*, Edinburgh, 1993.

Scott, Paul H., *Walter Scott and Scotland*, Saltire Society Edition, Edinburgh, 1994.

Scott, Paul H., and Davis, A. C. (eds), *The Age of MacDiarmid*, Edinburgh, 1980.

Scott, Tom, *The Penguin Book of Scottish Verse*, London, 1970.

Scott, Walter, *Poetical Works*, London, 1894.

Scott, Walter, *Waverley*, Penguin Edition, London, 1972.

Scott–Moncrieff, Lesley (ed), *The Forty–Five: To Gather an Image Whole*, Edinburgh, 1988.

Scottish Crofters Union and Royal Society for the Protection of Birds, *Crofting and the Environment: A New Approach*, Isle of Skye, 1992.

Scottish Green Party, *A Rural Manifesto for the Highlands*, Scourie, 1989.

Scottish Natural Heritage, *Sustainable Development and the Natural Heritage: The SNH Approach*, Battleby, 1993.

Scottish Natural Heritage, *Enjoying the Outdoors: A Programme for Action*, Battleby, 1994.

Sharpe, Richard, *Raasay: A Study in Island History*, 2 Volumes, London, 1977–78.

Shaw, Margaret Fay, *Folksongs and Folklore of South Uist*, Second Edition, Oxford, 1977.

Sheail, John, *Nature in Trust: The History of Nature Conservation in Britain*, Glasgow, 1976.

Sheail, John, *Rural Conservation in Inter-War Britain*, Oxford, 1981.

Shepherd, Nan, *The Living Mountain*, Aberdeen, 1977.

Shoard, Marion, *The Theft of the Countryside*, London, 1980.

Shoard, Marion, *This Land is Our Land: The Struggle for Britain's Countryside*, London, 1987.

Simmons, I. G., *Changing the Face of the Earth: Culture, Environment, History*, Oxford, 1990.

Simmons, I. G., and Tooley, M. J. (eds), *The Environment in British Prehistory*, London, 1981.

Simpson, Kenneth, *The Protean Scot: The Crisis of Identity in Eighteenth Century Scottish Literature*, Aberdeen, 1988.

Sinclair, David, *Shades of Green: Myth and Muddle in the Countryside*, London, 1990.

Smith, Alexander, *A Summer in Skye*, Byways Books Edition, Hawick, 1983.

Smith, Iain C., 'The Future of Gaelic Literature', *Transactions of the Gaelic Society of Inverness*, XLIII, 1960–63.

Smith, Iain C., *Selected Poems, 1955–1980*, Loanhead, 1981.

Smith, Iain C., *Towards the Human: Selected Essays*, Edinburgh, 1986.

Smith, Iain C., *Collected Poems*, Manchester, 1992.

Smout, T. C., *A History of the Scottish People, 1560–1830*, London, 1969.

Smout, T. C., 'Tours in the Scottish Highlands from the Eighteenth to the Twentieth Centuries', *Northern Scotland*, 5, 1983.

Smout, T. C., *The Highlands and the Roots of Green Conciousness, 1750–1990*, Scottish Natural Heritage, Edinburgh, 1993.

Smout, T. C. (ed), *Scotland Since Prehistory: Natural Change and Human Impact*, Aberdeen, 1993.

Smout, T. C., 'Trees as Historic Landscapes', *Scottish Forestry, 48, 1994*.

Smyth, Alfred P., *Warlords and Holy Men: Scotland, AD80–1000*, London, 1984.

Snyder, Edward D., *The Celtic Revival in English Literature, 1760–1800*, Cambridge, 1923.

Stafford, Fiona J., *The Sublime Savage: A Study of James MacPherson and the Poems of Ossian*, Edinburgh, 1988.

Steel, Tom, *The Life and Death of St Kilda*, Fontana Edition, London, 1975.

Steer, K. A., and Bannerman, John W. M., *Late Medieval Monumental Sculpture in the West Highlands*, Edinburgh, 1977.

Stephenson, Tom, *Forbidden Land: The Struggle for Access to Mountain and Moorland*, Manchester, 1989.

211

Steven, Campbell, *The Story of Scotland's Hills*, London, 1975.

Steven, H. M., and Carlisle, A., *The Native Pinewoods of Scotland*, Edinburgh, 1959.

Stevenson, David, *Alasdair MacColla and the Highland Problem in the Seventeenth Century*, Edinburgh, 1980.

Stevenson, Robert Louis, *Kidnapped*, Puffin Classics Edition, London, 1983.

Stone, Christopher D., *The Gnat is Older than Man: Global Environment and the Human Agenda*, Princeton, 1993.

Stott, Louis, *Robert Louis Stevenson and the Highlands and Islands of Scotland*, Aberfoyle, 1992.

Survival International, *Review: 21 Years of Survival International*, London, 1990.

Taylor, Rachel A., *The End of Fiammetta*, London, 1923.

Thomas, Keith, *Man and the Natural World: Changing Attitudes in England, 1500–1800*, Penguin Edition, London, 1984.

Thomson, Derick S., *The Gaelic Sources of MacPherson's Ossian*, Edinburgh, 1953.

Thomson, Derick S., 'The MacMhurich Bardic Family', *Transactions of the Gaelic Society of Inverness*, XLIII, 1960–63.

Thomson, Derick S., 'Gaelic Learned Orders and Literati in Medieval Scotland', *Scottish Studies*, 12, 1968.

Thomson, Derick S., *An Introduction to Gaelic Poetry*, London, 1974.

Thomson, Derick S., *Creachadh na Clarsach: Plundering the Harp: Collected Poems, 1940–1980*, Edinburgh, 1982.

Thomson, Derick S. (ed), *The Companion to Gaelic Scotland*, Oxford, 1983.

Thomson, Derick S. (ed), *Gaelic and Scots in Harmony*, Glasgow, 1988.

Thomson, Derick S., 'Alasdair MacMhaighstir Alasdair's Political Poetry', *Transactions of the Gaelic Society of Inverness*, LVI, 1988–90.

Thomson, Derick S., 'The Seventeenth Century Crucible of Scottish Gaelic Poetry', *Studia Celtica*, XXVI–XXVII, 1991–92.

Thomson, Derick S., *Gaelic Poetry in the Eighteenth Century: A Bilingual Anthology*, Aberdeen, 1993.

Thomson, R. L. (ed), *Foirm na h–Urrnuidheadh: John Carswell's Gaelic Translation of the Book of Common Order*, Scottish Gaelic Texts Society, Edinburgh, 1970.

Thoreau, Henry David, *A Week on the Concord and Merrimack Rivers*, Princeton, 1983.

Thoreau, Henry David, *The Maine Woods*, Penguin Edition, London, 1988.

Thoreau, Henry David, *Walden*, Everyman Edition, London, 1992.

Tipping, Richard, 'The History of the Scottish Forests Revisited', *Reforesting Scotland*, 8–9, 1993.

Tiryakian, E. A., and Rogowski, R. (eds), *New Nationalisms of the Developed West*, Boston, 1985.

Tomkies, Mike, *A Last Wild Place*, London, 1984.

Tomkies, Mike, *Out of the Wild*, London, 1985.

Tomkies, Mike, *Last Wild Years*, London, 1992.

Tomkins, Steve C., *The Theft of the Hills: Afforestation in Scotland*, London, 1986.

Tomkins, Steve C., *Forestry in Crisis*, London, 1989.

Toulson, Shirley, *The Celtic Alternative: A Reminder of the Christianity We Lost*, London, 1987.

Treece, Dave, *Bound in Misery and Iron*, Survival International, London, 1987.

Turner, Frederick, *Rediscovering America: John Muir in his Time and Ours*, San Francisco, 1985.

Watson, Adam, and Allan, Elizabeth, *The Placenames of Upper Deeside*, Aberdeen, 1984.

Watson, Roderick, *The Literature of Scotland*, London, 1984.

Watson, William J. (ed), *Scottish Verse from the Book of the Dean of Lismore*, Scottish Gaelic Texts Society, Edinburgh, 1937.

Welch, Robert, *Changing States: Transformations in Modern Irish Writing*, London, 1993.

Whitehead, G. Kenneth, *Hunting and Stalking Deer in Britain Through the Ages*, London, 1980.

Whitelock, D., McKitterick, R., and Dumville, D. (eds), *Ireland in Early Medieval Europe*, Cambridge, 1982.

Whyte, Ian, *Agriculture and Society in Seventeenth Century Scotland*, Edinburgh, 1979.

Whyte, Christopher (ed), *An Agaidh na Siorraidheachd: In the Face of Eternity: Eight Gaelic Poets*, Edinburgh, 1991.

Wigan, Michael, *The Scottish Highland Estate: Preserving an Environment*, Shrewsbury, 1991.

Wightman, Andrew D. (ed), *A Forest for Scotland*, Perth, 1992.

Wilmer, Franke, *The Indigenous Voice in World Politics*, London, 1993.

Wilson, A. N., *The Laird of Abbotsford: A View of Sir Walter Scott*, Oxford, 1989.

Wilson, Edward O., *The Diversity of Life*, Penguin Edition, London, 1994.

Withers, Charles W. J., *Gaelic in Scotland, 1698–1981: The Geographical History of a Language*, Edinburgh, 1984.

Withers, Charles W. J., *Gaelic Scotland: The Transformation of a Culture Region*, London, 1988.

Wittig, Kurt, *The Scottish Tradition in Literature*, Edinburgh, 1958.

Womack, Peter, *Improvement and Romance: Constructing the Myth of the Highlands*, London, 1989.

Wordsworth, Dorothy, *Journals*, 2 Volumes, London, 1941.

Wordsworth, William, *The Works of William Wordsworth*, Wordsworth Poetry Library Edition, Ware, 1994.

World Commission on Environment and Development, *Our Common Future*, Oxford, 1987.

Worster, Donald, *Nature's Economy: A History of Ecological Ideas*, Second Edition, Cambridge, 1994.

Youngson, A. J., *The Making of Classical Edinburgh*, Edinburgh, 1966.

Youngson, A. J., *After the Forty–Five: The Economic Impact on the Scottish Highlands*, Edinburgh, 1973.

INDEX